FARM
TO FORK

About the Author

Joe Stanley is a farmer, conservationist and writer and a passionate ambassador for sustainability and high standards in food and farming. Joe is often to be seen in the farming and national press advocating for positive change in our food system and explaining the realities of modern agriculture to wider society. He holds an honours degree in history from Durham University and a Graduate Diploma in Agriculture from the Royal Agricultural University, Cirencester. He has been honoured to receive both the National Farmers Union's Meurig Raymond Award and Associateship of the Royal Agricultural Societies for his farming advocacy. Joe is rarely to be found more than ten feet away from his trusty Jack Russell terriers, Ted & Toby (to whom he owes any small success).

FARM TO FORK

The Challenge of Sustainable Farming in 21ST Century Britain

JOE STANLEY

Quiller

To Kathryn: my rock, my love,
my most honest critic.

Copyright © 2021, 2023 Joe Stanley

First published in the UK in 2021
by Quiller, an imprint of Amberley Publishing.

This edition published 2023

British Library Cataloguing-in-Publication Data
A catalogue record for this book is available from
the British Library.

ISBN 978-1-84689-392-6

The right of Joe Stanley to be identified as the
author of this work has been asserted in accordance
with the Copyright, Design and Patent Act 1988.

The information in this book is true and complete to the
best of our knowledge. All recommendations are made
without any guarantee on the part of the Publisher,
who also disclaims any liability incurred in connection
with the use of this data or specific details.

Design by Guy Callaby

Whilst every effort has been made to obtain permission
from copyright holders for all material used in this book,
the publishers will be pleased to hear from anyone who
has not been appropriately acknowledged, and to make
the correction in future prints.

Printed and bound in Great Britain by TJ Books Limited, Padstow, Cornwall

Quiller
An imprint of Amberley Publishing Ltd

The Hill, Merrywalks,
Stroud GL5 4EP
Tel: 01453 847800
Email: info@quillerbooks.com
Website: www.quillerpublishing.com

CONTENTS

9
FOREWORD

13
INTRODUCTION

25
AUTUMN: SEPTEMBER, OCTOBER, NOVEMBER – *ESTABLISHMENT*

• Crop rotations • Crop varieties • Soil • Cultivations
• Stone picking and drystone walls • Planting
• Plant protection products • Climate change

83
WINTER: DECEMBER, JANUARY, FEBRUARY – *SHELTER*

• Longhorns • Winter routine • Daily routine • Crop pests
• Dairy • Calving • Boundaries • Drainage • Red Tractor standards

139
SPRING: MARCH, APRIL, MAY – *GROWTH*

• Turnout • Fertilisers and soil chemistry • Spring field operations
• Livestock and the environment • Sheep • Vets and animal health
• Livestock and disease

193
SUMMER: JUNE, JULY, AUGUST – *BOUNTY*

• Silage and haymaking • Beef production • Harvest • Summer shows
• Chickens • Farming and the environment

243
CONCLUSION

255
ACKNOWLEDGEMENTS

'Agriculture not only gives riches to a nation,
but the only riches she can call her own.'

Samuel Johnson (1709–84), English essayist

•

'Farming looks mighty easy when your plough is a pencil,
and you're a thousand miles from the corn field.'

**Dwight D. Eisenhower (1890–1969),
34th president of the United States**

FOREWORD

I T'S THE FIRST of May and I'm writing this while sitting at my desk, gazing through the farm office window, looking out across our farmyard. Grass is sparkling with early frost in the morning sun, swallows are circling and I'm conscious that soon I will hear the cuckoo in our water meadows. Year after year, different generations of the Downton cuckoo return from Africa to the same spot beside the river Avon. For me, like Joe, the rhythm of farming life is dictated by the seasons. Every season has its challenges, but, on my farm, May is the month of hope and optimism; winter is behind us, lambing completed and spring-born calves are benefitting from the first green shoots of spring grass.

I'm a tenant farmer near Salisbury in Wiltshire and a mum to teenage twins, but also president of the National Farmers' Union (NFU), representing 50,000 farming businesses.

I don't always read a foreword; such is my enthusiasm to get into a new book. All I really want to do in the words that follow here is to offer some personal reflection on why I believe farming matters – Joe Stanley opens the door to a wonderful personal account of life on a lowland family farm.

The combining impacts of Brexit and Covid mark a major reset moment for farmers and citizens alike. The Agriculture Act of 2020 is landmark legislation for England and the first of its kind since 1947. As yet few of us really realise how much new trade deals will influence our daily lives, what is in our fridges, our kids' school meals, or what is on the menu at the local pub.

As an island nation living through a global pandemic that brought our world quite literally to a standstill, many of you will be asking questions such as: 'Will we be more self-sufficient in producing the food we're good at in the UK?' Surely, there is no greater responsibility for any government than making sure it can feed its people with a ready supply of homegrown food. Can we get back to a more localised added value food system? What farming families like the Stanleys need are policies that reconnect our economy with rural Britain.

The lockdown in March 2020 saw the worst of human nature, as supermarket shelves emptied and people hoarded and stockpiled food. Many in government wondered if we would run out of food; we didn't, but political memories are short and one thing Covid-19 did was shine the brightest of lights not only on our national food security but on the wellbeing and recovery of many people, choosing to walk and exercise in the countryside.

The National Farmers' Union was founded in 1908 to restore farming's credibility with government, at a time when farming was going through the longest and deepest depression in its history, as imports of cheap grain and frozen meat flooded in from abroad.

Now, 113 years on and post-Brexit, the focus of the NFU has been endeavouring to ensure that food imported into this country is not produced to standards that are illegal here. In 2020 the NFU led a massively successful campaign on food standards with a petition that achieved over a million signatures in under two weeks.

Success was down to an unprecedented coalition of farmers, environmentalists, consumer groups, animal welfare experts and chefs like Jamie Oliver. The result was that agriculture is the only sector to have secured parliamentary scrutiny on all aspects of food imported in future trade deals via the Trade Agriculture Commission. Winning public support was no surprise; the UK was the first country in the world to enact legislation on animal welfare and has continuously added to it. Put simply, the people of this country care passionately about animal welfare and how their food is produced.

The evolution of agriculture, from the very first revolution in Neolithic times to modern day farming, has totally underpinned economic growth and success across the developed world. It's allowed cities to flourish and urbanisation to succeed, but that success poses the significant question: at what cost? We've become so disconnected from the food we eat that our diet and health, climate, environment and biodiversity have suffered at the hands of a world demanding ever-cheaper food. Covid itself is the outcome of a food system that has failed to respect the natural world.

Here in the UK there is a moral imperative for us to produce the food we're good at; we have a maritime climate that grows grass – we don't need huge feedlot systems. With the right incentives and the ability to revolutionise water infrastructure, we can produce much more of our own fruit and vegetables, rather than pressurising water-scarce countries for our own nutritional benefit.

Through my role as a trustee of Farm Africa I've come to understand the importance of inter-generational and international leadership to prepare the world for the next agricultural revolution. The UK has the chance to lead the world in climate-friendly farming, collaborating and brokering a new global approach to truly sustainable agriculture, ending our reliance on totally man-made fibres by growing not only sustainable food, but biodegradable fibres ever more sustainably on the earth, rather than continuing to deplete our precious finite resources from the inner earth.

History will judge our ability to solve how we feed an extra billion people on less land, with fewer inputs and less water, by 2030. Producing our food will always impact on our environment, whether it's plant or livestock based. The problems will not be solved by reports that simply don't do justice to the complexity of the challenge ahead and the policies that will be needed. These reports also, and sometimes wrongly, demonise the very people that are the solution – the farmers themselves; Joe Stanley and the farmers I represent, who are only focused on leaving their farms in an ever-better condition.

Joe's book is a must-read story about life on a lowland mixed farm. The book is one of hope and optimism, recognising the modern-day challenges that we as farmers face. But hope alone doesn't pay the bills. Government has a massive role in bringing the public and private sector together to build a new economic model for our countryside, creating new world sustainable farming cooperatives that can establish trading platforms for farmers to sell carbon and biodiversity net gain. But the foundation for success both here and across the world must be sustainable food production – the most important agricultural revolution to date is about to happen, and it's farmers like Joe that offer the sustainable solution to all of our everyday lives.

Minette Batters, NFU President
Wiltshire, April 2021

INTRODUCTION

FOOD IS OUR most intimate commodity and, along with water and shelter, our most pressing concern. We think of it at least three times per day (and I, as an inveterate snacker, considerably more). We bring it into our homes; we feed it to our children; it is the beating heart of our social interactions with each other; we look forward to eating out; we pride ourselves on our culinary skills when we eat in. Food is sustenance, comfort, joy, pleasure. We turn to it to celebrate and commiserate, on special occasions and in the everyday. Snatched meals wrapped in foil or three-course banquets cooked from scratch. Food is at the centre of our families. It provides structure to our lives. It gives us something to look forward to on a dreary workday morning as the clock ticks towards one. It is life.

But most of us know too little about the food we eat. For something we are so familiar with, and upon which we rely so greatly, how many of us can say that we are truly familiar with the food on our plate at all?

The modern food system is a remarkable network of global interconnections and supply chains valiantly attempting to feed a global population approaching eight billion. Consider the food in your own kitchen; it will range from relatively straightforward ingredients (such as vegetables, fruit, meat cuts or eggs) to more highly processed foods on a sliding scale from roasted nuts or canned tuna at one end to ready meals and confectionary at the other. As a general rule, the more processed the food, the more complex its story – its 'provenance' – becomes. It's easy to understand that the milk in your fridge is just, well, milk. Simple. (Though how much do you even know about how that staple gets to your morning coffee?) But that simple story becomes much more complex when you pick up, say, a dairy alternative which may contain a dozen ingredients sourced from multiple countries, produced and packaged in another before being shipped across further borders to its final destination. Two products fulfilling a similar role, but with very different back stories. The days when most of our food was produced locally and cooked fresh at home are long gone, and perhaps with it our concept of what food sustainability – our ability to produce something continuously in balance with our environment – means.

Society in much of the developed world has lost touch with the land from which our food comes. In 2014 a mere 1.5 per cent of the British workforce was directly involved with agriculture[1], compared with approximately fifty-five per cent in 1700.[2] Thus, the vast majority of Britons have no direct contact with the farms on which their food is produced, nor with anyone involved in its production. This has caused a disconnect between the food – which the majority of people source almost exclusively from large supermarkets – and those who actually grow it. Common are the anecdotes of children who announce that 'milk comes from Tesco' and are subsequently shocked and not a little squeamish to find

[1] Department for Environment, Food and Rural Affairs; Department for Agriculture and Rural Development (Northern Ireland); Welsh Assembly Government, The Department for Rural Affairs and Heritage; The Scottish Government, Rural and Environment Research and Analysis Directorate, 2015, *Agriculture in the United Kingdom 2014*, 109pp.

[2] Simpson, J., 'European farmers and the British "agricultural revolution"' in L. De la Escosura (ed.), *Exceptionalism and Industrialisation: Britain and its European Rivals, 1688–1815*, Cambridge: Cambridge University Press, 2004, pp. 69–85.

that it does in fact squirt from the teats of a cow! Most adults, at least, are somewhat better informed, but still there's a huge chasm in the understanding of many between the everyday ingredients with which we cook in the home and their provenance. For some, the disconnect is even greater: meals are either eaten away from the home or warmed up out of a packet, making the mental leap between what's being consumed, where it came from and how it was produced even wider. For many, the countryside is just something to be crossed in order to get to somewhere else, or even to see from a plane window as they head off to sunnier climes.

Addressing this disconnect matters because if you don't know about something how can you care about it? Moreover, how can you be in any position to discern between facts as you might come across them, and fiction – especially in the age of social media, where misinformation is rife.

Sustainability, meanwhile, has become the watchword of a modern world increasingly concerned by the clear and present danger of global climate change – though the concept itself risks becoming increasingly devalued, overused by everyone from politicians looking to curry favour to Big Oil firms looking to shift blame. Yet one fact is immutable: between now and 2050 – when the world's population is expected to hit ten billion – as much food will need to be produced as has already been grown in all human history and, for us to have a chance of living within our global ecological means, we'll need to do it **far** more sustainably than is currently the case, using less of our world's finite natural resources. Britain's farmers are at the forefront of addressing how this is to be achieved.

The purpose of this book is to describe from a farmer's eye view the production of the food you eat. What do we grow? How do we grow it? Why do we utilise the techniques we do, and why should that reassure you that the food reaching your plate is of the highest standard in terms of safety, quality, welfare and sustainability?

I am a third-generation farmer from a family farm in North West Leicestershire, on the edge of the picturesque Charnwood Forest. This means that my parents farmed here before me, and my paternal grandfather before them. I became a full-time farmer in 2009 alongside my parents. It's the family business. It's not unusual for children to follow in their parents' professional footsteps in any walk of life, but in farming it's perhaps more common than in any other industry. There is a certain sense of place and belonging when, like me, you were born into and grew up on the family farm. In those circumstances, it's not just your workplace, but also your home. There is also a high level of assumed expectation that children will continue in the farming tradition. However, my route into farming was not as predestined as might be expected: my childhood ardour for the profession cooled noticeably in my mid-teens and it wasn't until my mid-twenties (after a history degree and several jobs entirely outside the industry) that I decided to give it a go. All these years later, I am proud to be a member of this great industry.

But in those early years of my adult life, I lived in towns and cities and made friends who, like many of you reading this, have no background knowledge of farming or food production at all. My wife, indeed, could not be less of a farmer if she tried. My initial attempts to woo her on an early date through exposure to small fluffy animals led her to scream and run from new-born lambs which gambled towards her, looking for milk. The auguries did not seem propitious. But I would hope that, as a result of my somewhat atypical background, I have a slightly different perspective on our food system and am well placed to be your guide in this book.

So, who is the 'average' British farmer? I'm not sure there is such a thing. Agriculture is so remarkably diverse from Land's End to John O'Groats, from Great Yarmouth to Enniskillen, that it's impossible to put people in a neat box. From ages eighteen to eighty-eight (and older too), male and female, those who were born into it and those who followed their dream. The one thing they all have in common is a huge passion for what they do – it's not a job you can do if your heart isn't in it – and a pride for the food they produce. It isn't just a career: it's home, it's hobby, it's love. It's their place in the world. This can pose its own problems, but put a group of farmers together after a one-hundred-hour working week and they'll still talk about farming to the exclusion of all else. Sustainable and high-quality British food is the result of this pride, which I hope you can taste with every bite.

Farm to Fork will take you on a journey through twelve months on my farm – a mixed lowland arable and livestock farm on which we grow both crops (such as wheat) and breed cattle and sheep, in the relatively kind lower altitudes of the English Midlands rather than the uplands or hills of Wales, Scotland or the Peak District, for example. The farming practices in those climes are, by necessity, very different to ours, and are certainly well covered by other (frequently colder) authors.

What I hope to demonstrate as we move through the four seasons is what happens, and why, on a typical mixed farm such as mine – the type of farm from which much of your native-grown foods come, whether as meat, milk, bread or beer. Along the way I also hope to explain some of the detail of the farming industry, such as how government policy affects the way we farm; what our future outside the European Union means for us; and why I am proud to be a British farmer. In this way, I hope to leave you with a better understanding of how the food you eat reaches your plate; why you are fortunate to enjoy some of the highest quality produce in the world; and how you might consider modifying your shopping habits in future to support more sustainable farming methods.

For context, our farm consists of some 290 hectares (ha) or 720 acres (ac) of grass and arable fields. (A hectare is 100 x 100m, so 10,000m^2, or a little larger than a rugby pitch.) This makes us somewhat larger than the national average farm size of 80ha, but much smaller than many large estates which can run to thousands of hectares.[3] It's divided up into forty-three fields of all shapes and sizes, with an average area of 6.7ha. Across it are scattered rocky outcrops, copses, spinneys, woods and watercourses. Our fields are divided by a combination of wire fences, drystone walls and hedges. At the centre of it all is the farmyard, with house, cattle sheds and grain stores. The original farm and the oldest buildings (which are still in use, built from the local stone) date from the 1700s. Taken together, it's a beautiful part of the country and is, really, how you might imagine a classic British farm to look.

We have one full-time employee, thanks to mechanisation and specialisation. I can remember when we employed five full-time staff, and not long outside of my memory we would perhaps have provided jobs for life to ten or twelve. This means that the experience of farming in the twenty-first century is different to that of any other time in history. It has always been a communal enterprise, a group endeavour, a social experience as well as hard graft. Today, farming is frequently a lonely profession, despite the fact that through our mobile devices we are more connected than ever before (and what a godsend they are for farm safety). I can work twelve hours a day and never see another human. Perhaps in our drive for efficiency and technology we have lost something valuable, not just in farming, but in society too. This loneliness – plus long hours, low wages and frequent setbacks – has implications for rural mental health in the UK.

But I am lucky in having two constant companions by my side

3 Department for Environment, Food & Rural Affairs, *The future farming and environment evidence compendium*, Government Statistical Service, 2019, 122pp.

throughout my farming year to share the highs and lows and act as my very own dedicated morale officers – my two Jack Russell terriers, Ted and Toby. There is active (and no doubt never-to-be-resolved) debate in agricultural circles around just what is the best type of farm dog. Well, I nail my colours well and truly to the mast with my JRTs. Ted, a striking chap of black, white and brown, has been by my side for eight years at the time of writing, and comes from a long and noble line of star ratters bred on the farm. He was the only dog in his litter of three, and worked his way into my heart after I had declared that, bachelor that I was at the time, I didn't have time to care for a dog alongside my work and ineffectual attempts to woo the opposite sex. Ted put a stop to all that, and he's been my best friend and super-loyal companion ever since. (He was also a dab hand with the ladies, as my lamb-fearing now wife can attest.) Toby is Ted's much younger nephew, brown and white with a fluffy windsock tail, and similarly worked his doggy magic on my heart after I was **absolutely sure** this time that I couldn't possibly have a **second** dog at work. Toby is the boundless enthusiasm to Ted's stoic calm; the face-licker to his lap-curler; and they are both absolutely brilliant. They are also, perhaps, the only farm dogs in Great Britain which (even at Ted's rather mature age) need to be on a lead at all times when out in the fields, to head off the risk of their immediate disappearance upon sighting of anything mobile on ground, in water or in air. Terriers! It really is one of the perks of the job to be able to have my four-legged friends at work with me. And merely seeing them on the cover of this book is worth the effort of its writing!

An important point to make at the outset is that, across the approximately 218,000 farm businesses in the UK[4], there is a huge amount of variety. For such a small country, we are enormously

4 ibid

diverse in terrain, farming type and the foods we produce, while our long and storied history means that land tenure is often a complex mishmash of the ancient and modern.

Broadly speaking, a line can be imagined which bisects the country from north-east to south-west. To the right of this line is the nation's breadbasket, running from the Humber through the Midlands and down to the south coast. These are our prime arable and horticultural lands – mostly level expanses with deep, rich soils and a pleasant, temperate climate suitable for the growing of arable crops, fruit and vegetables. To the left of our imaginary line are the grasslands: rolling hills and valleys, the thinner soils of which are bountiful with lush, green grass, regularly watered by the ample rainfall blowing in from the Atlantic – though this generalisation does, of course, mask a huge amount of variety within that very arbitrary divide. I sit in the exact centre of the country, and indeed the Midlands continues to be a great area of traditional 'mixed' farming with a good mixture of land use types and farm diversity from sheep and dairy to arable and horticulture.

As for tenure, there's a variety of different means by which farmers hold their land: some own it while others rent – either on a short-term basis (from one to perhaps ten years) or on a long-term or even multi-generational standing – from landowners or institutions who don't themselves farm. These latter tenancies were common in the wake of the Second World War as landowners looked to lock in a long period of certainty following the tumult of those years, but new such tenancies are virtually unheard of today. The general perception that all farmers are landowners is therefore incorrect, and for many their biggest cost is the annual rent payment. This is particularly problematic for those only granted very short tenancies of as little as one to five years: in a business which frequently treats thirty-six months as a minimum horizon to make plans or breed livestock, many young people especially find themselves disadvantaged when trying to gain a foothold in a difficult industry. Between 2014 and 2017, the average British farm made a profit of £37,000 – when you consider the time, capital and risk invested, as well as the number of family members across multiple generations often reliant upon this single figure, that is not a considerable sum. In the same period, sixteen per cent of farms generated a loss.[5] Farming is too frequently an unprofitable endeavour, from which many of the questions around sustainability arise.

So, what do we farm in this country? Let's look at some headline figures. Agriculture occupies seventy-two per cent of the UK's land area (which is a lot). That's roughly 17.5 million hectares. At any one time, farms have in the region of twelve million cattle, thirty-five million sheep, five million pigs and 180 million poultry on their books. Around twelve million hectares of our farmland is pasture of one type or another; 3.2 million hectares are set aside for cereal crops; while around 150,000ha are each used for horticultural crops (fruit and veg) and potatoes. Fourteen thousand hectares are used to grow ornamental plants and flowers.[6]

British farmers produce approximately seventy-five per cent of domestic requirements for indigenous foodstuffs – that is, foods which we can grow here. For some of these, such as lamb, we produce a surplus which we export; for others, such as (especially) fresh fruit, we must import to balance supply and demand. Indeed, although we are seventy-five per cent self-sufficient in indigenous food, the UK is only about sixty-one per cent self-sufficient in all food[7] (down from seventy-eight per cent in 1984) because many staples of the British diet are increasingly non-native (think smashed avocados). We are now used to having permanent access to all the

5 ibid

6 ibid

7 National Farmers' Union, 'Self-sufficiency Day 2019: coverage and impact', 13 August 2019.

varied and wondrous ingredients the global economy has to offer at any time of year. Even native goods such as strawberries are now available all year round, imported from Egypt, Israel or Spain when out of season here. Indeed, it's in fresh fruit that British production is most deficient, growing as we do only some seventeen per cent of domestic requirements. With vegetables we fare somewhat better, at around fifty per cent, with staples such as potatoes and carrots being available throughout the year.[8]

Where does the rest of our food come from? The vast majority (seventy per cent) is imported from the European Union (EU), which in turn is recipient of sixty-two per cent of our food exports. Much of this is of course down to geography and history; as both our closest neighbours and those with whom we have (until recently) shared ever-closer political and economic ties, it's natural that they are also our closest trading partners (especially for perishable goods), while as partners in the EU, we have also shared common regulatory standards in food for forty years, hugely easing the frictions inherent in cross-border trade. The course we will now chart having left the European community, and the implications of that for food and farming in this country, we will return to later.

This book describes a farming year as lived by me, but it could describe twelve months on innumerable farms across the country. At the same time, one of the hallmarks of British agriculture is that there are almost as many different ways of farming as there are farmers. I don't claim that my methods are representative of all, but they are how we do it on our small patch of the countryside, and I include comments on how I hope to improve in future.

Similarly, I don't grow root crops, cultivate herbs, produce fruit or breed any of a dozen types of livestock which are done with great skill on other farms. I leave those topics to another author. But what I hope to demonstrate is the passion and care which

8 Defra, 2019, op. cit.

22

goes into producing your food on farms across the nation, whatever their specialty, as well as the world-leading standards to which we adhere whether on environmental sustainability, animal welfare or food safety.

I decided to tell my story through the four seasons, each with its inherently different character. Autumn is the season for planting crops; for establishing new life. The chill winds of winter see our cattle take centre stage as they come in from the fields and require constant attention through the short days and long nights as they birth the next generation. Spring sees fields come to life as grass and crops emerge from their slumber and turn sunshine into green matter as our calves experience their first days in the great outdoors. And summer, the archetypal and busiest farming season, sees machines take to the fields to gather in the sun-ripened harvest.

The farming year turns with metronomic regularity; yet, as you shall see, no two days are ever quite the same, and one of the great joys of the job is the huge variety it brings, as well as the privilege of working in the great outdoors, in nature's garden. And one of the challenges is that Mother Nature always plays her hand, be it good or bad. I hope you shall also see that farming is about much more than food. Britain's farmers are the stewards of our shared natural environment; the guardians of our historic landscapes; the trustees of our rural heritage; and I'm proud to be one of them.

This is the story of your food.

AUTUMN

• SEPTEMBER • OCTOBER • NOVEMBER

ESTABLISHMENT

*'No spring nor summer beauty have such grace
as I have seen in one autumnal face.'*

John Donne (1572–1631), English poet

CROP ROTATIONS

ON OUR FARM, we are highly typical of British arable farmers in growing a variety of different 'combinable crops' – wheat, barley, oilseed rape, beans and oats – all of which, as the name suggests, will end their lives before the blades of our combine harvester. In the UK, we can grow a single cash crop such as these in each field every year. It's not advisable to grow any crop continually in the same fields, so from one year to the next different crops will be moved around the farm – a 'crop rotation'. Some crops are more profitable than others; wheat, for example, is generally considered the most lucrative due both to its relatively high value and yield. But, grown continuously in the same fields year after year, I would quickly start to see a decrease

25

in yield which would become worse with each successive season. The primary reason for this is the build-up of soil-borne diseases specific to particular crops when grown in quick succession. For wheat, a prime example is the fungus 'take all' which can sap yields by as much as fifty per cent and for which there is no means of control.

To avoid this and other diseases, then, farmers rotate their crops around their fields; a simple three-year rotation might be wheat, barley and then oilseed rape, before returning to wheat in year four – though the 'longer' the rotation, with the greater number of crops, the more beneficial to general field health. In this way, our soils are kept healthy, and our yields hopefully high. Farms are thus invariably a patchwork of different crops offering different habitats at different times to insects, birds and mammals, rather than vast plains of 'monocropping' with a single species being grown as far as the eye can see – a classic image of the great prairies of the United States, Australia or Russia. Our many small, interlocking neighbouring farms, all with their own rotations, further enhance this beneficial effect and give great variety to our landscapes.

Even better for the crop rotation is inclusion of livestock such as sheep and cattle, which perform the dual tasks of grazing injurious weed species from fields without the need for chemical controls and add valuable organic nutrition back to the soil in a manner which synthetic fertilisers cannot match. Before the advent of such modern artificial inputs, grazing livestock were thus the vital element of a healthy crop rotation and earned the sobriquet of 'the golden hoof' as crops grown after livestock were invariably more bountiful. But, in the past century, the proliferation of artificial chemicals and fertilisers has led many traditional mixed farms to specialise in crop production to the exclusion of livestock from their rotations to remain profitable. We'll return to this later, but increasingly British farmers are realising that such market-driven specialisation was perhaps a short-term fillip and that a return to more traditional mixed farming – commonly today referred to as 'regenerative' agriculture – is desirable to replenish the health of our soils.

Another benefit of a wide and diverse crop rotation is that the weeds which compete with crops for nutrients, light and space are more easily controlled. Cereals such as wheat and barley, for example, are grasses, so grass weeds are difficult and expensive to control in those crops by means of modern chemical sprays because of the close relation between the crop and the weed. They are much easier to control in a crop of, say, oilseed rape – a 'brassica' genetically much different from the grass weed. Alternating between different crops therefore prevents an overwhelming build-up of injurious weed species in any crop as a broader range of herbicides can be used to manage their populations more effectively. In the UK, 'blackgrass' is an arable weed of particular concern, costing farmers an estimated £400 million per year in treatment costs and lost yields of some 800,000 tonnes of grain.

CROP VARIETIES

The major combinable crop groups are 'cereals' such as wheat and barley, 'oilseeds' such as the yellow fields of oilseed rape or blue fields of linseed that you may see flowering in spring, and 'legumes' such as beans or peas. They all have their different uses and markets. Wheat, of course, is the basis of flour for baking; barley is essential to brewing and distilling; oilseed rape makes a great domestic alternative to olive or palm oil, as well as being useful in many industrial processes; and we (all) love baked beans.

Each crop has many different varieties with different characteristics from which the farmer can choose depending on their preferences. Some varieties have better natural disease resistance than others; some are less likely to blow over in storms; some have higher yields; some varieties of wheat are better for milling into bread flour; others for biscuits. Some varieties of oilseed rape are better for cooking; others for industrial lubricants – and you don't want to get them mixed up. Some farmers are forever trying new varieties; others just like to stick with old favourites.

All have names; we currently grow 'Revelation' wheat, 'Tundra' beans and 'Diablo' barley, among others. All are bred by plant scientists working for seed companies who subsequently own the patents to the varieties, which are produced through a process of trial-and-error interbreeding. As a farmer, I then select the variety I wish to grow based on the characteristics I prioritise, and purchase an amount of seed from a merchant who has bought it on contract from a farmer who specialises in growing very pure 'seed crops'. For most crops and varieties, some of the seed from the first harvest can be retained by the farmer and planted again the next year (though some 'hybrids' are bred with limited reproductive ability to be 'home saved' in this way and must be bought fresh every year). So when you see a field of combinable crops, all the plants in that field will be of the same variety, selected for a specific purpose, with specific characteristics in mind.

A good illustration of this is barley: I can grow 'malting' barley or 'feed' barley. Malting barleys (there are many varieties) are bred to produce a good, consistent malt for beer and spirits; 'feed' barleys are generally bred for higher yield, but would be unsuitable for malting, and are processed into animal feed. Malting barley – providing, once harvested, it matches the strict criteria (which is not guaranteed) – is more valuable than feed barley, but will the premium (which varies from year to year) offset the lower yield versus feed varieties? This is one of the questions I grapple with when choosing my cropping; trying to guess what the markets will be like twelve months into the future!

Different crops also have different characteristics in the rotation. As mentioned, wheat is considered the most profitable and bountiful crop, but to achieve this it extracts significant nutrients from the soil, and achieving good yield also requires significant inputs, especially of nitrogen, which acts as the fuel to achieve rapid and significant growth. Beans, on the other hand, are one of the 'break' crops available to achieve a balanced rotation, and are somewhat kinder to the soil. They require no artificial nitrogen, for as a legume they have the remarkable ability to extract it directly from the atmosphere, some of which even remains in the soil for the benefit of the following crop.

SOIL

But before seed can be planted, I must prepare the ground. Think back to your school religious studies lessons, and the parable of the farmer and the seeds; it didn't end well for the grains thrown onto rocky or hard ground, and what was true in first century Judea is still true in twenty-first century Britain. You can't just chuck your seed hither and yon – you need a plan!

At the end of harvest, once the crop and any straw have been removed, I'm left with fields of stubble – the bottom few inches of the stalks of the previous crop sticking out of the soil where it has been cut by the combine harvester. The soil itself is – after nearly a year under the elements, having been pounded by rain, baked by the sun and variously run on by heavy machinery – rather hard and unyielding, and not an inviting prospect for seeds to grow in.

This is the time of year when as a farmer I'm able to press the reset button on my fields; when the previous year's triumphs and disappointments are finally cleared, and – shaken like a giant Etch-a-Sketch – I erase all evidence of the past twelve months from the landscape through the process of cultivation. It's a word which has entered our positive linguistic lexicon; to 'cultivate a relationship' is to prepare the ground for better things in future, and so it is every autumn on the farm. This is one of the big set-piece jobs of the year, and one of the most satisfying as you leave the farmyard at daybreak to return at nightfall having made your very visible mark on the landscape, turning golden yellow stubbles to fresh brown soil. It's one of the original hallmarks of our human civilisation; the cultivation of ground and the husbandry of crops as the basis of settled agriculture rather than the hunter-gatherer existence of our ancestors. I can't say these thoughts occur to me every time I jump in the tractor, but just occasionally on a perfect autumn's evening one can take a moment to reflect with satisfaction on the sense of my small part in the thin golden thread that is agriculture which weaves its way unbroken from distant past to present and – hopefully – well into the future.

Before we talk about the process of cultivation, let us discuss the medium: soil. Soil is our most vital resource, not just as farmers but as a species. There's a well-known line in the farming community which runs that humans, despite all our accomplishments, owe our existence to a six-inch layer of topsoil and the fact that it rains. This is true, and, when you think about it, quite scary. For all our technological advancement and supposed mastery of our planet, we're completely reliant on the soil beneath our feet to produce our food; without those few inches of earth, our so-called civilisation would all be for naught. Not all soil is alike; anyone who has ever dug an allotment or garden border will know that only a few inches beneath the rich, dark layer of the surface there is generally to be found a solid layer of gravel, stone or clay in which it's not possible to grow anything. That layer of fertile topsoil can often seem worryingly delicate.

Topsoil is a complex mixture of minerals and organic matter which is the result of the interaction between parent materials (for example, the erosion of rocks), soil organisms and the climate, and an inch of it can take centuries to create. Remarkably, there are estimated to be more living things in a teaspoon of soil than there are humans on the planet.[9] It's a living, dynamic resource about which we know remarkably little but into which a huge amount of research using cutting-edge technology is now being conducted into its physical, chemical and biological properties as the agricultural industry tries to work out how best to manage its most valuable asset.

Across my farm, the topsoil 'types' are incredibly varied. In some parts of the country the soils are quite consistent from field to field across a large area, but I was once told that glaciers retreating at the end of the last ice age by turns scarified and dumped soil and rock as they went in a tangled mess on what is now my gaff. As a result, most of my fields have at least two different soil types, and some many more. These range from very 'light' and sandy at one end of the spectrum, to loamy soils high in organic matter in the middle to very 'heavy' mineral-rich, clay-rich soils at the other. Some of my land has very thin soil with a large percentage of shingle and pebbles; other fields sport deep soils heavily congested with jagged granite rocks. These varying soils behave very differently, and require different approaches to farming.

Sandy soils have low organic matter levels and struggle to retain moisture in dry conditions due to the large spaces between their granules, and are therefore unlikely to produce bumper yields and are prone to drought – though are conversely difficult to waterlog and easy to work even in wet conditions. In contrast, very heavy

9 The James Hutton Institute, *What on Earth? Your soil health explained*, Aberdeen: The James Hutton Institute, n.d., 8pp.

clay soils are prone to waterlogging and can be difficult to establish crops in as they can become lumpy when dry or like putty when wet, but are more drought tolerant as they better retain moisture and are capable of delivering more significant yields in the right conditions. Medium, loamy soils are the best compromise between the two, and I wish I had more of them!

Many farmers believe that for too long our delicate soils have been treated too much like 'dirt', without the care and respect they deserve given their critical place in our precarious human ecosystem. It's certainly true that some farming practices are less careful of soils than others. Bare soils exposed on a slope and subjected to heavy rain will see rivers of brown water flowing off them; that brown water is the very stuff of life, and at worst it will find its way to the sea and be lost forever – though not before the nutrients held within cause pollution and sedimentation in our waterways. Well established permanent pasture on that same slope, subjected to that same rainfall, will see far less soil loss as the leaves absorb the energy of each raindrop and the roots and decaying organic matter bind the soil together. It's important to grow the right crop in the right place.

This was something I gave little thought to earlier in my farming career. I admit that I took it for granted that soil was soil, and it more or less stayed where it was (the perils of a history, rather than an agricultural, degree perhaps). I carried out my work, generally too busy to give it any deeper thought. But, as the years progressed, I started to notice clues that perhaps all was **not** well in paradise. Clearing field ditches would produce large mounds of topsoil to redistribute back into the field. There was that gateway which always ran brown during heavy rain, out onto the road. A drystone wall at the base of an intensively cultivated slope which, I idly realised one day, had three feet of soil built up against its base. Field drains, originally planted three feet deep, which now seemed suspiciously shallow. I always took it for granted that we were doing the best we could for our soil, and realisation only slowly dawned that perhaps these isolated observances were indicative of a general lack of thought which needed correcting. It was just happening so slowly that it was hard to spot at first, like the gradual deterioration in the health of a relative whom you see every day. Don't get me wrong; we weren't using and abusing our soil, uncaring of consequences. Like most British farmers, we appreciate its value and follow good practice to avoid damage. But there was clearly, I realised, **more** that I could be doing. This has started to guide my thinking in recent years; I now think of soil not as immutable, but as a delicate asset to be constantly tended. After all, it takes centuries to build an inch of it, but perhaps only hours to lose it.

Of course, there's much more to good soil management than just managing surface runoff, and it's a hugely complex living organism in its own right, packed full not just of microorganisms (many of which's functions we still don't understand) but other biota such as insects, worms and fungi which are vital to the fertility of our earth. Farmers need to manage the nutrient levels in their soils to ensure that their plants grow healthily, and through those plants their animals – and all of us – too. Soil is the basis of all things, the foundation of civilisation's pyramid, and the medium in which I work daily. It's strange; for all the big ideas and epochal concepts when it comes to soil, just the act of getting my hands dirty with it (which happens most days) or coming in at the end of a long day veritably caked in it (to my wife's lament) gives me an inexplicable sense of satisfaction, a visceral connection with the land which is one of the small private pleasures that comes from being a farmer, like a spectacular sunset which seems all for you, or the delight of seeing new life come into the world. Earth is a special element.

It's also something we keep an eye on. In the UK, farmers are required to sample their soils at least once every five years to keep tabs on the levels of various nutrients – primarily phosphorus (P), potassium (K) and magnesium (Mg) – and its acidity/alkalinity (pH). These are the basics of good crop production, vital for root growth, leaf growth and photosynthesis. A pH around 6.5 (very slightly acidic) is considered optimum for most crops. Move too far from this figure, and plants' ability to absorb and assimilate nutrients becomes impaired, regardless of how much of them is available. Crops absorb these minerals from the ground and subsequently farmers must top up back to healthy levels. But through testing we can see whether we do in fact need to apply such fertilisers, or whether there are sufficient stocks in the soil.

I try to sample a third of the farm every year, most easily done in the autumn or winter, when hopefully the ground is moist and easy to sample and before crops grow too high and become an encumbrance. Sampling is a case of walking a big 'W' pattern across each field with a bucket and a sampling spear and taking soil cores of about twelve inches; perhaps one every hectare. The cores are then all mixed together and a representative sample sent to a laboratory for processing. For P&K, this is done on an index: 2 is good, 3 or 4 is very high, 1 or 0 very low, with steps of + or – for each number; 2+ is a little high; 2- a little low. It's a bit … agricultural … but is a tried and tested system. Increasingly, farmers are starting to take notice of more than these basic minerals and pH when they sample their soils as our institutional appreciation of the medium improves, and in recent years I've begun testing for the organic matter (OM) content of my soils as well. As we'll see later, soil OM is becoming increasingly appreciated for the absolutely vital role it plays in the health and productivity of soil, as well as farmers' ability to play an active part in combatting climate change.

CULTIVATIONS

Cultivations can begin as soon as the crop has been harvested. The first issue to address is soil compaction, which primarily results from the passage of farm machinery through the year, squishing the soil and pushing the airspaces out of it, making it both more unrelenting to roots and more prone to waterlogging. It's thought that compacted soils cost British farmers some £500m per year in lost production.[10] To address this, in areas where we suspect compaction, we use an implement mounted on our tractor called a subsoiler, which consists of a frame with steel legs with winged feet which we pull through the ground causing the soil to heave and thus breaking up the compaction layer. This is slow work (imagine spending all day at 5km/h!) but an essential first step to ensure our crop has the best start in life. You may think that steel is pretty resilient (and it is), but such 'wearing metal' in constant motion through the ground experiences huge friction (and gets really hot), gradually eroding over the course of the day to a razor-sharp edge, and as such is in need of regular replacement with fresh bolt-on parts to stop the frame of the machine itself becoming damaged.

After this, we have two options. The plough is the archetypal cultivation instrument with which we're all familiar from our days reading nursery books about farming onwards. It's existed in one form or another for millennia and enabled productive agriculture to spring up around the world over the centuries. Indeed, it was one of Radio Four's choices for its groundbreaking *A History of the*

---

10 'How to crack down on costly soil compaction', *Farmers Weekly*, 21 August 2017.

World in 100 Objects series. Ultimately, the basic function has changed little over the centuries, whether pulled by one ox-power in ancient China or 300 horsepower in modern Britain. It inverts the soil, burying trash and weeds from the previous crop and bringing fresh, loose soil to the surface ready for planting.

Discs are a faster and cheaper alternative to ploughing, as instead of inverting the soil to a depth of anything up to twelve inches they are pulled along the surface and churn it up to a depth of only a few, loosening the top layer. And this is the important part of cultivation: seeds thrive in a fine, loose 'tilth' of soil. Try to plant into hard ground and the seed may not be covered by soil at all and be left at the mercy of the elements, scavenging birds and slugs, or will simply be unable to put down roots at all. The process of cultivation creates an actual 'seed bed' in which it's comfortable enough to grow with the simple application of rain. Why disc instead of plough? The major advantage of ploughing is in burying the residue from the previous crop (which can be a hindrance to the following one) along with weeds and their seeds to a depth which mostly precludes further germination. But some of those seeds can remain viable for years, lying dormant in the ground. Regular ploughing runs the risk of returning those seeds to the surface and negating much of the benefit gained from an expensive and time-consuming process, and with some crops leaving much less residue than others, discing becomes a low-risk and lower-cost option in those years. Farming is a game played on a long timescale.

These days, my farm is sufficiently small that it's rare for me to work late into the night. The long days of summer and autumn offer me all the time I generally need to get fieldwork done without having to resort to pulling an all-nighter, though sometimes impending bad weather might force my hand. When I was younger, and we farmed a much larger area, it was common to work late into the night, relying on the lights of the tractor to see by, before returning home at midnight ready for another 6am start. I was never a fan of this; fields invariably have obstacles such as trees and telegraph poles which can lurk in the dust and mist of the night, and it's much easier to make a costly mistake in these conditions. Most farmers have at least one story of 'the time they took out the telephones to the village'. Accidents happen – especially when tired at night, and it's hard to think of another civilian industry where working eighteen hours a day, week after week, is so normalised as in agriculture where it is by turns treated as both expected and a badge of honour. It's one of the reasons the health and safety – and mental health – record of farming is so poor. Those working in agriculture are eighteen times as likely to die at work compared to the national average.[11]

But even if I don't work into the night as many do, the days can be long and repetitive. At some point (about a fortnight into the season) all the music and all the news the radio has to offer have been listened to. This is where my canine morale officers put in some of their most solid work. Ted and Toby, in another demonstration of why Jack Russells are clearly the finest farm dogs, each fit perfectly one on each side of the cab in their beds (beat that, Labs). From their lofty perches, they take turns to snooze and keep watch for any four-legged threat which might require some of the swiftest barking action. Having those two with me is a great tonic to the pressures of the job, and the loneliness which comes frequently from such a solitary career. I often find myself deep in conversation with Ted about the finer points of the task I'm carrying out (he's got almost as much experience as me in these things) or commenting to Toby about the loveliness of the view (he frequently demurs). Having them with me forces me to get out

11 Health and Safety Executive, *Fatal injuries in agriculture, forestry and fishing in Great Britain 2019/20*, 2020, 10pp.

of the tractor every so often to let them stretch their legs, and gives me a minute to take a break and breathe in the fresh country air. After all, I'm lucky to be in a job which has it on tap; it's a shame to waste it. Dogs offer many farmers, isolated despite the technology of the modern world, a sense of great companionship, and they're vital members of the team. Which isn't to say you can trust them with your lunch. Both have been guilty, over the years, of devouring the contents of my lunch box when given half a chance and left unattended in the tractor. All I could do was laugh at their mayonnaise speckled snouts.

STONE PICKING AND DRYSTONE WALLS

A final job to consider before planting – and more familiar to some farmers than others – is 'stone picking' and, whether you're farming in 2021 BC or 2021 AD, this is a job done by hand. As I've mentioned, we have a huge variety of soil types at home, and that includes fields containing ancient Precambrian granite boulders quite literally up to and including the size of a family car. Luckily, most are not quite so large, but all are equally hard, and a constant of modern machinery is that it dislikes coming into contact with large lumps of stone when working. Cultivations such as the ones I describe above invariably turn over and expose fresh stone every year – quite remarkable when you consider the decades and in some cases centuries for which fields have been worked. But, through a geological process I don't pretend to understand, they seem to continue to rise to the surface to torment me anew year in, year out! (Unless somebody is coming in the night and spreading them unnoticed.)

If there isn't a proverb which warns 'beware of arable field with drystone wall', there should be, because those rocks have come from somewhere very local! In fairness, in a way I have it a lot easier than previous generations. My grandfather was heavily involved in destoning virgin agricultural land in the 1950s, creating fields which are still in use today and seem to have been hacked from the very living rock which still rises around them in jagged peaks. If you look over the stone walls which were created from much of the spoil, you can see piles upon piles of unused rock alongside massive boulders still bearing the scars of the charge holes and explosives used to split them. Today, the destruction of what would have been pristine natural habitat would never be allowed for agriculture (and rightly so) and I somehow doubt the effort would at any rate be worth the reward (even if a farmer could still get hold of explosives!) but they were different times, and the government actively incentivised farmers to clear land for food production in the wake of the Second World War. Indeed, colossal feat that it was, it was one of the reasons that my grandfather was eventually awarded an OBE for services to agriculture. In other ways, I have it tougher now than in the past (break out the tiny violins). In my grandfather's day, he could call on a workforce of a dozen men to swarm a field after ploughing, picking up rocks and throwing them in a passing trailer. Today, it can often just be me or at best two or three of us covering the same fields and removing the same number of rocks by hand. When they're too big to move, we bring in a telehandler to dig them out and carry them away.

It's great stuff though; the rocky fields of our farm are all girdled with traditional drystone walls, constructed at great effort over the centuries by a multitude of skilled hands, one painstaking metre at a time. We have mile upon mile of them (our share of the 95,000km across England and Wales), and they were built to last. Different parts of the UK have different wall-building techniques and different styles, some of it based around the raw material available, some of it around the task for which it was designed, but some of the differences down to plain regional colour in the same manner as the polyglot accents of the people who built them.

Ours are relatively simple affairs, with a shallow foundation trench beneath layer upon layer of slaty, sharp-edged granite facing stones sandwiching a core of smaller filling stones, finally capped off by a row of coping stones lain at 45 degrees to the horizontal, to a total height of perhaps 5 feet. And all without any cement, mortar or bonding of any kind. In places, you can still find ancient stone gateposts, single massive chunks of rock with rusted iron hinges painstakingly driven through and sealed with lead. Charnwood walls always strike me as somewhat more ambitious than those from other parts of the country; they lack the large 'through' stones which bind many of their regional kin together, whilst at the same time being consistently narrow from base to top, not like the more stable, pyramidal walls seen elsewhere. These are walls built with chutzpah.

I always consider that we're blessed to have these wonderful features in the landscape of the farm, for they're not common in Leicestershire nor much of the country to the south. Our farm sits astride the very western edge of the Charnwood Forest, an upland landscape more reminiscent of the Peaks than the lowlands of much of Leicestershire and the Midlands. So much so, that half of our rather modestly sized holding is replete with these patient sentinels, while the other has not a one, and relies instead on hedgerows for demarcation. Although built to last, inevitably time, the elements, tree roots, rabbit burrows and the occasional careening car take their toll. Believe it or not, but wall theft is even an issue, with those lining the quietest lanes disappearing over the years, no doubt to create rockeries and outbuildings in local gardens. Even the sturdiest wall will eventually need maintenance. Some of our drystone walls are in great shape; others are afflicted with a few conspicuous holes; but some, sadly, lie tumbled and shattered like low rows of jagged teeth on the skyline.

The truth is that the utility of walls as livestock barriers – their original primary purpose – is now much reduced with the rise of the ubiquitous barbed-wire fence, which is an order of magnitude easier, quicker and cheaper to erect. Wall building and maintenance is an artform, and too few people in the countryside now practise it, a situation accelerated by the dramatic reduction in the rural workforce in recent decades. It's tough, backbreaking work, usually performed in the winter months when other work is sparse. I tried my hand once on a tumbledown section of wall, and when I finished it somehow looked worse than the pile of disorganised stones with which I had started.

On the list of spending priorities, rebuilding walls has inevitably been in the 'nice to do' rather than the 'need to do' column in recent decades, when farm profitability has been so poor. Luckily, we've been able to make use of EU grants which have match-funded drystone restoration as part of the maintenance of our rural heritage in recent years. It's true to say that, on our farm and on many others, without the walls built in their unique local styles, the landscape would be a very different place, and this sense of place and heritage has always been something which the pan-national European Union, through its rural funding programmes, was keen to safeguard and promote.

It was hugely satisfying recently to plough a field containing a wall which was earmarked for repairs, stone pick it, and use those very stones to rebuild the wall. It really did make me feel at one with the land – to use its own natural resources in that way – and with my forebears who would have done that exact same task. But the truth is – even with financial help – such activity is expensive, with the result that miles of our walls, especially around arable fields where they no longer serve an active purpose, lie more as overgrown boundary markers than useful infrastructure. But I'm determined to keep chipping away, year after year, and it's a skill I'm determined to learn for myself.

PLANTING

So, now our field is prepared, how do we get the seed into the ground – variously known as seeding, planting or drilling? It should come as no surprise that things have progressed since the biblical days of scattering by hand (though I can still be found doing this most years to patch up a muddy area in a grass field or a bit I've missed in an arable field – it's good to keep grounded).

Seed comes onto our farm in 500kg or 1000kg bags. Most farmers buy seed, or treat their own saved seed from harvest, with a seed 'dressing' – a chemical coating. I can choose what sort of a dressing I want applied to my crop; some are micronutrients which are thought to speed up the germination of the seed and its early growth. Some are fungicides, which protect the seedling from diseases in the early stage of its life; and some are insecticides which the growing plant absorbs to defend itself against predatory insects. The idea of such dressings is to give our plants the best chance of a good start in life and to reduce unnecessary losses, using very small quantities compared to the use of a crop sprayer applying it as an aerosol at a later date. And as the seedling absorbs the dressing as it germinates, it's also immediately effective.

The basic principle of the 'seed drill' is a hopper mounted above either tines or discs, towed by a tractor, which open a slot in the earth for the seed to drop into, before covering the slot back over with soil, sealing the seed in its bed. Good seed-to-soil contact is needed to ensure that germination is high and this is why a fine seed bed is traditionally important: dry, cloddy conditions will leave many seeds in large air pockets with no motivation to sprout and grow. Conversely, seeds forced into very wet soils are more likely to rot than they are to thrive. The seed drill knows how fast the tractor is moving, and either a pneumatic device or an air fan transfers the seed from the hopper through flexible pipes to the disc or tine at a steady rate, ensuring an even seed distribution and neat rows. This is important, as crops which are too thickly planted will counterintuitively yield less than those which are drilled at the correct density, as too many plants too close together will out-compete each other for light, space and nutrients, as well as being more likely to harbour disease in their over-thick canopies.

I calibrate my seed drill for every individual crop, but also every variety within that crop, as they all have different characteristics. It's a point of pride to make sure that each batch of seed is calibrated to a high degree of accuracy – but also good economics; if you're even five per cent out, that adds up over a large area. Different crops have very different drilling rates: wheat might be sown at 150–200kg/ha; oilseed rape at 4–5kg/ha. Much depends on the date (the later the drilling, the more seed you may choose to plant as conditions deteriorate) but also the soil conditions. A perfect tilth requires less seed than a poor seedbed, and in some years it's just not possible to do a perfect job. These crops also subsequently yield very differently; on our farm a 200kg/ha investment of wheat seed might return nine tonnes of wheat per hectare at harvest; our 5kg of rapeseed perhaps 3.5t/ha. You speculate to accumulate, after all!

Drilling is the task in which I take the most pride. Many farmers will tell you that harvest is their highlight, but I take greater satisfaction driving into a bare field in the morning, and driving back out again in the evening having planted the promise of new life for the coming year. It can be nerve-wracking, though. Any mistakes are hidden until the seedlings start to break cover some weeks later, and are then plain for all to see for the next twelve months! As a self-taught operator, in my first year I made the error of not realising there was a delay between dropping the drill in the ground and the seed actually entering the soil. As a result, every single pass of the drill that year (and there were thousands across dozens of fields) left an empty patch of seedless ground which would have been knowingly observed by all my farming neighbours as they passed. Worse, at that time one of the farms we worked was directly under the flight path of East Midlands Airport, which I realised to my great embarrassment when I flew from there that winter. My mistake was visible to literally 20,000 feet, and all the 4.2 million holidaymakers who peered out the windows as they neared the ground that year. When I flew again that spring, I kept my eyes on my book.

As with an elite athlete or musician, practising any repetitive task hour after hour, day after day, week after week, leads to a certain element of skill, and so it is that, after many thousands of hours of operating farm machinery of all types, I'm pretty handy in a field, even if I do say so myself (would only anyone cared: it's somewhat less compelling to watch than London 2012 or the Last Night of the Proms). When we get familiar with any task, it just comes naturally; in tasks like cultivation, drilling or harvest, you can almost feel the ground beneath the machine, easily compensate for hills or curves, and sense through your seat when something is wrong, or from the slightest change in the tone reaching your ears. When I milked cows, I never did it often enough to get good at it, which meant it took me an hour longer than everybody else, no matter how much I applied myself. But with arable operations, when I might spend twelve hours a day, seven days a week, for a month straight, doing the same thing, you rapidly develop a muscle memory which instantly switches back on even a year later when you come back to do the same jobs again. You also get completely used to the rolls and bumps of every field, and find yourself compensating for them seconds before you cross them (like a budget Jedi), especially useful when doing a job like spraying, with a 24-metre boom stretched out delicately behind you.

Those who spend all their working lives around livestock develop similar intuition and can tell if an animal is sick or stressed just from the set of its back or angle of its ears; they can anticipate what it might do a second before it does it and react accordingly. You certainly learn about the zones of flight and blind spots which they have to enable you to better understand how to safely and compassionately handle them.

Reversing with a trailer is one of the basic skills you learn rapidly on any farm, and most farmers can go backwards as easily as they can go forwards! I do remember one of the proudest moments of my school years (betraying perhaps the fact that I was hardly a sporting sensation) was the day I had to reverse a minibus with attached trailer around a corner because my teacher had made such a hash of it as the class watched on for about twenty minutes. As a farmer's son, it was a piece of cake!

One of the most dazzling demonstrations of skill you'll witness in the food chain is to watch practiced hands picking fruit or veg in the horticultural sector. The speed with which they work is remarkable, able to pick as much as 30kg of soft fruit an hour, and to do that all day, five or six days a week, through the harvest season. (This is some forty-five per cent more than their British colleagues were able to manage – those who were willing to try – when measured in the summer of 2020 when, due to Covid-19, more domestic pickers were required.[12])

For decades, membership of the European Union has meant the vast majority of these workers have come as migrant labour

---

12 'Britain's fruit farmers hanker for return of foreign pickers', *The Sunday Times*, 23 August 2020.

from Eastern Europe, travelling to the UK for three or four months, working hard, and returning home with a good wage to show for their labours. (Contrary to popular belief, everyone is paid at least the national living wage, but bonuses for hitting piecework targets would take most earnings far beyond this.) Most of them returned, to the same farms, year after year. The end of freedom of movement with our exit from the EU has seen this longstanding relationship broken, with the pickers considered to be 'unskilled labour' not worthy of our jobs. But farm labour is far from unskilled. Just because it doesn't require an associated university degree or command a six-figure salary does not mean that the jobs, manual or otherwise, being carried out to produce your food aren't incredibly intricate to perform and require years of experience to do well. Most farmers and farm workers by necessity possess a wide variety of (usually undocumented) abilities from engineering and plumbing to veterinary skills and agronomy. It's one of the travesties of our modern society that many of the tasks most beneficial to the public body as a whole (from working the land to caring for the elderly to serving in our armed forces) are those least well regarded and least well remunerated. The challenge of sourcing sufficient labour is one of the major issues facing British growers in the years to come; in 2020, vast quantities of produce rotted in the fields for lack of hands to pick it. We can only hope that government alters its policies to allow more of this food to reach our plates in future, or risks seeing even more of our fresh produce imported from abroad.

As soon as the field is drilled, it'll be rolled by another tractor towing a set of unfolding hydraulic rolls sporting a hundred or so individual profiled roller rings which leave the field surface looking a bit crinkled. There are several reasons for this. Primarily, we're looking to conserve soil moisture for seed germination, and rolling the surface after drilling lightly compresses it and stops excessive evaporation in the sun and wind. It also helps ensure better seed-to-soil contact; again, for better germination. A rolled surface is also more difficult for one of our primary pests, slugs, to penetrate and eat the seeds before they can grow, and provides less humps and hollows for them to hide in during the day, aiding birds in finding and eating them. It also pushes rocks beneath the surface to reduce the danger they pose to the combine harvester's cutting blades come next summer.

We drill different crops at different times, and some are more forgiving than others. Oilseed rape must generally be sown in early August to ensure a successful crop and establish itself ahead of pests and frequent September dry spells. Winter barley is a September-sown crop at its best, while winter wheat most likes to be planted in October and November, but can be drilled as late as February. Winter beans, similarly, are happiest planted in November or December but can go in the ground much later. You'll also note the use of the word 'winter', for arable crops not only have many different varieties but also two major sub-groups: winter and spring.

Historically, crops were planted in the spring, which allowed livestock to graze the residue from the previous year's harvest over the winter, adding manure to the soil and keeping the weed burden low in the following crop. In the past, oats were also a much larger part of the national harvest due to the importance of horses to both agriculture and transport. In the twentieth century, changes in modern farming techniques – in particular, the invention of plant protection products (PPPs) – and a revolution in plant breeding have, however, led to a situation where most arable crops are now planted in the autumn and early winter, and wheat has become by far our largest national crop. The benefit of this is that winter crops, in the ground for longer and able to establish deeper root systems and more leaf area, are generally able to yield significantly more than spring crops, but require the cold of winter to enable 'vernalisation'; that is, the ability to flower in the spring. Winter varieties cannot be sown in spring (with very few exceptions) and vice versa.

Spring cropping windows for all crops are generally late February to early April. If we take spring versus winter barley, harvest will likely be in mid-August as opposed to mid-July on my farm, so you can see that spring crops grow incredibly fast. Despite being in the ground perhaps five fewer months than winter varieties, they harvest only a month later. The big risk of spring crops is that the ideal planting window is narrow and, if as a result of bad weather you cannot plant, there's no second chance for the year, and, in a time of drought, their shallower roots generally leave them more vulnerable. However, despite yielding less than winter crops, they also cost less to grow as they require fewer inputs of fertiliser and PPPs.

Ironically, the wheel is beginning to turn back towards how things used to be when it comes to spring cropping, as more farmers look to incorporate grazing livestock back into their rotations. Spring crops across at least some of the farm are one way to achieve this, as a grazeable 'cover crop' of deep-rooting legumes and herbs, or perhaps stubble turnips, can be established in the autumn with the intention of feeding cattle or sheep outdoors through the winter. Come February or March, the ground is cultivated and a spring crop planted for harvest which will experience the benefit of better natural weed control and the fertiliser inherent in the livestock manure deposited across the field. In this way a farmer can improve the health of their soil and in effect achieve two crops from a single field in one year: both livestock and arable. With the reduction in synthetic inputs the following spring crop would require, this points back towards a lower carbon, more sustainable way of farming than has perhaps become the norm in recent decades. One might even think that the farmers of the past knew what they were about! This is certainly something I'm now looking to incorporate more on our farm in future, an added bonus being that it breaks up the planting workload by spreading the year's drilling across two seasons, rather than compressing it all into the autumn.

For arable farmers, autumn is our busiest season. Harvest, yes, is a frantic time when all too often we race against the weather to cut our crops before rain or high winds. But the modern combine harvester is an absolutely remarkable machine with enormous capacity to 'get on' and clear a field of crop at speed. With one pass, its job is complete. As we've seen, establishing the following crop is a much more involved process involving multiple actions – none of them fast!

In a good day I can plough perhaps eight hectares (eight rugby pitches) and disc or drill perhaps twenty. For some farmers this would be more like an hour's work, for there's huge variety in machinery and field size across different farms. Smaller fields on more fragmented farms such as ours are less efficient. They are also generally less productive, as yields invariably drop around the edges of fields (the 'headland') by around twenty-five per cent due to issues such as overshadowing by trees, grazing by rabbits or compaction from the turning of machinery at the ends of each run. The drive for greater efficiency, coupled with the mechanisation of agriculture after the Second World War (and the subsequent increase in size of that machinery over the decades) thus saw the loss of many hedgerows and walls on farms across the country, including ours, where old maps show many of our fields now much larger than was once the case, with more trees once sprinkled across them, which were perhaps subsequently felled to remove what were at the time perceived as obstacles.

I have mixed feelings about this. While it gives me the chills to think of the many miles of hedgerow and wall lost to previous decades, with all their associated history, habitat and heritage, were my farm today to be in the same form as it was a century ago, it would be unfarmable in the modern sense. The efficiency of such tiny fields, designed for the horse and ox, would be uneconomical in the modern world of commodity agriculture. Important too to remember that farmers such as my grandfather were not acting in a vacuum or in secret; governments, both during the war and after, encouraged and even incentivised farmers to rationalise their holdings and boost production. And yes, even gave out honours for doing so! But today, things are very different. It would be illegal for me to remove one of my hedges or walls, and for many years farmers have in fact been incentivised to once again replace those same hedges that were lost in previous generations – such are the perversions of public policy.

The system of crop establishment I've described so far in this chapter represents a very traditional and reliable approach to seed bed preparation which would be familiar to generations of farmers the world over, and it's how we've done it at home for as long as anyone can remember – it works. But, increasingly, British farmers are evolving away from this traditional method towards what is hoped is a simpler, cheaper and – potentially – more sustainable means of establishing crops. Although it's not a new concept, 'direct' or 'minimum tillage' drilling is becoming increasingly popular as a way to improve margins on many farms by cutting out some of the expensive mechanical processes outlined above. At its most ambitious, it seeks to do away with the cultivations described in this chapter and allows the farmer to sow seed directly into crop stubble with big implications for fuel usage, time expenditure and – as I'll explain in greater detail later – the environmental issues which can arise from cultivations, including erosion and soil carbon emissions.

Such practices aren't just a case of buying a new piece of machinery, though; it requires a wholesale change in approach towards what is referred to as 'regenerative agricultural principles', a somewhat amorphous term to which different people attach different emphasis. But, in general, 'regen ag' points towards a mindset of improvement which is increasingly taking root in the soul of British agriculture. This concept posits that healthier soil leads to healthier plants and animals and, by extension, more productive and environmentally beneficial farming systems which require fewer synthetic inputs. The fundamentals of the concept are sound: taking better care of the soil, increasing crop diversity and introducing a greater role for livestock, organic manures and even trees and hedges. These are the basics of traditional mixed farming, at which Britain has always excelled. If, in recent decades, many farmers have been encouraged or even forced into adhering to the dictates of the market economic system in which we exist and have turned their hands to 'specialisation' to the detriment of our traditional mixed farming principles, we can hardly be blamed. For many years we have been urged always to produce more, cut costs, employ fewer staff – all while real incomes from farming decreased as food became ever more globalised and devalued as a commodity. In this way, many farms became devoid of livestock and were instead devoted to high-input high-output arable or horticultural production with a strong reliance on artificial inputs. As we are finally learning as a society, a race to the bottom on costs rarely pays dividends when it comes to our interactions with the natural world. Regenerative farming is nothing new; in many ways it harks back to 'how things used to be'. But as we move forward, good practice such as this must be supported financially when the sustainable thing to do is not necessarily the most profitable thing to do.

What does it look like in practice? There are no hard and fast guidelines, but reduced cultivations are a core principle for many farms, along with fast-growing 'cover crops' which are generally planted immediately after harvest directly into the stubble with the intention that their root systems do the work of mechanical cultivations in preparing the ground for the following (usually spring) crop, creating a friable surface layer which seeds can be comfortably slotted directly into. It's also thought that cover crops have the ability to 'fix' soil nutrients in place, which might otherwise be 'leached' by rain into watercourses. Advocates generally press that soil should never be left bare and exposed to the elements, but always be covered by organic matter – 'soil armour'. This, in turn, feeds the soil biology which boosts the resilience of the soil biome itself, leading to better water infiltration but also drought tolerance as organic matter concentrations in the soil increase, thus raising soil carbon levels. When taken in conjunction with wider crop rotations – including livestock or at least the addition of organic manures – the aim is that an increasingly healthy soil requires fewer costly synthetic inputs and even improves its productivity as a result in a virtuous, sustainable cycle which seeks to shift farming from the 'chemical age' of the past seventy years towards the 'biological age'. At its most ambitious, it even seeks to reintroduce trees into our food production landscape – 'agroecology' – rather than keeping them mostly to the margins, to harness what are seen by some as their beneficial characteristics in a regenerative, 'agroecological' farming framework.

With these manifest benefits, why am I not already adopting regenerative agriculture on my farm? Well, in many ways, I am: as a mixed farm we already enjoy the benefits of livestock in our rotation, and for some years have been attempting to reduce our cultivations to the extent possible, as well as experiment with cover crops and reduced synthetic input use. But there's no such thing as a free lunch, and each farm has its own unique challenges of soil type, terrain, competing interests and finance. Regen ag is a toolbox of options from which each farmer can and does draw, but I believe should be seen more as an evolution than a revolution in how we conduct ourselves in Britain. Moving at speed towards a purist interpretation of these options has – for many farms – resulted in high initial costs and reductions in yield and profit, costs which many farms are unable to bear and which sap short-term enthusiasm. I believe that the regenerative agriculture journey is an exciting path along which British farmers are only just beginning, each at their own pace. It's no silver bullet to the issues we face in food sustainability, but is one part of a larger challenge with which I as a farmer am keen to wrestle.

PLANT PROTECTION PRODUCTS

My farm is classed as a 'conventional' as opposed to an 'organic' farm. The latter, if not the former, is a term you are no doubt familiar with. A conventional farm is one which utilises artificial inputs such as nitrogen fertilisers and PPPs – more commonly referred to as pesticides. Organic farms, as you might imagine, attempt to operate with greatly reduced inputs of this type – although it's a common misconception that no pesticides are used on organic crops, or that no antibiotics are used on organic livestock. In fact, with the rise of regenerative farming principles, the conventional/organic binary is becoming increasingly unhelpful as a means to describe British farming in the twenty-first century, with many farms operating as a hybrid of the two, with the best of organic practice being adopted by their conventional peers. (One cannot simply self-identify as an organic farmer, however; there are strict certification procedures administered by official organic bodies to which an organic farm must be a member, requiring annual inspections and strict enforcement of organic rules.)

What are PPPs? They're substances used to control pests, weeds and diseases in growing crops and help ensure that we have a good supply of safe, high quality, affordable food. They contain at least one 'active substance' with one or more of the following aims: to protect plants or plant products against pests or diseases either before or after harvest, to influence the life processes of plants, to preserve plant products, and to destroy or prevent the growth of undesired plants or parts of plants. An active substance is defined as 'any chemical, plant extract, pheromone or micro-organism that has action against pests, or on plants, parts of plants, or plant products'.[13]

Essentially, a PPP is anything applied to our crops which affects their development, and is not necessarily a 'chemical'. Our food crops compete with 30,000 species of non-food plants, 10,000 species of insect pests and countless diseases. It's estimated that without the use of PPPs our ability to produce food would be reduced by at least one third[14], to add to the huge amounts of food waste already present in our food system. PPPs reduce unnecessary crop losses and improve productivity.

In the UK, the vast majority of farmed land is conventional. In 2019, of 17.5m hectares, only 485,000 hectares were under certified organic production – with sixty-three per cent of that permanent grass pasture. Only eight per cent (39,000 hectares) was under organic cereal production, compared to 3.2m hectares of conventionally farmed cereals.[15] I have huge respect for organic farmers who – in forgoing the majority of pesticides and fertilisers available to me – frankly have a tougher time of producing

13 'Pesticides', European Commission website.

14 'What we do', Crop Protection Association website.

15 Department for Environment, Food & Rural Affairs, *Organic farming statistics United Kingdom 2019*, 2020, 19pp.

profitable outcomes. That the preponderance of organic land is grass for raising livestock demonstrates the even greater difficulties inherent in organic arable. They rely to a much greater extent on a more diverse and widely spaced crop rotation, with more incorporation of grass and livestock as well as fertility building legumes (known as 'green manures') sandwiching 'cash crops' such as organic cereals or vegetables. They may also grow more than one crop in a field at a time ('polycultures' or 'companion cropping') in order that, perhaps, one leafy and low-growing crop suppresses weeds so that the other can grow upwards more strongly in a mutually beneficial manner – increasingly staples of the regen ag movement. But, as a rule, organic farming also requires greater use of cultivations and mowing/topping of fields to control weed populations, and therefore more expenditure of diesel fuel. (Minimal cultivations are highly reliant on herbicides to create a stale seed bed, often to kill the cover crops which are an important element of regenerative practices. Min-till organic is considered by some to be the holy grail of sustainable arable agriculture, but represents a huge practical challenge.)

As I've said, pesticides and antibiotics are available to organic farmers. With pesticides, the difference is that they must be 'natural' extracts as opposed to the synthetic active ingredients in conventional PPPs – though being natural does not necessarily make them non-toxic in the environment. Many antibiotics are common between conventional and organic farms, the main difference being that the 'withdrawal period' (imposed to ensure medicine residues have cleared an animal's system before its meat or milk enters the human food chain) is lengthened from conventional requirements, generally to twice the manufacturer's recommendations. Evidence does indicate, however, that organic farms do utilise lower volumes of antibiotics than their conventional counterparts.

Why isn't organic more common? Without access to the range of agrochemicals and fertilisers from which conventional farmers benefit, organic crop yields in highly productive countries such as Britain are generally about half what they could be[16], while milk yields are down by a third. But the data suggests that premium payments, combined with generally lower input costs, do make up this shortfall allowing organic farmers to hold their own financially against their conventional counterparts in most sectors. There is some truth that there's a certain amount of institutional scepticism and stereotyping about organic farming in the wider agricultural community, though this can be over-exaggerated. Ultimately, organic produce costs more to the consumer, and its niche position is a reflection of supply and demand. Most consumers are acutely price-sensitive, which can often make it difficult to nudge them to purchase high quality British versus often cheaper imported goods; to convince them to then spend an additional amount on organic is usually a step too far, and so it remains the preserve of the generally wealthier in society who can afford to shop with their conscience as they see it. Organic production is broadly accepted to have a lower environmental impact per hectare of production, though the data on a per unit of produce basis (with more land being required to produce the same quantity of output as conventional) is more uncertain. Uncertain again is evidence that organic food is fundamentally 'healthier' than non-organic, though it's somewhat stronger for certain products than others. In the round, organic farmers face a huge host of challenges and thoroughly deserve the premium they receive for the food they produce. If nothing else, it's telling that – as we've seen – many of the principles of organic production (which are the principles of

16 Soffe, R.J. and Lobley, M. (eds), *The Agricultural Notebook*, 21st edition, Wiley Blackwell, 2021, p. 652.

traditional pre-war farming) are being so enthusiastically 'rediscovered' and adopted by a new generation of conventionally based regenerative farmers. They must be doing something right.

Yet consumer sensitivity to the organic price point is the same issue – though more acute – faced by food production as a whole in the UK: the true costs of our high-quality food are not reflected in the shelf price, meaning that farmers are often selling **below** the costs of production and as a consequence are too frequently in dire financial straits. It's a political priority of governments around the world to ensure food is as cheap as possible (with often hugely distorting effects on economies), and the power of the major retailers in the UK specifically keeps food artificially cheap as they outcompete each other to drive prices ever lower. This is an important issue with implications for the whole of society to which we will return later.

The PPPs I use come in a number of broad categories: herbicides, insecticides, fungicides, molluscicides and plant growth regulators.

Herbicides control weed populations in a growing crop. In any farming system it's important to control weeds which compete with crops for light, space, water and nutrients. Herbicides can either be non-selective (they kill almost any plant they contact) or selective (they will only kill or impact specific types of plant and can be used to remove certain weeds from a growing crop without its damage).

Insecticides are used to target insect pests of crops; these pests may either damage the crop by consuming it or by spreading diseases which they carry. Some also lay larvae in crops which cause damage on emergence.

Fungicides are used to treat plant diseases which are generally carried on the wind or are present in the soil or leaf trash from a previous crop. Some diseases are untreatable once contracted, so some fungicides have preventative properties and are applied to avoid initial infection by common diseases.

Molluscicides are used where necessary to control slug populations in the early life of crops.

Plant growth regulators (PGRs) are used to both control the height of crops (which can fall flat if they become too tall) and their leaf canopy in order that the most efficient level of photosynthesis can be achieved, thereby maximising yield.

Until 2020 the UK was party to EU regulation on the use of PPPs, regulations which we have inherited since the end of the transition period. The European Food Safety Authority (EFSA) evaluates every active substance for safety before it can be used in the food chain. Each product must have been proven safe for human and animal health, and to not have unacceptable effects on the environment.[17] Such approvals are granted for a limited period so that re-evaluations can occur periodically. The key issue has been to ensure that Minimum Residue Levels (MRLs) of active ingredients in foodstuffs are strictly set so that there is a maximum safe level which is legally tolerated.[18]

In this work, the EU operates to the 'precautionary principle' whereby the burden of proof lies with the developers of an active ingredient to prove that there are no negative consequences to either human or animal health, or the environment, from their product. To quote an EU report: 'A precautionary approach captures the idea that regulatory intervention may still be legitimate, even if the supporting evidence is incomplete or speculative and the economic costs of regulation are high. Better safe than sorry.'[19]

The EU approach to PPP regulation therefore operates in a hazard-based framework (asking the question '**Can** this cause

17 'Approval of active substances', European Commission website.

18 'Maximum residue levels', European Commission website.

19 Science for Environment Policy, *The precautionary principle: decision-making under uncertainty*, Future Brief, Issue 18, 2017, 24pp.

harm?') rather than a risk-based framework ('What is the **likelihood** of harm occurring?'). To put it another way, if you took a hazard-based approach to swimming in the sea, you would likely rule it out on the basis that you **could** be attacked by a shark; that if this happened it would be very serious; and therefore the hazard is high. However, most people would take a risk-based approach to this decision, reasoning that the **likelihood** of being attacked by a shark is incredibly low and therefore the risk is acceptable.

My point is this: within the EU we adhered to some of the world's toughest legislation on PPP regulation and MRLs, legislation which we have adopted. There has always been an undercurrent of understandable concern in society and the media about the use of PPPs in food production, and scarcely a year goes by without a major news story seeking to cultivate renewed fears over their application, often based on very fragmentary evidence or none at all. In this country farmers have access to an ever-shrinking toolbox of PPPs as product authorisations are periodically reviewed and deemed no longer satisfactory under the precautionary principle. There are – as of 2019 – seventy-two pesticides legally allowed for food production in the United States which are banned in the EU and UK.[20] MRLs in US grapes are up to 1000x those allowed in the UK, while those for apples are 400x higher.[21] This is considered acceptable by regulators (and most consumers) in the US. The same reasoning lies behind the outlawing of biotechnology in European food production (though not European food) which is otherwise commonplace around the globe.

Whether I believe the EU or the US system is more desirable or defensible from a scientific viewpoint, what I hope to convey is that the regulatory system utilised in the EU (and adopted by the

20 Donley, N., 'The USA lags behind other agricultural nations in banning harmful pesticides', *Environmental Health* 18 Article 44, 2019.

21 'UK vs US farming: what's the difference?', *Which?*, 14 July 2020.

UK Health & Safety Executive, HSE, from 2021[22]) is among the strictest in the world. If I, as a farmer, am using a PPP in your food chain, you can be assured that there are no credible scientific grounds for concern. Whether you, as the consumer, make the personal decision that you still prefer the concept of reduced-pesticide organic agriculture, then that is fine by me – just please choose British produce!

Of course, it's not always so simple. For example: in the UK we are unable to produce sufficient quantities of the high-protein milling wheat which bakers demand for the consistent production of the classic British loaf. As a result, most bread is a blend of UK wheat produced under UK laws, and imported wheat produced under different regulatory circumstances and utilising, for example, PPPs that it would be illegal for British farmers to use. This is a constant source of irritation to farmers who see this as unfair competition whereby we are held to a higher standard than our foreign competitors. If such products are deemed damaging either to the environment or human health if used in the UK, why do we implicitly encourage their use abroad by purchasing grain (and many other foodstuffs) produced through their use? This is an example of the hypocrisy present at all levels of our economy, whether it's importing foodstuffs grown using supposedly hazardous pesticides, steel produced with a huge built-in carbon footprint or clothes sewn in factories using child labour. All too often, practices which would be intolerable within our own borders are considered acceptable elsewhere in the world – out of sight, out of mind.

What PPPs enable me to do is to produce a greater volume of food, more efficiently, for any given area, thus optimising my resource use efficiency and lowering the carbon footprint of each

22 'Regulating pesticides in the UK after Brexit', Health and Safety Executive website.

unit of food produced as a result. The greater number of conventional PPPs available give me the ability to combat more weeds, pests and diseases more effectively and reduce the amount of food waste I generate on-farm; that is, crops which had the potential to produce yield which was subsequently lost. In a world where people still go hungry, and in which the population is expected to rise by another three billion by 2050, I believe my ability as a farmer to produce the greatest amount of food that I can, utilising safe and environmentally benign PPPs, is a positive thing. But of course, this must be balanced carefully with my environmental obligations, and does not free the rest of the food chain (including you) from the responsibility to reduce waste: the food with the greatest carbon footprint is that which is thrown away uneaten. It's estimated that 9.5 million tonnes of food is wasted by retailers, the hospitality sector and households in the UK every year: this is a moral scandal.[23]

However, for me PPP use is usually a last resort. My grass fields very rarely receive any PPPs as I would generally prefer to use organic methods of weed control, such as topping or pulling by hand, due to their being more effective and cheaper in most cases than chemical alternatives. Indeed, I have grass fields I can honestly say have never received any PPP or synthetic fertiliser. So parts of my farm I farm organically, and very happy I am about it too. For me it's about having the right system in the right field. Indeed, as we've seen, there's much to be relearned from good organic practice, especially when it comes to wider rotations and the role of livestock. As I've alluded to, it's true that in the past half century farmers around the world have come to rely too much on chemical tools to drive short-term yield and profits, while being encouraged by both 'the markets' and government policy to do so. Much of

---

23 'UK households waste 4.5m tonnes of food each year', *The Guardian*, 24 January, 2020.

the good, solid agricultural practice which is by necessity at the core of most organic farming has been clouded by two generations of farmers told by chemical companies that innovation had finally broken the need to adhere to it; that science had finally triumphed over nature. This has proven (predictably) to be false, and certainly on my farm (and many others) I will spend much of my career fixing that which has been degraded, whether in biodiversity or soil health.

However, that the needle was too far in one direction for our long-term good does not mean that the concept of chemical use in agriculture is inherently flawed; pesticides have a valuable place in our food system, but we are now learning to use them more sparingly and with a reduced impact on the environment. Many of the products developed in less understanding times and used by my grandfather have been banned for decades (and rightly so) as have the methods used to apply them; such evolution is common in many industries. But we must be wary of overreacting to past errors by adopting an overly critical attitude to tools such as modern PPPs and in so doing stumbling into the realm of unintended consequences.

A case in point is a group of PPPs called neonicotinoids, meaning literally 'new nicotine-like insecticides', chemically modelled on naturally occurring nicotine – an authorised PPP in organic farming systems. 'Neonics' are highly toxic to invertebrates, and were widely used in EU agriculture from 2005[24], primarily as a seed dressing. We used them in particular on oilseed rape; as we've discussed, the growing plant then absorbs the active substance as it grows through its own shell and is protected from the pests which might prey on it at the earliest and most delicate stage of its life. For oilseed rape, this pest is the Cabbage Stem Flea Beetle (CSFB),

---

24 'Neonicotinoids', European Commission website.

tiny black insects with powerful back legs (enabling them to jump quite literally like a flea) which blow in on the wind in their swarms and devour whole crops of young oilseed plants quite literally overnight. Those crops which survive often find themselves host to dormant larvae which then eat their way out – *Alien* style – in the spring, killing the plant. For the early part of my farming career, neonic seed dressings kept my crops safe and CSFB was not something to which I paid much mind.

However, in 2013 the European Commission banned the use of neonics in oilseed rape over concerns that the toxin was still present in the crop during its flowering season the following spring. The fear was that bees and other beneficial pollinators (which we rely upon to fertilise many of our food crops) were being harmed by residual neonics when foraging in the bright yellow rapeseed flowers; that we farmers were inadvertently killing one of our most important assets. There were also concerns about the persistence of the chemical in the soil and the potential for it to be absorbed by other flowering plants.

Ultimately, the evidence was inconclusive as to whether this was genuinely the case in the 'real world' as opposed to in laboratory tests, but the EU's strict hazard-based approach to PPP regulation meant that from 2014 rapeseed growers were left without this vital protection for their crops. In fairness, many farmers were willing to accept the loss of neonics in rape due to the extreme seriousness of the allegations against it, and the large areas of the crop which were grown. And at first, most farms remained unaffected. Yet, slowly but surely, and spreading like a plague from east to west, by 2018 the CSFB menace had reached my fields in Leicestershire.

It's difficult to describe your livelihood evaporating before your eyes. As a farmer, I'm used to my income being hugely dependent upon and exposed to the vagaries and vicissitudes of the weather, disease and pests, over much of which I have little control. But to watch a swarm of flea beetle move into a young crop of rapeseed is like watching footage of locusts moving into a farmer's crop in Africa. The speed and destruction of it is on another level compared to what I'm used to in Britain. They travel on the wind, and thrive in hot, dry conditions – exactly those in which the delicately emerging rape crop struggles to grow, and exactly those which are now becoming increasingly frequent in September as the rape emerges.

So, in the absence of the neonic dressing, what can I do to save my crop? I could do nothing, and watch a significant investment in time and money be shredded in their tiny, uncaring jaws. Or I can spray the crop with a foliar-applied insecticide from my crop sprayer. We'll return to the mechanics of this shortly, but the upshot of it is this: one hectare of treated seed equates to approximately fifty-eight square metres of applied chemical, so low is the volume required to coat each seed; one hectare of **sprayed** crop equates (clearly) to the full $10,000m^2$ of that hectare, most of it falling wasted on either leaf or bare soil and not the target beetle.

There are very few insecticides left in the UK's armoury as a result of the precautionary principle. The main survivor is a class known as pyrethroids, which have become over-utilised because of the lack of alternatives. As a result, many of the main target pests have become increasingly resistant to them due to natural selection (CSFB included) which means their efficacy is low. In turn, this means (out of desperation) many farmers will use multiple applications of pyrethroid sprays in an attempt to control the beetles eating their crops. And although they may not kill the pesky flea beetle, they **will** kill many of the beneficial insects co-existing in that crop. In a further ironic twist, it's also legal to apply a neonic **spray** to the crop. Unfortunately, this is far less effective than the seed dressing, and does not have the persistency to protect the crop from successive waves of pests.

So, as a result of a well-intentioned attempt to protect pollinators from potential harm by banning a chemical seed treatment, oilseed rape growers across Europe are now left in the crazy position of utilising seventy-two times the amount of insecticide, as an untargeted foliar spray which is unable to distinguish between invertebrate friend and foe, and doing so multiple times with often poor results. To do this, farmers are having to use more diesel and more water in the sprayer. This is madness, and exactly what was warned would happen when the ban was first mooted. Yet, it was pushed through without a viable alternative control method in place, with devastating consequences both for insects and crops.

I spent the autumns of 2018 and 2019 locked in this grim cycle; the first year I hoped was an aberration; in the second year I halved the amount of oilseed rape I grew to reduce my risk, only to see that remaining area do even worse. Our yield dropped from an average of around 3.5t/ha in the years before 2018 to 1.5t/ha in 2019–20. Oilseed rape went from being one of our most profitable crops to a big entry of red ink in the ledger. As a result, in 2020 we dropped it entirely from our rotation – along with many other farmers. The national crop has dropped from 2.2m tonnes in 2017[25] to just over a million tonnes in 2020.[26] In fact, the UK has moved from being a net exporter of this valuable commodity to a net importer, with the imports (yes, you guessed it) coming from countries which still use neonic seed dressings: Australia, Canada, Ukraine – and even EU countries such as Poland, which have successfully applied for derogations to continue their use as a result

25 Department for Environment, Food & Rural Affairs, *Farming statistics – provisional crop areas, yields and livestock populations at June 2017 – United Kingdom*, 2017, 23pp.

26 Department for Environment, Food & Rural Affairs, *Farming Statistics – provisional arable crop areas, yields and livestock populations at 1 June 2020 United Kingdom*, 2020, 29pp.

of the perverse outcome described above. This raises the question of what we're hoping to achieve.

You might ask why British farmers continue to grow the crop under these circumstances. Some, especially in chillier northern climes, are still relatively unaffected. Others are attempting to grow their rape in innovative and experimental ways, using fertiliser planted alongside the seed to encourage rapid vigour or utilising appetising companion crops alongside the rape in the hope that CSFB eats the decoy instead of the crop. Still others are experimenting with grazing their rape with sheep over the winter in an attempt to eat the destructive larvae out of the stems before they emerge in the spring. Some even swear that by spraying their fields in livestock effluent or pig muck, the smell puts off the beetles. Plant breeders and scientists continue to search for non-chemical solutions. Some of these solutions work, some of the time. I can't but feel it's largely luck: what works for some one year, doesn't the next.

I stopped growing oilseed rape in large part because I could not justify the use of such large quantities of insecticide to produce a cash crop. It just didn't seem right. I will debate with anyone why I believe PPPs are an essential tool in the farmer's armoury to produce safe, high quality and affordable food. But insecticides are always the product I am most reluctant to use, and always the final resort after all other avenues have been utilised. Neonic seed dressings were introduced to avoid the sort of indiscriminate blanket spraying that their removal has brought back like a bad 1990s reboot. I, and many others, would suggest that their ban has created more problems than it's solved. This includes many commercial beekeepers, who struggle to find enough flowering crops in the spring to satisfy their hives now that so many farmers have stopped growing such a wonderful pollinator habitat. Certainly, I feel that my farm will lack its annual colour injection in future as I move from growing rapeseed to other, less valuable, crops. But I feel happier in myself that at least the decision has been made, and my environmental conscience is now clear.

One genuine issue around the sustainability of pesticide use concerns the 'resistance' outlined above; CSFB are not the only pest insects to have largely achieved it versus insecticides, while many weeds (such as the pernicious blackgrass mentioned at the start of this chapter) are also evolving to resist previously effective herbicides. Many would argue that resistance is indicative of the folly of attempting to control nature through chemical means; life finds a way. I would tend to agree that for too long many farmers have relied too heavily on chemical controls to support practices which have become too detached from traditional, cultural methods such as mixed farming: as a result some pests and weeds have been given the time and space to develop a significant element of immunity. I would refute that this is proof that PPPs have no place in 'real' farming: they are one vital strand in a sustainable system. But yes, some must relearn the ability not to lean so heavily upon them in future, while in the meantime we must find ways to deal with the problems we have created for ourselves.

Let us return to our drilled and rolled field, to which I'll be applying a 'pre-emergence' herbicide directly to the soil before the shoots begin to push through. This is the most effective means by which modern weed control sprays operate, essentially forming an invisible film through which any seedlings must grow at their most delicate. Non-target species (the crop) will be unaffected, while weeds will be killed or sufficiently stunted to allow them to be outcompeted and smothered by the crop. I will apply different PPPs to different crops, but also to different fields depending on the weeds I know from experience I will find there. Sometimes I wonder whether I really need to use these products, but I can assure you that wherever I might accidentally miss a patch, weeds rapidly outperform my crops and severely limit yield. It's not hard to spot a spray miss. An effective pre-emergence herbicide is perhaps the most important PPP application of the crop's life, and hopefully minimises expensive and yield-sapping complications further downstream by giving it an easy start. One spray at this stage may save several later.

Farmers apply PPPs through a crop sprayer, either towed behind or mounted on a tractor or with its own integrated engine and wheels. A sprayer is essentially a large water tank (mine is 3800 litres) with hydraulic booms which fold out to the sides to enable the farmer to cover a large area of ground with each pass (mine are twenty-four metres). Into the water tank, we apply our concentrated PPPs which are then heavily diluted to the appropriate level for application to our crop.

You'll be familiar with the sight of wheel tracks in arable fields – known as 'tramlines' in farm lingo, and famously seen in many a historical film set before tractors were invented! Once a crop is planted, these are the only parts of the field on which machinery will travel for the year, and if your sprayer has twenty-four-metre booms, the tramlines will be twenty-four metres apart; the rest of your machinery will also be bought to match this width. This ensures that as little crop is trampled as possible, and clearly the bigger the reach of your machinery, the faster you can complete any given job and the fewer tramlines (and trampled crop) you have. But on my farm, even twenty-four metres is more than big enough for some fields, hemmed in as they are by hedges, walls and woodland.

I'm only too aware that crop spraying is one of the most contentious activities carried out in modern farming, and I completely understand that to the casual observer it might seem like an excess of modern 'industrial' farming. Indeed, it is frequently characterised as such with varying degrees of informed misdirection, as when secretary of state at Defra, Michael Gove, famously (and to the irritation of his farming stakeholders) accused farmers of 'drenching [their fields] in chemicals'. It's certainly a stark phrase, but does not reflect the reality.

Most PPPs are applied at a volume between ten millilitres per hectare and two litres per hectare, diluted into either one hundred or two hundred litres of water per hectare. My most commonly used pre-emergence herbicide, for example, is applied at a rate of 0.6 litres per hectare, which means a total volume of concentrated PPP of around 0.06 millilitres per square metre. Such is the efficacy of modern PPPs that incredibly small volumes need be used.

Modern crop sprayers are also incredibly accurate; this is a combination of operator best practice and the technology available. As you can imagine, operating around the British weather can be very frustrating: generally speaking, PPPs cannot be applied less than two hours before rainfall, or onto already damp leaves. This means there are few mornings when dew does not rule out spraying, let alone impending rain. The ground must also be dry enough to carry the machine. Wind is usually the biggest factor limiting my ability to apply PPPs; I require still air to ensure the spray does not 'drift' onto non-target areas. Some applications, such as pre-emergence herbicides, actually **require** rain after application to activate them – but not too much, as that can damage the crop! Factoring in all these variables can mean that there are few days when there's an acceptable window for spraying. But on top of my weather-eye, I will always keep my sprayer boom as close to the ground or top of the crop as possible to further reduce drift. I also drive slowly, at the optimum speed so as not to create a vortex which will cause drift. I also have a selection of nozzles on my boom specific to different tasks or weather conditions; my primary nozzle set (of which there are seventy-two across the twenty-four metres) are optimised for low drift, and I can even add drift retardants to the spray mixture to further reduce it.

It's a requirement to have grass buffer-strips along all watercourses and minimum distances between the edge of a sprayed crop and features such as hedges; and some PPPs have bigger buffer requirements than others. All of this is intended to ensure our primary aim when applying pesticides, which is that it all goes where we intend and does not impact the wider environment. Modern sprayers are fitted with GPS and automatic nozzle shut-offs to ensure that there is never any overlap within the field; that the absolute minimum of PPP is used. I don't have this function, but as with many farm jobs, experience brings a steady eye and a quick hand! Exciting technology is even nearing the commercial stage which will actually spot individual weed plants among the crop and only activate each nozzle for as long as it will take to spray that single plant. Alternatively, small robots are in development which may soon traverse fields in groups and individually target weeds with either herbicide or an electric current, thus hopefully in the near future reducing our chemical use by an order of magnitude.

Have pesticides been overused in the past? Yes. Do British farmers employ best practice in their use today? Absolutely. Can the modern move toward more regenerative practices alongside new technologies greatly reduce their use? I believe so. Will they continue to be a vital strand of a sustainable food production system, at least for the foreseeable future? Certainly.

The exact date of crop establishment varies from year to year, largely as a result of the weather, but by the end of October we would hope to have most of our autumn sown crops in the ground. Within a fortnight we would hope to see the first green shoots emerge, and after three weeks would be basking in the glory of long straight rows of plants all exactly where we hoped they would be! This, however, is the point at which crops are most at risk of damage from one of my number one farming adversaries – slugs. Not the great big ones you might see in your garden or crossing a path, but teeny tiny ones which hide under stones or clods of earth during the day and come out at night to munch on the delicate green shoots. Some years the slug pressure can be extreme and you can watch a field go from brown to green and back again; other years you don't see a one. If slugs are present, they're controlled by spreading tiny solid pellets of molluscicide across the problem areas, much the same as you might use in your garden. Generally, this is done with a granule spinner attached to the back of a quad bike or similar small ATV. When a slug then happens across one of these pellets, it ingests it and subsequently dies. These pellets will survive a long time in the open before rain finally dissolves them, but in some years repeat applications are necessary: it's also in the wet years that slugs tend to be most active. The slug threat generally recedes as we move into winter and colder weather, and is anyway less acute once crops move beyond their early establishment phase and are able to survive a certain level of nibbling. One of the frequent jobs at this time of year is slug patrol with Ted and Toby: a good walk during the working day wrapped up in the righteous cause of crop protection.

So, our crop is now established and bedded down for the winter. One big challenge remains: the weather.

CLIMATE CHANGE

Farmers are famously obtuse about the weather. This is a criticism which, I think, is very fair and represents almost any farmer at any given moment in time. As you read this, I am no doubt looking up at the sky and tutting. But we have good cause. Consider spending your entire working life outdoors, and consider too your whole livelihood being dependent upon the predictable and benign actions of the clouds and winds under the heavens. This has been the lot of farmers for as long as there have been farms. There is no greater factor in whether we have a good or bad year. For many of you reading this, the weekly forecast may be more of passing interest than tangible concern; for farmers, it's the information by which we, or at least our crops and animals, live and die.

Some sectors are more insulated from the vagaries of the seasons than others, but nobody is immune. A mixed lowland arable and beef farm such as mine is at the more exposed end of the scale, but we are lucky at least not to be on the floodplain of any river. Recent years have seen many farms in low-lying areas submerged again and again (along with houses inexplicably but increasingly built in similar places) with terrible financial and ecological consequences. Essentially, the more you grow outdoors, the bigger your exposure to Mother Nature. The concept of indoor vertical farming is therefore very appealing (and would certainly reduce my stress levels) but not really feasible for anything except relatively small quantities of high-value crops such as herbs and salads. (Though there is now a floating vertical dairy farm in Rotterdam harbour, I'm told.)

For us, why does this matter? British farming has evolved over the centuries to take advantage of both our geography and our reasonably predictable and mild temperate maritime climate. In this sense, I take 'mild' to mean rarely too much of any one thing at a time and rarely to the extremes we see in other parts of the world. It's worth bearing in mind that London is of a more northerly latitude than Quebec, and Edinburgh more northerly than Moscow. Yet our existence as an island jutting into the Atlantic

Gulf Stream has always kept us from experiencing the extremes of heat and cold that they endure, while the epic droughts of Australia and wildfires of California are terrifying occurrences which we experience only vicariously through the international news.

Farms such as mine rely on warm, dry autumns, shading into late moisture, to establish our crops; sharp, cold winters to control our pests and diseases; warm, moist springs to give our crops the sunlight and moisture they need to grow; and hot, dry summers to enable us to cut our crops in peace. When this delicate balance moves out of kilter, it can have seriously adverse financial implications for farms. Hell; it can have seriously adverse implications for society as a whole, as can be seen throughout the great sweep of history with the rise and fall of civilisations too numerous to count, often on the whims of capricious weather gods. There's a reason the ancients prayed so hard to them.

Recent history too is busy with major weather aberrations which live long in the memory; extreme weather is not a uniquely modern phenomenon. I remember a July evening when I was fourteen when a thunderstorm of such huge intensity broke across the farm that for the first time in living memory our buildings were submerged in water – and we live atop a hill. We tried ineffectively to create a dam of straw bales around our harvested grain before it began to float out of the shed, and our dairy cattle were literally wading to their shoulders in their straw housing. Despite this, and the loss of electricity, they still needed milking that night with the help of the emergency generator once walls had been knocked down to release the water. Our grain I spent many days thereafter trying to dry. (To my surprise, this story was accepted as the reason I had not completed my French homework the next day; either Mr Brewster took pity on me, or admired what he considered to be an elaborate fabrication.)

But I can say with no equivocation that, from my position on the frontline of society's interaction with the weather, our climate is changing, and farming is an early casualty. When I first returned to the farm in 2009, and for some years thereafter, it was still possible to rely on the rhythms of the seasons that my father had inherited from his. You could predict to the week when the major changes would come, and our major operations would be planned around these. But my experience of the years since the mid-2010s have been of weather patterns becoming increasingly extreme.

In recent years, we farmed a local holding which ran through a shallow valley, some 150 hectares in all. One spring day, a freak thunderstorm moved through that valley, beginning and ending at the border with neighbouring farms. Hailstones the size of golf balls pummelled our crops, shredding them. The buildings on site were wrecked; vehicles were written off; branches were sheared from trees and sheep and wildlife who didn't find shelter were killed. It was a scene of the most appalling carnage of the type I did not think was possible in Britain; it was as if a twister had moved through the valley. At harvest, we were able to salvage about twenty per cent of the yield we would have expected had it not been for that ten minutes of climate hell. And, no, this being Britain and not Australia or the USA, we were not insured.

As a rule, autumn is now a washout, with rain which begins in late September and continues unabated into winter, which has lost its snow and frosts and become unrecognisably mild. The rain now seems finally to relent around late March, before the heavens launch into their now habitual drought which takes us into the summer, the only season seemingly still up for grabs: will the drought continue, or will we experience an early start to the autumn rains? Looking back only on 2020 (with Met

Office data stretching back to 1862), February was the wettest on record (with 237 per cent of average UK rainfall). We then experienced the sunniest (and fifth driest) spring on record, before experiencing the third hottest day ever recorded in the summer (the hottest being the year before). October then saw the wettest day ever recorded, with the month itself the fifth wettest ever.[27]

How does this affect the farms producing your food in practical terms? It doesn't just mean farmers with bad tans and wet clothes, though that is also often the case. We need dry weather at harvest to cut our crops; this isn't a 'nice to have', but an imperative: wet crops will not go through combine harvesters, and will soon begin to rot in the field. The same is true of forage crops for livestock: you cannot make hay if the sun is not shining, and that clearly has implications for the coming winter. In the autumn, seeding machinery will not plant seed into wet soil. So it was that the autumn of 2019 saw us fail to plant our crops for the first time ever; it wasn't until April that we subsequently were able to plant some spring crops, but the drought which followed until June (the third in three years) then burned away much that we had managed to drill, before a wet harvest added the sour cream to top off the already bitter cake. Indeed, in recent years early spring droughts have frequently made soil too hard to plant in, or too dry for seed to germinate.

Extreme wet conditions lead to livestock damaging the very grass upon which they graze, turning it to mud, while mild winters are harbingers of disease in both crops and animals. Droughts in recent years have led to the stressful sight of fields of grass turning pure brown as the sun beat down on them day after day, with our cattle grazing them to the flatness of a bowling green. In these

27 Met Office, 'A look back at 2020', 30 December 2020.

circumstances, additional feed is necessary, but many farmers found themselves without after a difficult hay season and a long winter. Extreme rainfall overwhelms rivers and field drainage systems, and machinery sinks up to its axles with little warning, causing huge difficulties to recover and damage to valuable soil structure, which is all too easily washed away by day after day of precipitation. Hard frosts are a valuable means of both controlling weeds and insect pests but also of allowing machinery to travel on fields to carry out vital tasks; but these are all too rare in my recent experience.

It's difficult to convey the feeling of helplessness you experience when the weather is against you; I certainly begin to feel very small, and realise that for all my planning, horsepower and modern technology, Mother Nature will still determine whether I succeed or fail. The autumn of 2019 was very tough to bear, with sheds full of seed going unplanted in fields cultivated in anticipation of drilling, but now utterly waterlogged. After any period of heavy rain, our fields need a couple of days to become workable, but the volumes we received that autumn and winter needed weeks to drain away, especially in the short cold days of that time of year. So extreme was the situation, that only two days after the birth of my first child that January, Ted, Toby and I were back on the tractor when an extremely narrow window of opportunity opened up. I have a very understanding wife, but nevertheless missed those irreplaceable early days.

Later that spring, the effort did not seem worth it, when so bad had the drought damage become to that particular field – which had struggled through the wet all winter – that I appeared on local news standing amidst my shrivelled and withered crop explaining what the **lack** of rain now meant for my financial future and the food produced from my fields. In fact, recent years have seen our farm repeatedly battered by the unfolding climate crisis; we have not had a good harvest since 2017 as a result of flood, drought and pests – many of which would be controlled by a Christmas-card-style winter. What's more, weather extremes wreak havoc with our wild flora and fauna: plants don't know whether they're coming or going when they start budding in the middle of a warm winter, while I've even been approached by wild animals crazed by thirst after the watercourses have dried up.

So as a farmer I am only too aware of the need for action when it comes to climate change, and as a farmer I am in the privileged position of being able to do something about this great challenge of our times.

British agriculture contributes ten per cent to our national greenhouse gas emissions.[28] This is a much smaller figure than frequently quoted in the media, which often prefers to use crude international averages which are much higher. Compare this with the twenty-seven per cent of emissions which come from transport; twenty-four per cent from energy; seventeen per cent from business; and fifteen per cent from residential emissions. When you consider that agriculture utilises more than seventy per cent of our land area in the UK and provides more than sixty per cent of our food – a rather important resource – that ten per cent seems to me a reasonable starting point. But – and despite farming's emissions having reduced by sixteen per cent from 1990 levels – we must do better, and in combatting climate change and moving toward a more sustainable food system every farm will have its part to play. Agriculture has the ability almost unique in the economy to act not only as a source of GHG emissions, but also as a sink – to be a part of the **solution** to climate change. It's in this spirit that the National Farmers Union (NFU) has committed its 55,000 members to the ambition of achieving net zero emissions

---

28 National Farmers' Union, *Achieving net zero: Farming's 2040 goal*, 2019, 12pp.

by 2040 – ten years earlier than the government's pledge for the wider economy. For me, the potential to embrace this challenge is empowering, exciting and important.

But how do we propose to go about it? As you might expect from such a huge challenge, the answer isn't straightforward. Perhaps we merely farm less in this country and thereby pollute less; simply turning more of our productive land over to nature – 'rewilding' – and in so doing also regenerate more of our own biodiversity? Or perhaps we could place greater emphasis on organic farming? Or plant vast areas of new trees to lock up atmospheric carbon? I would suggest that, although all of these approaches have their place, such binary solutions ignore the huge complexity of our food sustainability challenge. As demonstrated with my travails around oilseed rape and neonics, the danger is that we merely 'greenwash' our domestic policies while offshoring our environmental footprint and conscience abroad to nations with much lower environmental standards – in the same vein that we export our 'recycled' plastics to be burned, buried and dumped into the sea, out of sight, out of mind. Our future landscape will no doubt contain more wild spaces; more trees and more farms leaning closer to organic practice, but we mustn't be fooled by the siren calls of those who would suggest that any of those options are the single solution to our problems. I am a fan of the term 'sustainable intensification', with productive agriculture existing alongside ecological needs; a landscape-wide network of unfarmed but highly managed land which is wildlife friendly alongside productive fields. But what, then, do I hope to do to reduce my climate impact while still producing plentiful great British food?

These actions will fall into three broad categories: boosting productivity and reducing emissions; sequestering carbon; and investing in biofuels and renewable energy.

The first category covers a huge range of possibilities which will be different on every farm, to do more with less. As an arable farmer I can invest in more precision technology to further optimise my use of artificial inputs, whilst utilising more organic manures to improve soil health and structure. Perhaps I can further reduce my cultivations to cut fuel usage and increase soil carbon storage, or consider whether new crop varieties (potentially, in future, utilising biotechnology) may enable me to reduce my use of PPPs and fertiliser. I could leave less productive areas for nature and concentrate food production in my best fields. As a livestock farmer, I could consider whether feed additives may reduce the methane emissions of my cattle, or whether I could focus on their genetic breeding to select for those who grow most efficiently, or with the least emissions. Even by changing the way I graze my fields I can improve the efficiency of my livestock and help increase soil carbon levels.

Carbon sequestration is a topic we will return to in more detail later, but this is perhaps the most important issue you have never heard about. Yes, farmers are in a position to plant more trees (we have planted significant new woodlands all over our farm in recent decades, contributing to the National Forest of nine million new plantings) and we all know that trees can be good for climate change, by removing carbon dioxide (CO_2) from the air and locking it up. The many miles of hedge on my farm perform the same function. But our soil has the potential to absorb so much more, whilst still producing the food we need. It's calculated that permanent pasture stores 83 tonnes of carbon per hectare in the soil, compared to 66 tonnes beneath woodland. (Though this doesn't account for the 57 tonnes also stored in the trees – though at some point those trees will either die and rot or be burned, releasing their carbon.) By farming with an eye to carbon sequestration – 'carbon farming' – it's thought that British farms could remove up to five million tonnes of CO_2 from the atmosphere every year. This might involve less disturbance of the soil by actions such as ploughing, or by applying some of the practices described earlier in the book such as cover cropping or encouraging more livestock into arable rotations to increase soil organic matter and soil health, which is key to building stocks of soil carbon. Alongside this are exciting developments in the carbon credit market, with some polluters 'offsetting' their emissions via on-farm sequestration.

As for renewable energy, farmers are clearly in a position to produce grains which may be used in biofuels (the petrol in your car will be a ten per cent biofuel mix from 2021, cutting oil use), or biomass (such as straw) which absorbs atmospheric carbon as part of the biogenic carbon cycle before being burned for heat and power in the place of fossil fuels – the burning of which releases CO_2 which was previously locked away permanently in the ground. Alternatively, many farms are investing in anaerobic digesters, whereby cattle manure, grains and food waste products are fermented and turned into organic fertiliser, natural gas, heat and electricity. Already, farmers produce enough renewable energy to power ten million homes, primarily from solar and wind power installed in our fields and on our shed roofs! In the coming decades we must expect to see more solar panels and wind turbines springing up in our fields alongside more traditional crops as renewables become an ever-larger part of our national energy mix.

British agriculture's ambition to become a net-zero industry by 2040 is an exciting challenge, but also just the start of what we can achieve: carbon negative food. We have the potential not only to offset our own emissions, but also to act as a sink for the wider economy. What we need to achieve this is the support of the great British public to buy our produce and help champion sustainable food production, to help break the relentless race to the bottom in our global food system. Climate-friendly food is possible; many British farms are already producing it: support us and help turn the tide in the climate battle.

WINTER

· DECEMBER · JANUARY · FEBRUARY

SHELTER

'Winter is coming.'

George R.R. Martin, *A Game of Thrones*

LONGHORNS

LIVESTOCK ARE AT the heart of our farm, just as they've been at the heart of healthy, balanced agriculture for millennia. We've always kept cattle, with sheep a more transient presence. Dairy cows were a mainstay in my grandfather's time, disappeared when my father returned home in the 1970s to be replaced with beef, and then reappeared in the 1980s once again until 2005 when the herd was dissolved for a second time. Today, the farm is home to a herd of pedigree Longhorn beef cattle, and, for the first time in more than a decade, sheep have made a return to our pastures as well. A farm is not immutable, but responds to the demands of the times and passions of its occupants.

And for my parents, passion is the word when it comes to our Longhorns. The herd was started from scratch in 1989 as a direct result of my starting school. Until then, I was the centre of my mother's world, but with my entry into education she suddenly had a Joe-shaped hole in her days. Coming from a livestock farming family herself, she had always wanted her own project, and this was the opportunity to realise that ambition and take her mind off the daily absence of her little boy by starting her own herd.

At the time, we had dairy cows, but she wanted to begin something different. But which breed? Britain has a proud and distinguished history of livestock breeding. We have thirty-four 'native' breeds of cattle (and fifty-seven of sheep, eleven of pigs, sixteen of horse and four of goat) – genetically unique breeds sharing the same characteristics and appearance, which are recognised as being historically 'British'. Native breeds are associated with particular regions or counties and were generally bred to thrive in specific weather or terrain: hardy upland breeds, for example, versus the easier life of the lowlands where productivity was key.

These native breeds are an invaluable, irreplaceable part of our national heritage in a way similar to our great historic buildings or the collections of our museums, but remain a living and active part of our farmed landscape. Fourteen of these cattle breeds and twenty-five of the sheep are considered rare, with some of those critically endangered. (Of our native pig, horse and goat breeds, almost all are rare or endangered.) But these are not wild animals, being hunted to extinction or casualty to human habitat destruction or pollution; it may surprise you to learn that farmed animals can be so endangered. Why is this? The majority of the livestock in this country are no longer pure native breeds, but those imported from (primarily) Europe in the second half of the twentieth century with characteristics better suited to profitability in the consumer marketplace at a time when farmers were being pushed to produce more, faster, cheaper. These 'continentals' are either larger (and therefore can carry more meat), quicker growing, lower maintenance, provide more offspring or are able to produce more milk.

The best example of this is the ubiquitous black and white dairy cow. They are now almost exclusively of the Holstein-Friesian breed – as the name suggests originally heralding from Holland and north Germany. First arriving in the wake of the Second World War, they have now almost entirely displaced traditional native breeds such as the Dairy Shorthorn, primarily on the basis that a pedigree Holstein-Friesian averages some 8500 litres of milk per year, versus 5500 litres for the Shorthorn. The two world wars were dark times for our native breeds, and numbers fell precipitously as government encouraged farmers to kill their livestock and turn pasture into arable land to maximise the demand for simple bulk calories during the years of blockade and rationing. Coupled with the rise of post-war market economics, many breeds never recovered from this unfortunate policy, and today some have fewer than 150 breeding females remaining with dangerously narrow gene pools to draw on.

When my mother was looking for the breed she wanted in 1989, she decided for a native British type. Her agricultural hero is Robert Bakewell, the eighteenth-century farmer and pioneer who was one of the driving forces of the second great Agricultural Revolution, an essential precursor to the more widely known Industrial Revolution of the nineteenth century. Bakewell too was a Leicestershire farmer, based at Dishley Grange on the outskirts of our nearest town, Loughborough, five miles distant. One of his great contributions was the improvement of existing livestock breeds, turning them from mongrel jacks of all trades (producing relatively modest volumes of milk **and** meat while also spending much of their lives as draught animals pulling ploughs and carts) and selectively breeding the best with the best to produce more productive, specialised animals. The Longhorn is one of his great contributions in this regard, a superb beef animal which helped to feed the rapidly industrialising workforce of the late eighteenth century and beyond. In choosing the Longhorn, it was and continues to be a thrill to have this connection to our local history. Farming is often not just about pounds and pence, but about heart and pride: for us, the Longhorn is a living embodiment of our local and national heritage and we are proud stewards of its future.

The cattle themselves are majestic and striking beasts: predominantly brown and white, each one has unique markings, from almost completely white to almost completely black and everything in between – but always with a white stripe down their backs from head to tail. As their eponymous name suggests, their principal feature is great sweeping horns which show similar variety – most of ours have downward-curving bonnet horns, which sometimes can even meet under the chin! (Some even threaten to grow into their faces and need to be carefully trimmed.) Others jut sideways, or sometimes our girls have one of each. Bulls have the smaller horns, which tend to be short and stubby and stick straight out from their heads. Horned cattle are rare in modern agriculture – especially among the more commercially minded imports from the continent – because they require more careful management and greater space. But despite what can be a fearsome appearance, our Longhorns are very good-natured and generally placid; perhaps it's because they know they're beautiful. Dealing with the horns can be a faff, but it's an important part of the heritage of the breed. Our herd name is Blackbrook, taken from the swift-running stream which cuts through the centre of our farm; such things are another anchor in each farm's sense of place.

In 1989 Longhorns were a rare breed still recovering from their mid-century nadir, but their fortunes have improved over the years and they are now well out of danger and an increasingly common sight in the British countryside – a conservation success story. Their proliferation in conservation grazing projects and directly sold meat boxes is evidence that the best way to conserve our native breeds is to use them as they were intended! The attempt to give my mother something else to focus on after I went to school was also successful; it wasn't long until I would find myself frequently waiting at the end of the school day to be picked up, forgotten as she had become completely engrossed in her new passion! In fairness, it wasn't a long journey to my primary school; its playing fields backed onto our farm and I remember to this day how excited my classmates were when Dad once brought some calves and lambs to the playground to be smothered in giggles and hugs, or how the school nativity even featured real-life sheep to meet the baby Jesus. One dreads to think of the volume of paperwork which such gentle antics might generate today.

We have around 150 Longhorns, run as a 'suckler' herd. This means that we breed our own calves and they will stay on their mothers' drinking milk for as long as they want before they make the transition to eating grass and other solids; it's the traditional image of the British cattle herd. We have around fifty breeding females and the remainder of the herd consists of bulls, calves and youngstock – that is, last year's calves who are not yet ready for breeding. We hope that every breeding female will have one calf per year; twins are reasonably common, with perhaps a pair in fifty births. (To clear up a common terminological question – a heifer is a female which has not yet given birth to its **second** calf, at which point it becomes a fully-fledged cow.)

As a beef suckler herd, we take most of our cattle from birth to death. Our females are our most valuable asset, and we hope they will be with us for many years, providing calves to build our business upon. It's not uncommon for our cows to reach the age of twelve-plus, having given us nine or ten calves. For the most part, our females are therefore retained for breeding and are not sent for beef: that is primarily the lot of our bulls. From fifty births, you would generally expect an even split of bull and heifer calves in any given year, but that doesn't translate into twenty-five bulls heading to the butchers and twenty-five heifers entering the herd.

We are pedigree breeders, which means that each animal is registered as a pure-bred Longhorn, not cross-bred with any other cattle breed. Cross breeding is a bedrock agricultural practice – whether in livestock or plants. As Bakewell showed, it enables you to bring together genetic traits from different breeds to create something better than the sum of the original parts. It's quite possible to cross a Longhorn with, say, a continental breed to create something which looks not quite like either but combines traits of the two (hopefully positive). Such a cross bred isn't a pedigree, but a mongrel. To retain the genetic identity and heritage of distinct breeds such as the Longhorn, only pure-bred animals may be registered as Longhorns on the central breed database and recognised as such. As a breeder of such pedigrees, we sell to other pedigree Longhorn breeders to either expand their herds or inject fresh genetic diversity into their breeding programme. In any given year, we sell a number of our heifers and bulls not for meat but for breeding. Different breeds command vastly different prices; unfortunately, Longhorns are near the bottom of the monetary scale! While some prime specimens of other breeds can sell for hundreds of thousands of pounds, a good price for a Longhorn bull might be five thousand; a cow or heifer half that. The older the animal generally the cheaper it is, having less productive life left to it. What makes some breeds more valuable than others? It isn't scarcity; some of the most common breeds are the most expensive, while a non-pedigree animal is only worth what you can sell it for for meat. I think of it like art: some of the prices just don't make logical sense, but if enough people with enough money decide they want something …

Of the twenty-five heifers we breed per year, we might keep twenty and sell five for breeding. If we don't consider one good enough to keep or sell, she would go for beef. Of our twenty-five bulls, we might keep three or four for breeding, sell half a dozen to other breeders and the rest would go into the food chain. So, despite being a beef herd, beef production isn't our primary focus; for those farms where it is, there are different ways to achieve that goal. Some farms also operate as grass-based suckler units, breeding their own calves (whether pure-bred or cross-bred) and taking them all the way through to slaughter. Others don't breed their own calves at all (thus avoiding the associated costs and complications) but instead buy in young animals (known as 'stores') which they then 'finish' to slaughter age and size. Others, therefore, will specialise in only producing the youngstock to supply such finishing units, though many come from dairy farms who sell their male calves in this way. Some beef finishing units will operate more 'intensively' than we do, keeping their stores inside and finishing them on a high-protein diet of forage and grains rather than grazed grass, speeding up the fattening process. Others will be one hundred per cent pasture fed, taking even longer to mature than our more hybrid system. Beef cattle are around two years old when killed but this does vary hugely between systems, breeds and even individual cattle within herds.

Every year there's a certain amount of 'churn' in the herd, with older cattle being lost to be replaced by younger animals. Sometimes you do sadly discover a dead cow who has passed on unexpectedly from natural causes, but this is not desirable. Animals reaching the end of their useful lives will generally be sent to slaughter before they expire; perhaps due to an inability to fall pregnant, or a joint which begins to go, affecting their mobility and causing them pain. Ultimately, farms are businesses and cannot carry extra mouths indefinitely if they are not producing an income. There's also nothing kind about keeping animals in a poor state of health.

Our cattle all have names, and every year has its own letter. In 1989 my parents began with 'A' (their first calf named Acorn) and we've been moving through the alphabet ever since, having completed it once and now finding ourselves back in the Es, Fs and Gs in the early 2020s. And, yes, my mother even endeavoured with the difficult years – U, X and Z – but with a certain amount of creative accounting: U-Genie and X-Calibur, for example! But, to us, each animal is a personality, an individual. When we milked dairy cows, my favourite was number 181, Lenny Olive II. She was the friendliest, snuggliest cow I had ever met, always keen to come over for a scratch behind the ears before she went into the parlour, always with a sympathetic look when one of her peers pooped on me. With our Longhorns, it's U-Ropa, one of our oldest ladies (now pushing twelve) whom we bottle fed as a calf when we sadly lost her mother. As a result of that bonding experience, she learned to trust us more than most calves, always looking out for her next meal! But she still has a great affection for us, loves to be fussed, can't be flustered – but will not do anything she does not absolutely want to do. Sometimes she's a 600kg immovable object, standing in the middle of the farmyard, gently chewing as she eyes you with silent mirth.

In common with most British livestock, our cattle have a pasture-based existence. Once again, this is a function of the perfect conditions of terrain and climate which have always made it such a superb country in which to farm cattle, sheep and other animals. A large part of our farm is simply not suited to growing crops; the soil is too thin and the rocks beneath are too numerous. Grass and roaming livestock are perfectly suited to these conditions, and many of our pastures have not been disturbed in decades. Even if we wanted to, we couldn't put our entire farm down to arable, so livestock will always have an important role. Across the UK this also holds true: sixty-five per cent of our total farmland is pasture unsuited to the production of anything other than grass[29], but perfect for the rearing of top-quality livestock.

We house our Longhorns for perhaps three months of the year over winter, depending on weather conditions. There are multiple reasons for this. First and foremost, removing the cattle from the fields in what are traditionally the wettest months of the year saves our grass from being churned into mud. In this state, not only do we lose the grass, but there's a greater risk of losing the soil as well without the vegetation to bind it together. Secondly, grass doesn't grow over the winter. What little there is will also be low in nutrients such as the sugars which are produced when grass photosynthesises in the warm days of spring and summer, each blade acting as a miniature solar panel turning sunlight into energy.

Although cattle such as ours are bred to be hardy and are fully capable of remaining outdoors in most conditions, it's certainly more pleasant for them to be inside in driving rain or deep snow – they leave you in no doubt of that when they queue at the field gate! And of course it's easier for us to look after them through the winter if they are indoors; better to be working in a dry shed than outside in horizontal sleet. This is especially the case given that we aim to have all our cows and heifers calve between January and March; calving can be a risky time, and it's useful to have everyone indoors where we can keep a close eye on them and intervene with ease if necessary. We also bring our cattle indoors because we can; not every farm has the sheds to do so.

---

29 National Farmers' Union, *The facts about British red meat and milk*, 2020, 15pp.

What does our farmyard look like? Like many British farms, we have a mix of buildings going back centuries, all overlaid and interwoven. The granite-built farmhouse dates from the eighteenth century, as do the low stable blocks around it, long since repurposed many times from calf pens to an art gallery. We have three former dairy sheds still extant on the premises – from the 1950s, 1980s and 2000s. All are now repurposed to other things. Our great old nineteenth-century stone barn, once used to store forage for the winter, has housed our grain drier since the 1970s, itself now long since past its best. We have corrugated tin 'Dutch' barns from the 1960s, built on the foundations of even earlier constructions, alongside grain stores built piecemeal around the same time from concrete breeze blocks and asbestos roofing. And wherever there was once wet concrete, there are the indelible signed initials of whoever worked on the farm at that time, most long since forgotten. (The paw prints of Ted and Toby I have managed to distribute liberally in recent years, immortalised forever in 'stone'.)

To look around many a British farm is akin to viewing an archaeological dig or an historic building: the knowing eye can see the various layers one upon the other as the place has evolved over the decades or even centuries. Here, I can still see the old ramp up which milk churns were rolled into the back of the horse and cart, now consumed by a later wall. There, I see the old sleepers and tracks ripped out of the old Charnwood Forest Railway in the 1960s and repurposed as braces for a shed wall. I'm reasonably sure some of the grand oak beams in our oldest shed originally hailed from the Augustinian nunnery dissolved by Henry VIII, the ruins of which lie a mile from our yard. Farms are thick with history.

Like many farms, we work within the confines of the buildings we've inherited over the generations. The poor financial returns of the last twenty years have seen little significant new investment, and as a result much of our equipment has now outgrown the sheds built to house its predecessors. One of our three grain stores is accessible to only our smallest tractor – and only if you unscrew the radio aerial mounted on its roof. Our fifteen-tonne grain trailers are now too big to tip up in sheds designed for implements half their size. Our combine harvester is capable of cutting more grain in one hour than our drier can process in twenty-four. On many farms like ours across the country, everything just feels a bit tight; a bit second (and third and fourth) hand; a bit strained around the seams. I would dearly love to build a brand new grain store, fit for the modern day, efficient to use and better able to store my grain – our valued income – safely and securely. But, as a predominantly tenanted farm of modest size, we just can't afford to do it and must struggle on with what we have. At least it has character.

WINTER ROUTINE

It's December, and all our cattle are inside. We've divided them up into groups based on sex, age and calving date – as well as individual personality. They will have come in from the fields over the course of several weeks as the weather begins to turn and the grass stops its growth. By this point, they will need little encouragement to come inside, and the older animals will know that they can expect a move to warm indoor lodgings as the mercury begins to drop – open the gate and they will fairly run to the shed themselves.

It's now that we'll generally 'wean' our calves off from their mothers, at around eight to ten months of age. By this point the calves are significant beasts in their own right and have long since given up on their mums for milk, moving over to grass themselves.

There are still, it must be said, though, some tears at this point. Even if placed into pens nearby, both the mum and calf will call to each other until hoarse for a few days before they settle down once again. It's a bit hard on the heart and the eardrums, but at some point this has to happen for the mum to focus on her next calf, due in a few months' time.

The heifer and bull calves will be separated and grouped according to rough age and size. This is an important occasion; they will likely stay in these groups for many months. You may think that bulls especially are prone to fighting if in groups, but when they grow up together they actually get on really well. Problems only arise if new animals are introduced, or even if a longstanding member of the group is removed for any length of time and then reintroduced – 'Who's this guy? Get 'im!' They have short memories, and shorter fuses.

Our cows will be split into groups broadly based on calving date, but here personalities are also important: just like people, our cattle have strong minds of their own, and some, frankly, are bullies! Groups of cattle always need to establish a pecking order so that everybody knows where they stand, and these individuals will always come out on top – sometimes to the detriment of others who get in their way. Obviously, when confined indoors and especially when pregnant, this sort of behaviour isn't on, so we make sure that the known troublemakers are grouped off either alone or with other girls we know they can rub along with. So there's politics, even with cattle. At the most extreme, we have culled cattle who are just too bad tempered to own safely.

There's a wide range of materials that farmers use to bed livestock down: sawdust, woodchip, sand, even rubber mats. Like many, we use straw, the dried stems of our arable crops – primarily wheat and barley. This is a great example of the circular economy which exists on a mixed farm, with the arable and livestock enterprises working in symbiosis with each other. At harvest, straw is a biproduct of our cropping which would otherwise be chopped and returned to the soil, but instead we bale and store it for the winter and then spread it out in our loose sheds to provide comfortable and warm bedding. Several times per week we will introduce fresh half-tonne straw bales into the pens as needed, as the cattle add their manure! Over winter the straw beds therefore get deeper (and more comfortable!) as more fresh layers are added, before being cleaned out in the spring. At this point, it's become nutrient-rich farmyard manure, which is returned to the fields for spreading, completing the symbiotic circle begun the previous harvest.

'Conserved forage' – that is, silage and hay – is the mainstay of our and of most housed cattle in the UK. This is grass which is preserved in the summer for the long nights of winter. Hay, you are no doubt familiar with: this is grass allowed to grow tall and stemmy in the summer, before cutting and drying in the sun until there is virtually no moisture left in it. It's then baled and stored undercover until needed. Silage is a more modern development whereby lush younger grass is cut and collected before it's allowed to dry, either baled and wrapped in plastic or 'ensiled' in a silage 'clamp' or 'pit' (essentially a large bunker of either earth or concrete panelling) and covered with large sheets of thick weighted plastic to keep the air out. In these anaerobic conditions, the grass ferments as a means of preserving it. Both hay and silage will last for years so long as they're kept in the right conditions, meaning that the benefits of our bountiful British grasslands can still be utilised even in the depths of winter.

Although some farms will only ever feed their animals one hundred per cent grass products, most supplement that forage with other foods. A common one, which we made use of when we had dairy cows, was maize – which you may recognise as corn on the cob. Farmers will grow this on arable land and harvest the entire plant (which can grow to ten feet tall) and ensile the resulting fodder in the same way as grass, giving a high-energy feedstuff especially suited to high-output dairy cows. At the other end of the nutritional scale, straw can also be fed to cattle, acting more as a stomach-filling roughage in the same way we might eat bran. They usually eye it with as much enthusiasm.

Many farms will also feed 'concentrates' or 'compound feeds', which we call 'cake'. As the name implies, this elicits a much more excitable response when dispensed. These are fed in small quantities as supplements to their forage-based diets to provide an extra burst of energy to newly calved and suckling mothers, to augment growth rates in youngstock once weaned or to bulk up bulls to their optimum size. They consist of ingredients including cereals, sugar beet pulp (a waste product of British sugar production), malt residue (a waste product of brewing), molasses (a by-product of cane sugar production), peas and beans, plus vitamins and minerals.

Many of these products also contain imported soya, a crop which does not grow well in the UK and is primarily imported from much hotter countries such as the United States, Argentina and Brazil. Soya is a protein-rich natural rocket fuel for high-intensity livestock; for its nutrient density, it's also relatively cheap. The concern frequently raised about its production, however, is that intensive soya is one of the drivers of global biodiversity collapse – especially in countries such as Brazil, where opaque supply chains often make it difficult to know whether soya is sourced from areas of illegal deforestation. This is clearly a concern, and I am an advocate of replacing as much soya in animal rations with UK-grown proteins such as peas, beans and lupins as possible. We only buy concentrates that contain all-British ingredients. But many farmers don't have that luxury; the price they are paid for their produce – the 'farmgate price' – is dictated to them, and is kept as low as buyers can get away with – or even below the cost of production. That's why soya still retains a significant role in UK livestock diets (particularly pigs and poultry, rather than cattle) as the alternatives are not economically viable or as nutritionally dense. It's also worth bearing in mind that the majority of UK soya imports are used in the human, not the animal, food chain, so this isn't a straightforward farming sustainability issue but – as so often – one for wider society.[30]

Most frequently, concentrates come as small compressed pellets, and are highly palatable to livestock. All is quiet first thing in the morning until the cattle who are in receipt of concentrates know there's a human mooching about putting their boots on, at which point they start noisily demanding breakfast. They also know to start mooing about thirty minutes before the end of the working day, when their tea comes out.

There are other unlikely foods which livestock are known to eat too; when we had dairy cows, we often fed them carrots and potatoes rejected from the human food chain for being too bendy or too big. You haven't experienced farce until you've seen a cow smoking a parsnip. We crush (in our eighty-year-old feed mill) some of our own barley to feed our beef finishing cattle; another example of the symbiosis of a mixed farm. We crush the grains to make them easier to digest, otherwise we just see lots of wholegrains in their poo which then sprout again in the fields when spread as muck! (Think sweetcorn …)

And, yes, for avoidance of doubt, cows (and all ruminants) do have four stomachs. (Well, actually they have one stomach split into four compartments, but who's counting.) The reason for this is that grass, their primary foodstuff, is very difficult to digest and

30 Sustainable Food Trust, 'Are dairy cows and livestock behind the growth of soya in South America?', 26 January 2017.

extract useful nutrients from (humans couldn't do it with our measly single stomachs) and so they've evolved a highly efficient means of doing so with multiple stages. One of these involves the burping up of partially digested grass (the cud) and rechewing it. Ruminants have literally no manners.

DAILY ROUTINE

The average winter day begins at 7:30am which is more or less bearable depending on the weather (it's easier to be enthusiastic on a warm summer's morning). It must be said that there's a certain sense of foreboding on a frozen winter's morning to know that water troughs will be iced over and pipes will most likely be solid, necessitating either extensive (and gentle) thawing with blowtorch or kettle, or the bucketing of water from a tank to every pen while slipping on ice! Admittedly it's also not the **early** start that we used to have when dairy farming, when 4:30am was the norm. But at least the commute is short. (When working in London, I inexplicably managed to find myself a three-hour-per-day round trip from box room to office, which translated to about five miles in straight-line distance!)

The first job, especially in the calving window, is to turn the shed lights on and check whether there have been any calves in the night or whether anybody is in the process of calving. If all is quiet, it's a case of wheelbarrowing the cake to the groups that have them and scooping them out by hand into their feed troughs. It might be the 2020s, but many jobs on many farms are still done manually, rather than by machines. Ted and Toby would likely take this time to do their first rodent sweep of the day or locate some particularly tasty calf poo from the night before.

By this time, the accusatory eyes of those still waiting for their breakfast would drive me to the telehandler to begin cutting fresh silage from the clamp, or to unwrap the plastic net from a hay bale before depositing it into the feed passages in front of them. From this point onward, all is well with the world as far as our cattle are concerned, and you'll likely not hear another peep out of them for the rest of the day. Visitors are often surprised by the quiet – happy cows are quiet cows, and when somebody does make noise it's usually a good idea to go and check on them.

Next on the list of jobs is 'bedding down' any of those groups needing fresh straw. This is a task which our cattle take to with relish; seemingly even in the bovine world there's nothing more satisfying than clean sheets. Drop a whole bale into their pen and they'll gleefully spread it around themselves, using their horns to toss great heaps up into the air. They have thicker skins than me, though; barley straw is one of life's great torments if it goes down your top. An itchier substance has never been created by human hands (a function of the spiky and sticky awns which cling to the seed heads and come away in the straw). But, for cattle who think nothing of scratching themselves aggressively on barbed wire, it clearly has little negative effect.

With these morning tasks complete, the rest of the day is taken up with the huge range of jobs which a mixed farm creates, even in the depths of winter. But at around 3pm, we would then do a final sweep, topping any silage up for the night as necessary, feeding the evening cake, and then shutting up shop for the night around 4pm as the final light begins to fail. These are the shortest working hours of the year (although it's a seven-day-a-week job); come spring, summer and autumn we might work fifteen or more hours a day, so in a way the winter presents somewhat of a break.

One of the most frequently used pieces of equipment on the farm is the cattle 'handling system', a collection of passageways and integrated pens in one corner of our largest shed into which we can lead a group of cattle to more easily and safely handle them. Through a series of closing gates, the passageway gradually becomes narrower until the animals can only pass through it individually. The pens and passageways are all solid sided to make sure that the cows can't see what's going on outside the system and become startled. The whole thing also curves to the left, as (believe it or not) cattle are more comfortable when turning to the left. As they walk through, swinging gates can be opened into side pens to split animals off from the main group, while the main race eventually leads into the cattle 'crush', an alarmingly named device which is simply a box into which an animal can step and be held immobile by a neck restraint and sliding door behind. A scoop can then be brought up under their chin to keep their head steady if needs be. This enables safer (for us) and lower stress (for them) up-close examination, especially by the visiting vet if medical care is required. The last thing anybody needs when trying to inject a cow is for her to be jumping around or risk standing on your foot or kicking you. It's also an easy means to weigh the cows, as keeping tabs on their weights (for beef cattle, especially) is an important part of the data which farmers collect on their animals. Is each one growing as fast as it should? If not, why? Perhaps they're sick, or being bullied from taking their fair share of food. It's important to keep an eye on these things, so we have a digital weighing platform built into the floor of the system onto which each animal steps every time it goes through.

A modern handling system like this is of huge benefit to any farm; until recently we made do with a loose collection of gates which were not satisfactory, but thanks to an EU investment grant which part funded the project (on animal-welfare, human-safety and farm-productivity grounds) we were able to make this very welcome investment, which will be of value for decades to come.

CROP PESTS

One of the few jobs required on the arable side of the farm during the winter is keeping an eye on the various pests which can think of no greater delicacy than the crops I so carefully planted back in the autumn. It's great to get out and about with Ted and Toby over the winter especially on a gin-clear, frosty morning. I'm not sure they always realise it, but the lot of a farm dog is one of the luckiest – no nine-hour wait at home for them while their human goes to work. Just the endless horizons and possibilities of another day on the farm. Which is just as well, because Ted has a penchant for destroying the post when it drops through the door – best to keep him out of the house.

The main pests at this time of year are crows, pigeons and rabbits. Crows tend to target young plants as they emerge from the ground, so November-planted beans are perhaps the most at risk at this time of year as they finally push through. Crows are incredibly smart, and will work their way down a row of emerging plants, guessing where the next one will be even if they can't see it. Common wisdom holds that the damage always looks worse than it is – and you'll rarely see more than a dozen crows at work at any one time – but it's still pretty galling to see seeds emerging from the ground after all that hard work and effort on both their and my behalf only to be pulled up by a vagrant corvid. The other major airborne git is the pigeon, which is particularly fond of oilseed rape. Pigeons move in huge clouds which sometimes seem to obscure the very sun, before settling onto a field and proceeding to chomp their way through the leafy crop canopy.

There are a few things which can be done about this. First and foremost is usually high-volume harsh language and waved arms followed by a full-speed pair of Jack Russells with bottoms close to the ground. However, over the years I've discovered that the utility of Ted and Toby to permanently discourage our avian visitors is distinctly limited; they perennially struggle even to encourage the single well-fed urban pigeon living in our garden tree to decamp for more than a few minutes, quite apart from the hordes we get in the countryside.

The standard solution is a gas banger, effectively a spark-plug armed cannon charged with propane and ignited by a car battery. These are often to be found dotting my fields during winter, all with their own timer ensuring they only go off during daylight hours. Farmers may be famously awkward, but even the most obstreperous might draw the line at nocturnal gas explosions arousing the midnight ire of neighbours. The birds inevitably get used to them, though, so they need to be moved regularly. They also sadly and increasingly need to be hidden or protected in a cage; I'm always amazed at the lengths some people will go to to locate and steal a clapped-out old car battery – usually trashing the banger in the process.

Regular visitors to the winter countryside may also be no strangers to the incongruous sound of gunfire, the tried and tested means of moving flocks of pigeons along, or of the slightly more modern rockets which can be used to the same end. But because of poor old Ted I've been forced to abandon this tactic, unwittingly instilling into him a huge fear of gunfire and rockets specifically.

Other modern tactics in the escalating war with pigeon-kind include lasers (for scaring rather than vaporising), stereos playing the hunting cries of birds of prey, and kites in the shape of said birds on rigid poles which jerk around in the wind, somewhat unconvincingly. These latter perhaps fall into the same category of utility as 'neighbourhood watch' signs as far as deterrence goes; often I've found that pigeons will eat everything up to and sometimes including the square metre around them. Sometimes, you just can't go wrong with the good old-fashioned scarecrow dressed up in torn and stained old clothes. Though I'm not sure you'd believe me if I told you sometimes even these are stolen, leaving a somewhat forlorn and naked scarecrow.

Rabbits are another major pain and can cause serious damage, especially around the edges of fields. When younger I took a certain amount of satisfaction in trying to control them with my rifle (kids and firearms are a uniquely agricultural phenomenon) but as I've got older I've completely lost the taste for it and can't bring myself to pull the trigger, for all the good it ever did. In recent years I've tried to keep them off my crops by digging in rabbit fencing instead – wire mesh which runs underground to stop them burrowing under it. It's an expensive solution which has, to be honest, yielded mixed results. Frankly, damage and loss to pests is just a cost of doing business in farming, and there's often little that can be done other than trying to make yourself feel better by letting off a rocket or firing a laser (and there's not many jobs in which you can make that claim).

DAIRY

Until 2005 we milked around 150 cows three times per day. They lived indoors for approximately eleven months of the year being fed a highly enriched diet based upon grass silage but incorporating large quantities of maize as well as more concentrated feeds such as distillers' grains (a by-product of the brewing industry) and rape-meal (a by-product of oilseed rape processing.) Our average yields were huge at around 13,000 litres of milk per cow per year. This was not down solely to diet, but to a large extent on the breeding of the cows (for high genetic merit and milk yield) as well as their high welfare (unhealthy cows are unproductive and unprofitable). But yes, keeping them indoors and feeding them a high-input, high-output diet was key to achieving those very high yields in a way that wouldn't have been possible had they been outdoors, grazing naturally. We also bred our own replacements (unlike some dairy herds, which might buy theirs in as adults) and these heifers were largely raised outdoors before they began milking.

This is a good opportunity to address the label of 'intensive' or 'industrial' farming, which is frequently levelled at modern agriculture, often at high-output dairy such as this. I'm not naïve enough to claim I can't see the point that people are making when they use that term; there's no doubt that the scale and mechanisation of agriculture have vastly increased in the past fifty years. I can understand the view that keeping dairy cows indoors for such long periods can seem 'unnatural' or deleterious to welfare. The image of a cow grazing outdoors is more appealing in the mind's eye than the alternative. But I would suggest that the industrial criticism – as such it is – is a misleading accusation intended only to stir uneasiness in society. After all, what does industrial mean? 'Very great in extent or amount … an activity in which a great deal of effort is expended.' Given that agriculture covers some seventy per cent of the UK, and most farmers (organic, conventional or something in-between) walk through the door exhausted most evenings, I would agree with this description wholeheartedly; it could apply just as much to my conservation activities as it does to my farming ones. The power of words is in how they are utilised, and when it comes to our food, they are often weaponised to prey on our emotions.

There's risk in both over-romanticising an imagined past and in anthropomorphising the animals we farm. In Britain, our food has never been safer, cheaper nor farmed to such high standards and norms of animal welfare. As for the accusation that keeping dairy cows indoors for much of the year is cruel, I might suggest that they don't experience it as such. Happy, healthy cows are productive cows. I can remember when we used to keep our milkers outside on pasture through much of the year; rounding them up with a quad bike for the twice-daily trek back to the milking parlour was a common source of lameness from trips, slips and pebbles, and when the weather was grim they'd be hustling to come indoors. This isn't to criticise the many British dairy farms that do keep their cows outdoors; different businesses mould their systems around the resources (especially land and buildings) they possess in pursuit of that all-important profit margin: in the 2000s we chased top yields; others adopt a lower-cost, lower-output approach and perhaps end up in the same (or better) financial place. But modern intensive cattle sheds are luxury housing for cows, ensuring their every whim is catered for to ensure maximum productivity, from comfort in lying down, to cooling when hot to stimulation when bored. Unlike us, cows don't necessarily appreciate the view from the field, but they do appreciate having a full stomach and hassle-free life.

This isn't to deny that incidents of poor treatment can occur – just as they can on the least intensive of farms, or that the global excesses of the food system aren't pretty hard to stomach and seem to offer diminishing returns. Parts of the globe have been truly blighted when the free market has taken total control of farming, pushing it far beyond what is desirable when living, sentient beings are involved. In some countries, 'factory' farming does seem to be a fair description of conditions. But, here in the UK, we generally strike the right balance – to my mind – between the needs of feeding people for an affordable price and the environmental and welfare consequences of that – though that doesn't mean that we can't strive to be better.

Why is agriculture driven to be ever-bigger, ever more

mechanised, ever more industrial? Because society demands cheap food. Aston Martin can afford to still use traditional craftspeople to stitch, sew, mould and assemble its cars because they command such an astronomical price. A mainstream manufacturer couldn't afford to use such labour-intensive means and still sell an affordable vehicle. And so it is with food. Survey after survey shows that – in Britain particularly – people value 'cheapness' (sometimes expressed as 'value') above all other considerations when it comes to the food they eat in the home. (Eating out is another story, when 'experience' trumps price.) The supermarkets know this, and with their vast market power act accordingly. When was the last time you saw a significant rise in the price of milk? When we exited dairy production twenty years ago, it was because we couldn't turn a profit being paid around twenty pence per litre. A decade later the price was much the same[31], a situation which continues to drive many farmers out of the sector, but others to expand cow numbers in hopes of grasping greater economies of scale – with the same being true across much of the rest of farming. (A third approach is the time-honoured method of family farmers working ever-harder for less money and never employing staff or taking a break. This is heartbreakingly common and contributes to many of the physical and mental stresses on farming families.) But, as farmgate prices continue to stagnate (and are today in most cases much lower than they were fifty years ago) many farmers are running just to stand still. Food is simply not valued enough in much of society, and the gravity-defying act that we manage to achieve in the UK is that we have some of the highest production standards (and costs), while managing to produce the third cheapest food in

31 Agriculture and Horticulture Development Board, 'UK farmgate milk prices', updated 29 April 2021.

the world per capita.[32] This generally leaves farmers with only some six to eight per cent of the food value chain. Often, we are producing your food and selling it **below** the costs of production. When we consider food sustainability, here is the root cause of so many of our problems. It seems to me insane that bottled water is more expensive than milk – especially in a country where tap water is safe, cheap and plentiful.

Milking was never one of my favourite jobs; you either take to it or you don't, and as a thirteen-year-old thrown very much in at the deep end it was probably a bit rich for my blood. My Friday night started at 8:30pm (after having religiously, if I recall, watched the first half hour of *Xena: Warrior Princess*). Our milking parlour consisted of a 'pit' four feet deep, to either side of which was space for ten cows to stand at an oblique angle, their udders accessible at chest height. Hanging in the pit were ten milking 'cluster' units, four stainless steel cups with pulsating rubber inners connected to a vacuum system which by turns squeezed each teat while sucking the milk away through a system of filters, before dropping the milk into a big chiller tank which was constantly agitated (much like myself.)

Each group of ten would walk in and take their place before having their teats dipped in iodine and wiped clean with paper towels to sterilise them. The clusters were then attached by hand; some cows were a nightmare to attach, as their bags were either low to the ground or their teats were massive and a struggle to insert. They usually took my faffing in good humour, though. While one side of the parlour was milking, I would bring in the next group of ten on the other side and clean them up. When each cow ran dry (having given perhaps thirty litres in a single sitting) a computer would automatically cut the vacuum and pull each

32 'Why the UK has such cheap food', *BBC News*, 1 October 2018.

cluster off via a length of string attached to a reel. Each cow would then have its bag sprayed with iodine to avoid any infection entering the open teats, before being released back into the shed. Doing this three times per day, they knew the drill, and needed little encouragement: dairy cows want to be milked; if they aren't it's like having a very full bladder. That's why some dairy farms dispense with person-operated systems and instead utilise robots which carry out this whole procedure automatically when a cow walks into them when **she** decides it's time to be milked. It's impressive to watch such a robot carrying out all the actions described above completely autonomously, but with a price tag of £100,000–£120,000 per machine (with one machine per fifty to sixty cows) it was presumably always thought I was the cheaper option starting at ten pounds per night.

Back then, there was no Ted or Toby, but my loyal milking companion was Lilly, our one and only German Shepherd. She'd been bought as a puppy after a spate of break-ins on the farm to act as security, but was unfortunately blessed with a lovely temperament. Around strangers she could usually be found on her back, tail wagging. But she was good company while milking the cows, calm and well-behaved around the animals, her pay-off being a bit of milk spilt on the floor at the end of the night.

The milk in our bulk tank would be collected every day by a milk tank lorry, the contents sucked out via a long flexible hose connected to the valve at the base of our tank, mixing it with the loads already collected from other farms. The driver would then take it on to the milk processor, where it would undergo various tests to ensure its safety and consistency; for example, that there was no trace of antibiotics or that it hadn't been adulterated with water. (A sample taken at the farm would also be checked; if one farm's load had contaminated the entire tanker, the farmer would be liable for the whole shipment.) Cattle being treated with antibiotics were kept in a separate group which was milked at the end of the night and the milk from that group was dumped into the slurry tank, from where it would be spread onto our fields. It was critical that no mistakes were made here, as any antibiotics used in the food chain have a minimum withdrawal period before which milk or meat from that animal cannot be sold. I once made the costly mistake of forgetting to take the pipe out of the tank before milking this group, and was forced to dump an entire day's milk down the drain. Lilly was the only one not upset at this turn of events.

At the processor, the milk is then filtered, pasteurised (heated to ensure that harmful organisms which may be present are killed) and homogenised (the cream which would otherwise float to the top is, under pressure, uniformly distributed throughout to give it a smooth taste and consistency). Nothing is added or removed in these processes. To create skimmed or semi-skimmed milk, a centrifuge is utilised to remove the appropriate amount of butterfats. The milk is then bottled and dispatched to retail outlets.

We didn't bother with any of this and simply filled a jug from our bulk tank every day. Sometimes it had stuff floating in it, sometimes it didn't. Oddly, my parents never bothered to refrigerate this daily jug – presumably comfortable that an endless supply was available – thus it was left warming on the kitchen counter every day. My grandfather came to the farm daily and did likewise – and he lived until he was ninety-six, so it probably didn't do us any harm. (Which is more than I can say for his car: one day I filled the jug for him and rather densely just stood it in the boot before he drove away. Subsequently, I always associate the Honda Accord with the smell of rancid milk on a summer's day, a smell which never entirely dissipated.)

As I've said, milking and I never really got along. Far from ideally, I've always been somewhat allergic to cattle; they have a tendency to trigger my childhood asthma when in the close proximity of, say, a milking parlour of 150 sweaty cows. There was also a particular milking smell which stuck to me for at least twenty-four hours after each job (not ideal when attending school the next day; children hardly need an excuse to be cruel, do they?) And of course, standing behind and below 150 richly fed dairy cows was an open invitation to be, quite literally, dumped upon from height. Almost nobody likes to experience the sweet smell of urine as it jets down their back, or the feeling of liquid ordure being deposited in their hair. Occasionally a skittish individual would also give me a liberal kick to the head; I remember on one such occasion, I was stopped at school the next week and questioned as to whom (boy) I'd been in a fight with to receive such a throbbing black eye. The teacher seemed unconvinced by my cow-based explanations and triumphantly put me into detention for both fighting and fibbing. Such are the perils of being a farmer's child.

And, yes, if you were wondering, I have milked a cow by hand: and, yes, it's hard work which causes your hands to cramp within minutes. How our forebears ever managed with their three-legged stools and buckets before the advent of modern technology I have no idea.

CALVING

One of the big highlights of farming is bringing new life into the world and watching it grow, and watching livestock being born is something special. As a child I used to love taking eggs which our chickens had abandoned and putting them in the incubator, only for weeks later after all hope was seemingly lost to watch them begin to rock gently back and forth, before their tiny beaks began to miraculously peck their way through the shells, finally freeing themselves, exhausted, bedraggled, damp but alive. We've had litters of kittens, puppies and flocks of tiny lambs on and off over the years, but calves have been a constant on the farm for as long as my family has been here.

Our dairy cows used to calve all year round, but we calve our Longhorns between January and March; as a suckler herd, this gives our mothers access to ample spring grass at turnout when quality is at its best, while calving indoors over winter makes for ease of care. Because we also compete with our cattle at agricultural shows, it helps that they're born as early as possible in a calendar year to give them the most opportunity in their classes! (It's a bit like September-born children being slightly advantaged by age in their start date at primary school!)

We predominantly use bulls to inseminate our cows, which means having a number on the premises at any one time to keep our genetic diversity sufficiently wide – although inbreeding to one extent or another is a perfectly normal practice in agriculture, so long as it's restricted to the animals and crops. An alternative to using bulls is the practice of artificial insemination (the **agricultural** AI) whereby frozen 'straws' of semen are inserted by a technician directly into the uterine horns (our cows have horns at both ends) when the cow or heifer is in season. The gestation period of a cow is around nine months, so bulling generally occurs in the spring or early summer to hit our winter calving window.

We know whether our cows are pregnant or not by, firstly, observing them: if we see them served by the bull, we'll make a note of it. With a reproductive cycle of twenty-one days between ovulations, if the bull subsequently shows interest in her again after three weeks, we know she was not successfully served. If he doesn't, we would hope to see a calf some 283 days later. In the intervening period, to be certain that she was successfully served and has held the pregnancy, we will have her pregnancy tested by a vet. There are two main ways of doing this in beef cattle: the rectal examination and ultrasound. The former sounds alarming but is a tried and trusted technique! From around six weeks into the pregnancy a trained and experienced individual can ascertain, from feeling through the rectal wall for tell-tale signs around the uterus, whether the cow is pregnant or not (with the use of lubricant and an arm-length plastic glove). This might sound rather dramatic, but to a cow an arm in the rectum is neither particularly unusual nor uncomfortable. In the same way a doctor can diagnose a remarkable range of ailments from the rear, so can a vet. In recent decades, the more NHS-friendly ultrasound method has also been introduced into farming, allowing a greater degree of sophistication such as sexing and being able to identify twins. If the cow is not pregnant, it's also able to identify potential reasons why. But, similarly, the ultrasound is inserted into the rectum rather than run around the belly like in humans (and smaller animals such as sheep). Our vet uses a head-mounted screen like a pair of VR goggles, which has the advantage of being less likely to get pooped on than a laptop on a nearby table! In a beef suckler herd, the sole role of a cow is to produce one calf per year. So a cow which consistently fails to get into calf for reasons which are not identifiable and rectifiable will, sadly, be culled. Our cattle aren't pets, and can't be kept indefinitely if they aren't contributing financially.

When a cow is ready to calve, she usually lets you know. Generally, her udder enlarges with milk (bagging up) in the days preceding the big event, and she'll become restless and constantly swish her tail, or stand with it partially raised. If she remembers what's coming from last time, she's likely bracing herself. We try to separate anyone who looks likely to calve off into their own pen so they aren't disturbed, and then leave them to it. Livestock have a preference for calving at night, and many's the time that you'll arrive at 7am to find a couple of new arrivals from the night before. It's the main reason we fitted a pair of hi-resolution night-vision cameras to the cattle shed roof. Many were previously the nights that multiple after-dark visits to the maternity unit were necessary to check on things, stumbling around with a torch, standing in poo and (when I was young) jumping at every shadow or noise on the way. Now, any member of the team can just tap on their smartphone and check that all is well with our mothers-to-be and intervene if necessary.

The first sign that a calf is imminent is generally a trail of pre-birth mucus from the vulva, followed by the beginnings of what looks like a big fluid-filled balloon. The poor girl will be heaving and grunting by this point, and hopefully the water bag (containing the calf) will burst and you'll be able to see the calf's pointy front hooves emerging, followed by its snout and head (often with tongue sticking out), usually all covered in the membranes of the burst bag. Once she clears the head and, finally, the front shoulders, the calf falls out as gravity takes hold and the little gem drops to the straw, the umbilical cord already detached. The cow will spin around and start to aggressively lick the newborn with her incredibly rough, sandpaper-like tongue, stimulating it into taking its first breaths. She'll keep working at it until she's got him or her spotless, consuming all the mucous, remains of the water bag and (eventually) the placenta. Sometimes, the cow will get a big mouthful of it and then whip her head around, spraying blood and general 'fluids' all over the place. You do not want to be standing near when that happens. (Unless you are a Jack Russell, in which case you think it's a veritable delicacy. Animals can be grim.) Within five to ten minutes, the little calf will already be on its unsteady feet, stumbling around after its mother and even trying to take its first mouthfuls of milk. It's remarkable how rapidly mobile and self-empowering most members of the animal kingdom are in comparison to us humans, the apex species of the planet!

A good, easy birth can be over in as little as an hour or two (also something we poor humans could learn from). However, it's not uncommon that the farmer will need to intervene in order that the calf can be delivered successfully. If a cow (especially a young heifer who has not been through the experience before) has been visibly calving for a number of hours but isn't progressing, it's usually advisable to insert a hand into her vulva to see what situation the calf is in. Sometimes their legs are twisted back and need manipulating forward for the birth to continue; sometimes the calf is upside down; sometimes it's backwards. This is especially dangerous, as the there's a real risk that the calf will drown before it can be safely delivered. In these circumstances, it's often wise to assist. Where possible, this consists of pulling on the legs of the unborn calf, usually with birthing ropes, in an attempt to expedite its delivery. Most farms have a device like a ratchet which fits over the hips of the cow and through which the birthing ropes pass. Then, in time with her contractions, the ratchet can be tightened to keep constant pressure on the calf and keep it moving in the right direction. But it's **really** important to work with the cow, and not to tear her by applying too much pressure.

When the calf drops out, it's absolutely covered in slippery goo and its head may still be covered in the birthing membrane. If it seems unresponsive, it's important to clear its airways and force its first breaths. This is achieved by vigorously rubbing its chest and perhaps sticking a length of straw up its nose to initiate a first sneeze! If there's concern that it may have fluid on its lungs, two of you might pick it up by its back legs and swing it gently to help it in draining out; this can be challenging with a slippery calf weighing maybe thirty-five kilogrammes with its mother bustling around you. Sometimes, all of this is not enough. More than once I've given mouth-to-mouth resuscitation to a newborn calf – with variable results. There's nothing sadder than a little life lost at the point of birth. When this happens, we clear the body away quickly so as not to upset the mother.

In extreme circumstances, there's just no way the calf is going to be born naturally, and at that point we call in the vet to perform a caesarean. This is one of the most remarkable things you'll witness on a farm. Imagine the sterile hospital setting for a human c-section: with a cow, the procedure is performed with her standing upright in the crush under a local anaesthetic, with some iodine rubbed along her shaved side. The vet then makes the incision which seems to run from spine to underside and starts pulling all sorts of things out to get access to the uterus. I remember holding **various organs** in my hands at times over the years to keep them in place as the cow has stood calmly, chewing her cud, a steady trickle of blood running out of her. I could never be the person with the scalpel; it's all I can do to keep calm as an organ holder. The calf is then pulled out, and the cow rapidly stitched back together and put into a quiet pen with her new charge, plenty of clean straw and ample disinfectant sprayed about the wound. With our fifty-odd cows, we maybe have one c-section every two or three years, but, amazingly, never has the wound become infected or problematic.

It's vital that the calf takes its first drink in the first twelve hours to take advantage of all the antibodies in its mother's colostrum, the thick protein-rich milk she produces for the first few days after birth. With most calves this isn't a problem as they find their way to a teat eventually, but some struggle. They'll suck on their mother's underside, on the side of her udder, on her chest … they're just a bit slow. In these cases, you physically take hold of the calf and help it onto a teat; if that doesn't work it's a case of milking the cow by hand and then 'tubing' the milk directly into the calf's stomach from a bottle by inserting a plastic tube down its throat. This job isn't much fun for us or the calf, but sometimes you just have to make sure it's getting the milk it needs at this early stage. Commonly, dairy calves are removed from their mothers after they've consumed their colostrum and raised separately on powdered milk while the cows go straight into the parlour.

Different cows react differently to this whole experience; most naturally take to their new role as mother and just know what to do, even if it's their first calf. Some are very laid back about you handling their baby; others are very protective and can be quite aggressive. You **always** need to be careful around mothers and calves, especially if you are out enjoying the countryside and find yourself in a livestock field – and especially if you have a dog with you. Please do make a point of staying well away from them. We did once have a heifer, though, who clearly did not relish the experience. Having finally been helped to give birth, she turned around to behold this new presence in her life, struggling to his feet, put her nose an inch from his and just bellowed 'Moooooooooooooo!' at him over and over again. I think she may have been in shock, or perhaps lamenting her lost carefree youth. This was a memory which came to me with a quiet smile (a luxury not afforded to my poor wife at the time) at the birth of our own first child some years later; happily she coped somewhat better!

When calves are lost, it's important to 'dry' the cow off, as she will have bagged up with milk ready for her new arrival. We'll typically milk her valuable colostrum and freeze it for future emergency use, then feed her a low-energy diet (primarily straw) to reduce her milk production. Sometimes we might concurrently happen to have newborn twins and their mother may be struggling to feed them both; we might be able to transplant one of these to the cow who's lost her calf; or perhaps we have a calf who's lost its mum at birth and we can get the two to meld. This is a very hit-

and-miss process; cows are often very reluctant to adopt a calf they suspect isn't theirs, and can even become violent towards it. If we do end up with an orphan, it's a case of tubing it with our reserve colostrum before moving it onto powdered formula milk, which we then bottle feed until we can encourage them to drink from an open bucket. Raising an individual calf in this way is very time consuming, but at the end you tend to have a friendly animal for life, just like the aforementioned U-Ropa. She'll be an exception to the rule that we don't carry 'pets' after they reach the end of their productive lives; we're so fond of Ropey that we couldn't bear to send her off to slaughter before her time.

What happens to animals that **do** die on the premises? They must be disposed of properly; we can't just bury them. We call (whom we colloquially refer to as) the knacker man who arrives in his lorry within twenty-four hours. This chap has a sad job I don't envy, loading his vehicle with animal carcasses. Although an invaluable service, it's not a pretty sight or smell, especially in the summer. It goes without saying that these carcasses can't enter the food chain, and they're taken instead to be rendered, an industrial process which uses heat and pressure to sterilise and stabilise animal material, killing any harmful microbes. While the majority of the rendered animal is lost as water, what is left are fats and proteins which go into a wide variety of further uses. Livestock which die on-farm are considered 'high risk' material and their rendered by-products are only permitted to go into biofuels and solid fuel alternatives, but rendered by-products from other parts of the food chain such as the waste from slaughterhouses can end up as chemicals, pet food, fertiliser and biogas. Almost no part of an animal goes unused; the versatility of the carcass is staggering.

As for our happy, healthy calves, within a few days, and after they've found their feet and bonded with their mum, we'll move them from individual pens into a bigger pen with all the new mothers until spring arrives and they can move outside as a group. It's great to see the calves move about as a gang, as they skip, race and play together, tails high in the air. Ted and Toby are also big fans; a calf's milk-rich poo is, it would seem, the ultimate canine delicacy. Let them out of your sight for a minute at this time of year, and you can usually find them selectively deaf and hastily chewing down big mouthfuls of this sticky treat before you can get to them. It is **grim**, and puts all the expensive hypo-allergenic kibble I carefully select and buy for them into perspective.

You may note the unsightly big yellow ear tags which all cattle possess. These do somewhat spoil the aesthetics of our lovely traditional beasts, but are a legal requirement. In beef calves they must be fitted within three weeks of birth, in much the same process as a human piercing. These tags are designed to last the lifetime of the animal and record important data such as the unique herd number and that animal's unique individual ID number. On one of the tags there's room to write a name in indelible ink. Each animal also has a passport which must be applied for from the government's British Cattle Movement Service within four weeks of birth. This piece of paper will follow the animal through its entire life, recording each movement off-farm, whether to be sold or even if they just go down the road to an agricultural show. Some of our cattle are better travelled than me, with passports to prove it. This is all done to make sure that we have through-life traceability of every single animal in the British food chain so that the consumer can have complete confidence in the provenance of the food they eat. These levels of surveillance are also a reaction to the disastrous foot-and-mouth disease outbreak of 2001, when sparsely recorded animal movements contributed to its rapid spread around the country.

Currently, British farmers are going through the process of updating this traceability and passport system from paper-based to electronic. Most sheep have had electronically readable chips in their ears since 2010, and the intention is that cattle and other animals will move in that direction soon. Not only should this increase the ease with which animals are traced, but lead to improvements in on-farm management as farmers are better able to store and manage a range of data from genetic information and growth rates to medical records. For a profession insistent that 'the cloud' is something which brings rain rather than data, these are exciting times.

BOUNDARIES

We've spoken about my love of drystone walls and the important role they play in the landscape of my farm. Alongside them, sometimes literally, we also have the classic British farmland hedge. We have many miles of hedges hemming our fields, and along our roads and lanes. These act as boundaries, livestock fences, windbreaks, habitats, carbon buffers and landscape features. There's a lot going on in a farmland hedge (and, not infrequently, a certain pair of Jack Russells looking for something to chase).

It's thought that these wonderful living organisms have been a feature of the British landscape in one form or another for thousands of years, but it was after the Enclosure Acts of the eighteenth and nineteenth centuries that their numbers really multiplied as landlords ejected tenants from open, commonly held land and in many cases planted hedges to delineate their new private holdings. (Many of these newly disenfranchised farmers then migrated to the cities, to be fed in turn by the agricultural revolution of which this social change was a part.) Strange as it may seem today, the bucolic farmland hedge can therefore be seen as a symbol of both economic progress and social injustice.

The second half of the twentieth century saw widescale damage wreaked on hedges up and down the land, as war and its aftermath led governments to encourage and even incentivise farmers to rationalise their holdings by removing hedges to increase field sizes and improve efficiencies. The mechanisation of agriculture led to many fields becoming too small for modern practices. It was not uncommon to see hedges still being removed even into the 1990s, and I know from old farm maps that we used to have many more in our fields a century ago, along with their associated trees. Priorities and values were different in different times; today, farmers are replanting hedges at an unprecedented rate, and existing hedges have been protected in law since 1997.

Today, farmers across the UK manage around 800,000km of hedge, which equates to some 120,000ha in area.[33] They typically consist of hawthorn or blackthorn (with their vicious spines), with ramblers like guelder rose and bramble (with their vicious thorns), and alder and dotted with trees such as field maple, hazel and sloe. In short, you don't want to fall into a hedge. In summer they burst into flower in a patchwork of colours, before giving over to a multitude of berries and other foodstuffs for the long winter months and the foraging birds and mammals which also make both the hedge and its root systems their homes. Hedges are also natural corridors for such wildlife to move through in safety from wood to wood, field to field, hidden from watchful eyes and sharp talons.

Hedges aren't universal across my whole farm, but are concentrated in the mid and lowland areas with their deeper soils and less readily available hard granite rocks which make up the drystone walls of the higher reaches. People very much made use of the materials at hand when delineating fields in the past;

33 National Farmers' Union, 'Managing hedgerows for carbon storage', 2021, NFUonline.

where no rock was available, they planted hedge. The East Midlands, though, are the national home of the farmland hedge, with four kilometres in every square kilometre of land – the most in the country.

Just like walls, our hedges require maintenance to keep them in good condition. Left unmanaged, they grow too high and too thin at the base and more like rows of stunted trees, making them little use either as a barrier or windbreak to livestock, or for the fauna which would normally call them home. This management is usually carried with a hedgecutter mounted on a tractor – a spinning flail on the end of a long hydraulic arm. The aim is to keep the hedge in manageable proportions and good condition. This job is only carried out between September and February to avoid the main breeding season for nesting farmland birds, some of which use our hedges as comfortable homes. Of course, not being entirely au-fait with the Gregorian calendar, they don't necessarily know that they need to vacate the premises with their eggs or chicks by the first of September, so many farmers will leave as much leeway as possible into the cutting season before beginning, and will always be on the lookout for nests.

Hedge cutting can be a very contentious issue, and I certainly won't defend some pretty poor practice which can be seen on some farms where hedges are reduced year after year to very small, neat boxes often no higher nor wider than a kitchen worksurface, all for the sake of 'neatness'. To me, it doesn't look good and I can't imagine it's a particularly attractive environment for our native fauna, nor provides much winter food. Thankfully, such practice is declining; on our farm, hedges are cut at most once every two years to give them as many months uninterrupted peace as possible. It's great that some of ours are fifteen or twenty feet high, and half as wide across. I'm not a fan of cutting until well into the winter, as it's wrong to flail the berries off branches before the birds have had a chance to take them. The flailing itself can seem damaging, but hedge has a remarkable ability to regrow and compensate and is all the better for it.

So if birds may still be nesting in September, and berries may be better left for the autumn, why don't all farmers wait? It's important to remember that our fields are our incomes; with most crops planted between August and October, and our winters becoming increasingly wet, the potential is there to damage soil and crop by waiting until the latest possible moment, or for a hard frost which may never come. For many (especially those who may rely on contractors with big workloads) the work must be done before crops are planted. It's an imperfect system, yes, but most intentions are moving in the right direction. Personally, I like to see a scruffy, tall and wide hedge. Not only are they good for nature, but they can store more atmospheric carbon beneath their roots. The soil at the base of a hedge is often considerably darker and richer than that within the field, a sure sign of this. It's estimated that the carbon stored in the above-ground biomass of a smaller hedge is around fifteen tonnes per hectare, rising to thirty or forty tonnes for bigger hedges, with similar amounts stored below ground. Taken nationally, it's thought then that hedgerows store some 4.8 million tonnes of carbon scrubbed from the atmosphere while also providing a myriad other services.[34]

But when a hedge does get out of shape, and too thin at the base to fulfil its original task, it can be lain. This is a process which can also cause alarm to the uninitiated, as it seems that a precious farmland habitat is being cut down wholesale. But it's a time-honoured tradition which is perhaps best described as creative destruction. Essentially, much of the bulk of the hedge is removed, with the main stems cut nearly through and then leaned over

34 ibid

towards the ground and secured with stakes and binders. This creates a livestock-proof, living barrier and promotes regrowth from the base of the hedge (rather than the upper branches, now removed) and ensures the long-term health and longevity of the boundary for at least another fifty years. Hedge laying is, as with wall building, a skilled (and laborious) endeavour (with thick gloves a must); it's also a cash-hungry undertaking unless those skills are held in-house. As a result, many farmers similarly rely on grant funding from environmental stewardship schemes, of which there is never enough. Once again, sustainability on both the big and small scales boils down to cost and the amount of black ink in individual accounts.

Happily, in recent years – and with the help of those grants – we have invested in new hedges on the farm, putting right some of the wrongs committed in past decades. It's one of the most rewarding day's farming you can have to establish a new line of hedge 'quicks' (I don't know why they're called that, as both the process of planting them and their subsequent growth rates are far from speedy). But, as with planting a tree, you really are investing in the future when you plant a hedge, dibbing each one individually into its little hole, dropping a cane in and then wrapping both up in a protective guard. Earlier this year I was planting alongside a road, and it was great to hear the positive comments from passersby. If I'm going to make a permanent change to the landscape, I want it to be a positive one. And as the saying goes; the best time to plant a tree was yesterday – the second best time is today.

One of the most heartbreaking sights on the farm is when I see – all too frequently – long stretches of ancient hedge which have been ripped out of the ground by speeding motorists who lose control of their vehicles and career through them into my fields. Yes, the most important thing is that those individuals are unhurt, but they leave behind them jagged gaps which will never truly heal, even if replanted with new plants. When you're out driving in the countryside, please always remember that speed limits aren't a target, and that you never know what might be around the next corner: water, ice, a cyclist, a tractor, a horse; let's just all get home safely (and leave my hedges alone!).

Both drystone walls and hedges are expensive and time-consuming means by which to delineate fields. Nobody is going to construct new walls in the twenty-first century (sourcing the materials alone would be mind-boggling) while hedges can take decades to be properly stock-proof. This is why the barbed-wire or wire-net fence has become so ubiquitous. Two people can erect hundreds of metres per day by simply knocking in the wooden posts and stapling the wire taught along it. It might not look as nice, it might not contribute to the heritage of the landscape, and it might not serve as a biodiverse habitat, but the wire fence does the job of keeping your livestock secure for a fraction of the cost of a new wall, or even in many cases of restoring an old one. Even where I do plant new hedges, they need the protection of a wire fence for many years before they're mature enough to act as a barrier to livestock. What's more, our Longhorns are – it must be said – pretty rough characters. With their thick hides and wide horns, they're well able to knock walls over with their itchy bottoms, or bulldoze holes through even mature hedges with their horns. In reality, we need to 'back-fence' all of our walls and hedges to protect them from our cattle.

Erecting a decent wire fence is a skilled job too, for if you don't do it right the wire goes slack and the whole thing becomes a highly visible and sad testament to poor craftsmanship, but it's not on the same level as the traditional arts of wall-building or hedge-laying. In the past, every timber post would have been knocked in by hand but for the most part these days we use a mechanical post-knocker which drops a weight atop the sharpened stake and drives it into the earth. We have a lot of rocks, which means we also snap a lot of stakes, but that's just one of the challenges that comes with living in such a picturesque area. Sadly, the big trade-off of the wire fence is its longevity: although the wire is pretty indestructible (though the inevitable snaps and cuts from poachers and militant ramblers make it ever harder to keep taught) the softwood timber posts of today are pretty shoddy affairs which rarely last a decade before rotting off at the base and needing to be replaced; livestock fencing on a farm of our size is like painting the Forth Bridge. This, in contrast to the proud old oak posts, some a century old, cut from our own trees and still as good as the day they were painstakingly knocked in which can still be found in places.

Something which has made a reappearance on our farm in recent years is electric fencing. This consists of insulated plastic stakes, stabbed into the ground by hand along which is strung electrically-conductive tape or wire, connected to a battery or solar panel which keeps the system energised. It's a quick, cheap and flexible means of fencing. This flexibility is key, allowing farmers to subdivide fields without going to the costs and permanence of erecting wire. In a similar, but very hi-tech vein, are 'virtual fencing systems' which may well be the way of the future. Each animal wears a GPS-enabled collar which emits a warning sound or an electrical impulse when they cross an invisible boundary set via smartphone. Trials indicate that — especially in the vast uplands where flocks cover huge areas – this is a system which could really work and allow disfiguring (and expensive) wire fences to be dispensed with entirely.

Every farmer has painful experience of electric fencing. In response to the inevitable question 'Is it working?' comes the inevitable response 'Touch it and see' – though usually we gingerly touch the wire with a long blade of grass in an attempt to spare our nervous systems slightly. But somehow, and I don't know how, at some point in the year you almost always end up straddling an electric fence thinking it's off when it isn't. There's also the perennial experience of opening the curtains to find sheep or cattle wandering about on the lawn after the battery went dead at some point in the night, followed by 'But I only just charged it!'

Winter is the time for all the boundary work we've talked about. Although the days are shorter, the fields are empty of animals which means you can take old fences down and replace them at leisure. It's also the time that hedge plants and trees (which are grown in nurseries for a couple of years before I buy them) need to be transplanted, before they start to shoot in the spring. For the same reason, it's the season that hedge laying or coppicing occurs, whilst they're dormant in the cold months. Walls, well they can be messed about with at any time, but with much of the farm in hibernation over the winter, it's a good time to catch up on such jobs. In recent years the extreme wet winters and extreme dry springs have made even boundary work difficult; it's either too wet to get tractors onto the fields, or the ground is too hard with drought even to knock posts in, which snap as if hammered into rock. It's also very easy to lose a newly planted hedge in a dry time; it's important to keep the plants watered and free of competing nettles and brambles until they find their feet.

A final word on hedges. I frequently see accusations that farmers are still 'grubbing out' historic hedges to enlarge their fields. Although there's always going to be isolated incidents of people in any walk of life doing things they shouldn't, the law is clear – such things are illegal and the trend is now to plant and replace, not destroy. What breaks the heart is to travel the country and see ancient farmland, woodland and hedges ripped out to make way for 'development'. It's happening around us here in Leicestershire all the time, and nobody seems to make comment on it, as if such things are just 'progress'. Yes, we need new industrial units and housing, but the impulse always seems to be to build on greenfield sites rather than the vast areas of brownfield in our towns and cities which stand ripe for redevelopment at no cost to the natural world. At least I'm putting right what went wrong on my patch in the past; it'll be a lot harder to replant a hedge through twelve inches of concrete in future.

DRAINAGE

This may not seem the most promising topic to read about, but I assure you it's more interesting than you might think, and a major preoccupation of almost every farmer in the land. You may not realise it, but the majority of productive farmland across the country sits atop an intricate system of drains carrying excess water from the fields and depositing it in boundary ditches, and thence away into watercourses and, eventually, the sea. Were these drains not to exist, much of the farmed land in the country – particularly arable land – would lie wet and unfarmable, or at the very least be much less productive than is the case. More than this though, well-drained soil is better for the environment as it allows water to percolate into it more readily carrying whatever fertilisers have been spread on the field, rather than seeing run-off carried directly into watercourses, along with the soil itself. Well drained soils are also better able to manage the flow of water coming from farmland, releasing it more steadily during rainfall events and thereby mitigating potential flooding downstream in urban areas. In the East of England, huge tracts of our most productive arable and horticultural lands have, over many centuries, been 'reclaimed' from the below-sea-level marsh they once were in some of the most remarkable feats of hydraulic engineering ever to be seen in these isles. Today, drainage dykes and canals delineate fields in the same way hedges and walls criss-cross mine, with the water physically pumped away to the coast. Over many years, untold resources and effort have been expended on improving the productivity of our farmed landscape, all buried under the soil, out of sight.

Were you to strip the surface from many fields, you would see a delicate latticework of drainage channels like the veins of a leaf. These have been laid down over many decades, often piecemeal, by different hands in different generations using different materials and techniques. Most farms have paper plans of their drainage schemes – like mine – on yellowing paper often patched with browning sticky-tape, showing beautifully crafted hand-drawn maps of fields created by people with no formal training in art but who, through frequent practice, created a new genre of precise expression. In coloured pen and pencil, they sketched out (in exacting detail) the locations of all the pipes installed, their directions of flow, their lengths and distances from landmarks for future rediscovery, and any old pipes which they've happened across or assimilated into their new works. These are some of the most treasured and precious documents on any farm: they're true pieces of landscape history, without which we would be blind.

The oldest systems we have are 'stone drains' which date from the nineteenth century or earlier and are little more than channels dug in the soil to a depth of perhaps four feet and partially filled with local rocks before being backfilled with soil. Water would find its way down to the rocks and percolate away to boundary features such as streams. Remarkably – despite their great age – many of these still run today, though they are so old that they appear on no map, so that stumbling across them is always by happenstance.

In the nineteenth century technology took a step forward with the mechanical production of the clay drainage tile. Once again, mile upon mile of trench was laboriously dug, by hand, but now hollow clay pipes (the most popular size being perhaps four inches in diameter by twelve inches in length) were lain, one after another, in the base of the trench with the idea that water would percolate inside the pipe and run away into boundary ditches dug – by hand – around the edge of many a field. As with drystone wall building, the sheer scale of the effort involved in such an undertaking, and the precision with which it was carried out without any of our modern aids, never ceases to escape me. It's thought that fifty per cent of the farmland in southern Britain was drained in this way in the late nineteenth and early twentieth centuries as our Victorian ancestors strove to improve the world around them and boost the productivity of their land. Many of these pipes continue to run, even today.

Fast forward once again to the 1970s and 1980s and the inevitable appearance of plastic, this time in the shape of great rolls of flexible, perforated pipe. But by this point, large mechanical excavators on tracks with laser levels move across the landscape digging the trench, laying the pipe and covering it back over in one ponderous motion – though now also covering the pipe with a layer of permeable gravel in order to aid the throughflow of water. I can just remember the final time we had one of these machines on the farm in the early 1990s; I was certain it must have emerged from the pod of Thunderbird 2.

A huge amount of my time every winter is taken up in the maintenance and repair of our old drainage systems to keep them functioning. Some are many decades old, but the body of the system dates from the period after the Second World War until the 1980s when generous government grants were available to help install such things. Since the end of that aid, the amount of land drained or re-drained in the UK has fallen precipitously due to the high cost – £2500–£3500 per hectare. It's not that the cost isn't justifiable; it's just that for tenant farmers, those who are unable to borrow against the value of their land, it's a huge amount of money to find after decades of low agricultural profitability – especially if they are on short-tenure lets, when a drainage scheme might have a payback of decades. As a result, 'make do and mend' is generally the order of the day.

In winter I'll hire a digger and set off into the mists with Ted and Toby every morning for several weeks, returning at dusk. The primary job is to repair any drains which have become blocked, resulting in a build-up of water pressure until the pipe ruptures and bubbles up on the surface. Blockages occur as a result of infiltration of pipes by sediment or roots, or sometimes when earth movements (from our damned heavy machinery) knock the old tiles out of their careful alignment. Very rapidly, running surface water will liquefy the soil and kill the crops in its path, as well as causing erosion, sometimes digging deep channels in loose earth. Digging down, repairing the damaged section, and seeing the water flow freely once again before covering the pipe over is one of the most satisfying jobs I do on the farm. The entire system operates without any human input or power source, but solely through the laws of physics. I just love it!

The other major task to carry out is cleaning out the field ditches. Smaller pipes discharge into larger mains and thence into the ditches, which carry the water off to streams and rivers. These ditches, over time, also become clogged with waterborne sediment and general debris such as leaves and stones (as well as, unfortunately, an increasing amount of fly-tipping and human trash, with more and more people in recent years clearly believing that the countryside is the place for dumping their rubbish). Eventually, the water level in the ditches can rise above the level of the pipe outfalls. So with the digger I gently scrape the ditch out, slowly working my way around each field until the water flows freely. And there is no more satisfying sight in farming than discovering a previously unknown outfall and finding that it still discharges! I've discovered over the years that our drainage maps are woefully incomplete, having either been lost or never existing in the first place.

Basic maintenance has sadly suffered in the last decades as our little family farm expanded to chase big economies of scale, and take on big equipment and fewer staff. Time-consuming but 'non-essential' tasks like this took a back seat, year after year. In the past, we employed a man who had been with us his entire working life. During the winter, his sole responsibility was to disappear into the mist, like me, but with a shovel and a scythe rather than a digger. He would clamber into the ditches and – by hand – clear mile after meticulous mile of sediment, bramble and fallen branch every year to make sure that problems never developed: a little and often. What a shame that, in our modern world, that attention to detail has been lost, along with the knowledge such people once had of every inch of the farm. After more than ten years of my own labours, I am only now beginning to finally get to grips with my task, to know the location of every outfall and pipe. To uncover the hidden ditches which run in the high hills at the far extremities of the farm, carrying water to ancient slate-lined cattle drinkers, fed not by mains water, but by the rain from the sky filtered through my soil. I love working on the pipes and drains of my farm, hands dirty and wet, because in a strange way it feels like I'm connected to the very pulse of the land – my land – with water the very lifeblood of food production literally coursing through the ground. And, today, only I know where everything is; it's a privileged feeling of connection and place.

RED TRACTOR STANDARDS

I'm proud to produce food to some of the highest standards in the world in terms of animal welfare, environmental protection, quality, safety, traceability and ethics. As a British farmer, I'm lucky to operate in an environment where the legislative baseline of such standards is so high as a result of decades of incremental improvements, societal expectations and voluntary endeavours. The British public is similarly lucky to have such high-quality food as a given. Our membership of the EU has had a large role to play in this – but it's also true to say that many of the joint rules and regulations which should apply across the whole bloc have not always been adopted by other member states with the rigour of the UK. An example of this was the EU-wide banning of battery-caged laying hens in 2012. While British poultry farmers spent £400m investing in higher-welfare 'enriched' cages in the decade before the regulation was implemented, many European countries made little attempt to comply by the deadline, raising fears at the time that the UK market would become undercut by cheaper, lower-welfare eggs from the Continent.[35]

High standards are at the core of everything we do in British agriculture. This gives us some of the safest, highest quality food in the world, yet food which remains both the cheapest in Europe and the third cheapest in the world as a proportion of disposable household income, behind only the United States (with its comparatively unregulated food system, vast scale and eye-watering levels of financial support) and Singapore (which is so tiny, wealthy and densely populated that it largely imports its food). High food standards come with high production costs, and it's a constant struggle for me to turn a profit on the food I produce.

35 'The end of battery farms in Britain – but not Europe', *The Independent*, 27 December 2011.

But you'll struggle to find a British farmer who thinks the solution to that conundrum is to engage in a race to the bottom on food standards in order to cut those costs. We know that isn't what the British public wants, it's not sustainable and it's not how we want to farm.

The issue of food standards blew up in a big way in 2020 as a result of our decision to leave the EU. With our official exit in January of that year, government was finally able to conduct negotiations as an 'independent trading nation' and looked to prioritise a bilateral deal with the United States – working feverishly towards that goal in the final year of the Trump presidency. There was legitimate concern that – outside the umbrella of the EU, a world-trade superpower with its 450 million citizens – Britain would be forced to accept American agri-food goods produced to standards it would be illegal to farm to here in return for deals around sectors such as financial services. Indeed, many members of the governing party had openly touted the importation of the cheapest food from around the world as a key Brexit aspiration, dismissing concerns around standards as 'protectionism'.

You will be familiar with the outcry around issues such as chlorinated chicken and hormone-treated beef, which became the rallying cry of those opposed to such a lowering of our import standards. Although proponents of such imports argued (mostly correctly) that such food is not palpably **dangerous** from a safety standpoint, others countered that the real issue concerns the lower welfare of such systems which allow lower production costs, in turn undercutting higher-quality British farming. On chlorinated chicken, the point is that the stocking densities of the birds involved are much higher than those allowed in the EU/UK, with rules around the cleanliness of their habitats much lower or even non-existent. As a result, a chemical wash of the chicken carcass is necessary to neutralise dangerous pathogens such as salmonella and campylobacter after culling, whereas our higher welfare standards mean that only potable water is allowed to cleanse the bird after death. Essentially, chemicals are used to compensate for the lower welfare standards of many poultry enterprises in the US (and elsewhere) where birds end their lives filthy and covered with bacteria. In the UK, we treat the causes of such pathogens via higher standards and welfare, rather than fix the symptoms via chemical washes.

The questions around 'hormone beef' are more subtle; in the US there are few rules restricting the use of a range of artificial growth hormones which enable cattle to grow up to thirty per cent faster than naturally in the UK. These were banned across the EU in 1981 due to concerns about their impact on human health. The Americans (and others) argue that there's no conclusive evidence of a risk to human health from consuming these hormones, and there's been an ongoing battle between the US and the EU in the World Trade Organisation (WTO) ever since over the European ban on the import of hormone beef. Ultimately, the WTO – which some might suggest operates to the lowest common denominator in many areas – has tended to rule with the Americans, but the trade power of the EU has kept the issue at arm's length for decades. The hope of the American government is that, split from the protection of the EU, the UK will be forced to capitulate to their demands and accept hormone treated beef as part of any future trade deal. Under whichever president, America is a food-producing and exporting superpower and requires trade partners to accept its produce as a basic precondition of any deal. This is equally true of many of the other nations with which we are currently prioritising trade negotiations, such as Australia and Canada; the threat to our food standards is not restricted to any one agreement.

But, when it comes to our food standards, chlorinated chicken and hormone-treated beef are but the tip of a large iceberg. One of my key concerns is the terrible over-use of antibiotics in the global food chain. It's estimated that by 2050 anti-microbial resistance (AMR) could cause the deaths of up to ten million people per year.[36] Such a scenario was the driver behind the voluntary initiative of UK livestock farmers to reduce our purchases of on-farm antibiotics by nearly fifty per cent between 2014 and 2018, with new targets subsequently set to reduce usage yet further. In the United States and Canada, on-farm antibiotic use is five times higher than in the UK. The average US beef farm uses seven times more antibiotics than the average British.[37] There, they are used as preventative treatments (to stop animals from potentially becoming sick) and as growth promoters (to increase their productivity). Again, in the UK we take the position that good husbandry prevents the need for antibiotic use, and that only where animals do become unavoidably sick should such drugs be used. As far as using antibiotics to boost growth rates (and therefore profits), to me that just seems the epitome of unsustainable short-termism: cheaper food today for a health catastrophe tomorrow.

But it isn't just in animal products that there are huge differences between British production and that of much of the world; we've already seen that our competitors have access to a much greater range of plant protection products than we do in the UK, while of course genetically modified foods are common in much of the rest of the world, while still banned from production in Europe (though not, hypocritically, from importation). Such GMOs give farmers a huge competitive advantage. And this is before we get into the ethical questions of whether we should be buying food produced

36 Review on Antimicrobial Resistance, *Antimicrobial Resistance: Tackling a crisis for the health and wealth of nations,* 2014, 16pp.

37 Alliance to Save our Antibiotics, *Farm antibiotics and trade deals – could UK standards be undermined?,* 2020, 26pp.

in the ashes of some of the most biodiverse regions on the planet; from parched desert feedlots of 30,000 cattle and more; or imported cane sugar often produced using highly questionable labour standards when British farmers can grow our own sugar beet in the green fields of home.

We operate under some of the strictest regulatory standards in the world, but also go above and beyond this. The vast majority of the food produced here is grown under the voluntary 'Red Tractor' scheme, the logo of which I hope you recognise from your weekly shops, often seen alongside the Union Jack. As one of the 46,000 Red Tractor farmers across the country, I submit myself to additional requirements on areas such as animal welfare, food safety, traceability and environmental protection to ensure ever-improving standards in our food chain. Red Tractor labelled food is bred, grown, reared and processed in the UK in a way you can trust.

Every Red Tractor farmer has a copy of extensive obligations which we are required to adhere to, going above and beyond the regulatory minimum. These requirements range from having emergency plans in place to deal with a wide range of scenarios, to drilling down into the detail of how the welfare of our animals can be improved, how the safety of our use of PPPs can be optimised, or how our utilisation of antibiotics can continue to be reduced through better planning and practice.

For livestock, the 'Five Freedoms' are at the core of this. These are freedom from thirst, hunger and malnutrition; freedom from discomfort due to environment; freedom from pain, injury and disease; the freedom to express normal behaviour for their species; and freedom from fear and distress.

Every year I will have an annual on-site audit of my records and inspection of my animals and buildings to make sure everything is as it should be. Is there any evidence of rodents in my grain store? Are my animals clearly happy and healthy? Am I taking steps to ensure high biosecurity, and high security of my (explosive) nitrogen fertiliser? Have I been keeping good records of PPP applications, and ensuring that everyone is appropriately trained to the tasks they perform? Am I certain that no foreign bodies can enter the food chain? There's a long list of items which needs to be checked off before I am given the green light to continue to sell as a Red Tractor farmer for another year (all the way down to whether Ted and Toby have been treated with a wormer to prevent cross-infection of the livestock!), and I find it helpful to have that annual inspection to keep me sharp and not let issues escalate.

In theory, adherence to such a scheme should yield a premium for my produce by producing above the legal baseline, but in reality it's a scheme which has enjoyed such widespread acceptance and success throughout the food and farming industry that these voluntary standards have now essentially become the new baseline which is expected as a minimum from supermarkets and food manufacturers; good luck opting out of the scheme and trying to sell a load of wheat or cattle into the food chain. Essentially, British farmers have accepted the increased costs and burdens of being inside the Red Tractor scheme as a means of providing the British public with a better-quality, trusted product.

Red Tractor is not the only such assurance scheme you may see for British foods on your shelves, however. There are others such as the LEAF Marque scheme, RSPCA Freedom Foods, the Quality Standard Mark (QSM) scheme or Pasture for Life which all demand additional requirements on top of Red Tractor standards either around welfare, the environment or eating quality, as well as organic certifications such as from the Soil Association or Organic Farmers and Growers. Individual retailers may also have their own certification marques – in addition to those on imported foods such as 'Fairtrade' or 'Rainforest Alliance'. This can become confusing, but essentially indicates ever-increasing levels of oversight and cost for the farmer which (unlike Red Tractor) they hope will return a small premium on the goods they produce.

I hope, therefore, that you'll look out for the Red Tractor logo when you're in the shops and look to support British farmers. If surveys are to be believed, we Brits aren't unduly concerned about the **safety** of the food we eat, which seems a remarkable thought. But I would suggest this is actually a good thing; it demonstrates the faith which we all place in our food chain in this country, in large part as a result of the good work carried out around traceability and standards through the Red Tractor scheme, instituted in the wake of food scares such as BSE/CJD ('mad cow disease') and salmonella in the 1990s. When food safety scares do emerge, they quickly shoot to the top of the news agenda, but now are seemingly always concerned with imported goods; analysis of the horsemeat scandal of 2013 will demonstrate that none of those tainted products were British but instead ultra-cheap, ultra-processed imports. Clearly, food (such as it was) produced to such low price points was unsustainable without significant fraud in the supply chain, fraud which is becoming increasingly common as genuine ingredients are replaced with sometimes hazardous substitutes, often under the auspices of organised crime. You get what you pay for, and society must find a way to ensure good quality, sustainably produced and nutritious food is affordable to all. My aim as a farmer is to ensure that you can have complete trust in the produce you buy under the Union Jack, and as long as you keep buying it I'll keep growing it.

SPRING

· MARCH · APRIL · MAY

GROWTH

'Spring is the time of plans and projects.'
Leo Tolstoy (1828–1910), *Anna Karenina*

TURNOUT

AFTER WHAT CAN seem an interminable succession of short, wet days bookended by cold, blustery nights which see you arriving at and leaving from work in the dark with chapped lips and cracked hands, there's always a point when you suddenly realise spring has begun to arrive. Whether in late February or into March, one morning the sky seems a little brighter, the air a little crisper, the sunrise a little finer and the subsequent day a little warmer. As a gentle south-westerly breeze begins to replace a roaring north-easterly gale, the birdsong seems a little more pronounced and you suddenly see the fields begin to grow a little greener as hedges, trees and crops sense the change in the natural timbre and put on a spurt of early spring growth. The long sleep of winter is finally coming to an end, and life is returning to the countryside. Exactly when we can start to think about turning the girls back out into the fields after their winter staycation is a matter for the conditions, rather than a calendar date. But hopefully by early March the ground underfoot is dry enough and the weather warm enough to consider letting the first groups out of the sheds. From a business perspective, the sooner we can the better, for as long as each animal remains indoors it's consuming expensive feed and bedding. On the other hand, until the days lengthen and the sun becomes stronger, grass growth is still anaemic in the early spring so some outdoor supplementary feeding is likely to be required for a few weeks, especially for the mothers looking after little calves.

After three or four months indoors, the cattle are ready to get back out there. It's one of the great sights of the year when we throw open the doors and clear the way for them to race out into the field; the mothers (who have been through this before) will lead the way jumping and skipping and bucking their heads around as they race up the track and towards the green, green grass. The calves will follow behind as an uncertain, skittery pack, having never been outside the confines of the shed into the wide world before. The antics continue in the field, as the cows burst through the gate and stream away in all directions, acting quite out of character and younger than their sometimes double-digit years. Thence follows a lot of digging, snorting and (most likely) a fresh round of fighting until their excitement is finally drained. Any telegraph poles in the field will take a battering, the wires oscillating across the field. Today is also the litmus test as to whether the repairs you made to the fence over the winter will hold! After an hour, though, calm descends and they turn to the more important task of getting some grass down, and at the first sign of rain they'll be standing at the gate, lowing to be re-housed!

An ongoing issue with cattle is their feet – their hooves must be trimmed once or twice a year to stop them becoming overgrown. Cow's hooves (like their horns) are made from keratin, the same protein from which our fingernails are made. (It's also the same material from which rhino horn grows. What a tragedy that those animals are killed for the supposedly mystical qualities of such a mundane substance.) Just like our fingernails, a cow's hooves also need to be trimmed. Especially after a winter spent on soft bedding, they experience little wear and tear, and the poor state of a cow's feet can be a common cause of lameness, an uncomfortable condition which can see an animal hobbling around as if walking on hot coals.

Like many herd owners, we employ a professional foot trimmer to come in to do this skilled job. The cattle stand in a hydraulic crush which squeezes around them to hold them steady, and then tips over to the horizontal so that all four feet are off the ground and at chest height. Actual cow tipping is quite a sight, to be fair, and until they get used to it the cows can be quite alarmed by the experience. Using a combination of clippers, a small electric angle grinder and files, the foot trimmer then cleans each foot and cuts away the excess hoof in less time than it takes to make a cup of tea. You don't want to be standing anywhere near when the keratin flakes are flying off the angle grinder – unless you're a certain pair of Jack Russells, of course, who seem to think they are manna raining from heaven to be gobbled as quickly as possible. I worry about those two sometimes, who seem to spend their lives hoovering unpleasantness from about the farm. The box then slowly tips the cow back onto its feet, and she walks away, rather nonplussed about the whole experience.

I know every inch of my farm, as does every farmer their own. I know where the soil always gets slightly sticky in that field corner, or where that rock sticks out the ground which risks writing off the mower every year, and where the homes of this or that wild beast can be found. Our animals too, know the landscape in which they spend their lives. It's why we can open the shed door, stand back and just let them find their own way to the field at turnout. This is not unique to us; much of the livestock to be found across Britain is 'hefted' to the landscape in this way: generations of the same family lines tread the same tracks and fields, drink from the same troughs, and find shelter under the same overhanging branches. Mothers teach their calves the lie of the land and the best way to get from A to B, where the best grazing is, or where they feel most safe to stop and rest (all farmed animals are, after all, prey at heart.) Over the course of a year, you'll see livestock treading the same paths – say, that between gate and water trough – over and over again in single file, until they wear a narrow track into the grass. The inherited routes of those tracks won't change over the generations.

Hefting is most pronounced in the vast upland tracts of the country where extensive sheep grazing dominates. There, thousands of sheep will know the rough confines of their own farms and will never stray too far from the areas they are familiar with. There is a deep level of inherited memory in those otherwise quite simple sheep, which on all too many farms was cruelly wiped out in a single day during the foot-and-mouth epidemic of 2001 when mass culling of entire flocks and herds was used to control its spread. Generations of genetic experience was lost at a stroke, and it took many years for fresh flocks and herds to traverse the landscape with the practised ease of their forerunners, a loss which could never be compensated for financially.

Not every farm enjoys the value of hefting, of course: some farms operate 'flying herds' where animals spend only a portion of their life on any one holding, and perhaps will never venture outside in that time. But, for us, with most of our cattle born and spending their entire lives in the same few fields and sheds, it's one of the intangible benefits of the way we farm.

In order that our cows will calve around the turn of the new year, in late spring we'll introduce the bull into the field. He'll have been housed indoors in his own pen for some months, so as we clip a nose ring and drape a halter over his head and horns to take him outside, he'll start to snort and bellow, foam flecking from his hollering mouth. It's a struggle to keep him under control as you head for the gate, his massive energy and power literally quivering through him as he walks, staccato like, his natural impulse to run being curbed by the tiny metal ring in his nose. Then, through the gate, halter off and – finally – unclip his nose and take a couple of rapid steps back as he rears up, full of testosterone, on his haunches and thunders off across the field to the swirling group of cows and calves who greet this new addition to their field by charging in turn towards him. Chaos then ensues as the melee moves back and forth across the field, the bull introducing himself in turn to everyone present, before eventually the scene settles down and calm returns once again. It's quite a sight.

Bulls are generally bestowed with rather grandiose names – or, at least, those are that show promise from a young age. A good breeder can spot potential in very young animals, and may name them appropriately: my mother has named her chunkiest-looking calves such things as 'Conqueror', 'K2', 'Odin' and 'Uruk-Hai' in anticipation of greatness, which has generally been fulfilled. Conversely, occasionally a calf which did show little initial promise will subsequently blossom into an impressive adult, but may have a less than imposing name such as 'Dougal', initially destined as he may have been for a Sunday roast.

Our bull will be left out in the field with his new gang of females there to fulfil his main role – siring the next generation of calves. The impact of a single bull on the future of any herd, but especially a pedigree one, can be huge, with the hope that he will pass on his best traits, combined with those of the cow, to his calves (and by successively breeding the best with the best over generations, a general improvement in the herd can be seen). It's vital that we can trace his pedigree back multiple generations (such things are recorded by the livestock breed societies) to satisfy ourselves that no bad breeding might lurk in his genetics to spoil an entire generation of the herd: one bad cow can only throw one bad calf at a time; but a bad bull can sire dozens, leaving an indelible hoofprint on the future which may take years to remove. Some farms will only carry a single bull, but others will run multiple bulls over the course of a season to keep genetic diversity in succeeding generations high; there will also be a great deal of thought put into which specific cows run with which bull: certain traits should be beneficial if mixed (and the converse), while an element of inbreeding is acceptable and even desirable in livestock, but can only be taken so far.

Some, especially dairy farms, will not carry a bull at all, turning instead to AI, artificial insemination, a technique which we have already mentioned. The major benefit of AI is the huge flexibility and diversity it gives a breeding programme. There are certain superstar bulls in every breed renowned for their physical and genetic attributes: think of them as the leading athletes or supermodels of their species. AI allows any farm to be able to purchase 'straws' of their frozen semen to inseminate their cows, but without the cost of buying the bull, were that even possible, while leasing has fallen out of favour due to increased awareness of the risks of transmitting disease from herd to herd. And instead of owning and using a single bull, you have access to dozens of possibilities every year – they have glossy catalogues you can leaf through over breakfast to choose your man! As a result, some bulls have thousands of offspring in circulation at any one time, all over the world. The Blackbrook herd has exported Longhorn semen as far afield as the United States,

Australia and New Zealand.

Different breeds of cattle (and other livestock) can be crossed to combine (hopefully) the best attributes of both. We currently have a cow conceived by AI from a purebred Longhorn mother who is half Longhorn, half Belgian Blue and named, appropriately enough, Blueberry. As a 'crossbred' she cannot be registered as a purebred of either breed. But in her we looked to combine the exquisite taste of Longhorn beef with the faster and bigger growth characteristic of the Belgian Blue. As it turned out, she has such a great personality that we couldn't bring ourselves to send her to slaughter and instead kept her for breeding to see how her progeny turned out when she's crossed with pure Longhorn semen, reducing the Belgian Blue in their genes to only twenty-five per cent. This is the sort of trial and error which has been the bread and butter of progressive cattle breeding since Bakewell's days.

Semen used in an AI breeding programme can also be 'sexed', so that it's guaranteed that calves born using it will all be female. This is clearly of great use in the dairy sector, where each cow must calve once a year to keep her in milk but where only females are of use as herd replacements. The farmer may use high-quality sexed dairy semen on the top fifty per cent of their herd to ensure enough female replacements from their best cows, and unsexed beef semen on the bottom fifty per cent, the calves from which will then be sold on to a beef farmer for rearing; as crossbred dairy and beef animals, they will be much more productive than pure dairy bulls in the meat trade. A large percentage of British beef is produced through this symbiotic system.

The power of genetics offers some exciting possibilities for the future of sustainable agriculture. While in recent decades livestock breeders have been able to choose from a wide catalogue of traits mostly associated with high performance (such as milk yield and ease of care) talk is increasingly turning to mapping and promoting other characteristics such as feed conversion efficiency (how fast a beef animal can grow to killing weight) or methane emissions (whether certain genetic lines produce fewer greenhouse gases, GHGs, than others for every litre of milk or kilogramme of meat produced). This is equally true of crops: more thought is now being given to breeding varieties with a focus not just on yield or grain quality, but on disease and pest resistance and drought tolerance. In a world where we must produce more food more sustainably as the population grows and resources shrink, it will be more important than ever to harness the natural genetic potential of the species we farm. This will include safeguarding those rare and native breeds – of both plants and livestock – from around the world should we one day realise that they carry genes invaluable to our changing circumstances and needs.

To date, the choice of any trait has been a result of natural breeding programmes little different to those of our first farming ancestors millennia ago: breed two plants or animals together and see what random mutations occur in their offspring while hoping for the best. (This is an outcome also achieved by subjecting seeds to radiation or chemicals in some breeding programmes.) Yet modern biotechnology gives us the potential to formalise and expedite this trial-and-error approach by sequencing the genes of a particular species and learning which express what traits. With this knowledge, scientists can make small but significant alterations to the gene sequence of the plant or animal to enable it to predictably express (or suppress) a particular trait or traits, rather than slog through generations of hit-and-miss breeding to reach the same result. This has clear implications for the sustainability of food production: perhaps oilseed rape better able to naturally withstand attack by cabbage stem flea beetle (thus reducing the need for insecticides), cattle which naturally emit less methane (thus reducing GHG emissions) or wheat better able to withstand the rigours of drought. Any of these innovations would reduce the impact of agriculture on the natural world.

This technique – gene editing (GE) – is controversial and frequently confused with genetic modification (GM), the difference being that GM introduces foreign DNA into the selected organism (transgenesis), while GE merely alters existing genes (mutagenesis). They are two very different technologies, though perhaps it's that word – technology – which makes so many people uncomfortable when it comes to living organisms – especially in our food chain. The use of biotechnology is currently banned in European and British agriculture (though not in our imports, nor in our medicines), yet in the post-Brexit world our current government seems keen to introduce GE in an attempt to differentiate their approach from the European precautionary principle model, derided by some as creating a 'museum of agriculture' which risks seeing the Continent fall further behind their global competitors. Many farmers are keen to embrace GE to achieve greater environmental sustainability, if not profitability (recent history shows that advances in technology rarely give financial benefit to farmers). If growing GE crops can reduce input use, boost soil carbon sequestration, help withstand the extremes of climate change and even be optimised to deliver better nutrition to the consumer, what's not to like? But many farmers are not keen: they argue that biotechnology is a false solution to our sustainability conundrum, and that farmers will become addicted to GE in the same way they did to chemicals in past decades, using them as a crutch when better regenerative farming practices are what's really needed.

For me, the truth is somewhere in between: biotechnology is no panacea to the problems we face, but is likely to be one important strand in addressing them if implemented properly and with the support of the public. We shouldn't be afraid to have the national discussion around GE in agriculture; to my mind it would be foolish to discount any tool from the toolbox without intelligent debate or good reason, when all too often opponents of biotechnology fall back on emotive arguments such as 'scientists playing God' or raising the lazy spectre of 'frankenfood' without acknowledging the very real benefits which they could afford in conjunction with an increased focus on regenerative farming principles. I would like to see less ideology and propaganda and more honesty and pragmatism when addressing the challenge of food sustainability in an ever warming, more crowded world – a world in which predominantly comfortable and well-fed Europeans have significantly more latitude to dismiss potentially revolutionary solutions to resource depletion and hunger than those who stand to benefit most in other continents.

FERTILISERS AND SOIL CHEMISTRY

One of the first jobs which we come to in the spring is applying fertilisers to our overwintered arable crops. Most farmers find it a relief to finally be back out on the tractor after what can seem a very long, dark winter cooped up mostly around the farmyard. As the sun starts to shine and the mercury to rise, it's great to get back into the fields and watch the vistas stretch away to the horizon.

There are two types of fertiliser: organic and inorganic. As we've discussed, the major source of organic fertiliser on my farm is manure, either deposited directly onto the fields by cattle or stored over the winter and spread by machine in the spring. Other farms will use what's at hand to them: some may have diversified into housed chickens and will be able to spread copious amounts of nutrient-rich chicken litter on their fields; others, pig manure. Dairy farms – especially those that don't use deep straw beds such as ours – produce large quantities of liquid manure, or slurry. Cattle poop is pretty loose – especially when the production team is fed on a rich diet – and, combined with the copious volumes of urine, it's estimated that a dairy cow can produce in the region of eight cubic meters of manure per year. As Jeff Goldblum observed in Jurassic Park: 'That is one big pile of shit'. This slurry is collected as part of the daily routine on dairy farms, later to be applied to the fields as organic fertiliser. Traditionally, it was stored in large open lagoons and sprayed onto fields with simple 'splashplate' slurry tankers, but increasingly such open lagoons are being replaced with covered structures and the product itself is being 'dribbled' onto or even injected into the ground to reduce ammonia emissions. Some farms have invested in vast organic digesters which use such animal waste to create heat and electricity, with a very nutrient-dense solid fertiliser as a by-product.

Not all organic fertiliser is 'animal based', however; we also make use of human biosolids from waste treatment plants. What we all flush away must end up somewhere, and regional water companies periodically must empty their lagoons and dispose of the contents! When it reaches us by the lorry-load, it's been dried and decontaminated – but, my word, does it still stink! It's easy to become rapidly unpopular with the neighbours when applying this stuff on a hot day, but it's a valuable fertiliser and makes a virtue of an inevitable by-product of human civilisation.

It's worth remembering the value of organic fertilisers; at the start of the nineteenth century, farmers were realising that the productive capacity of their soils was insufficient to the task of keeping up with the rapidly expanding and urbanising population. Livestock and crop rotations could only do so much to keep rapidly expanding farmland fertile. The solution came in the unlikely form of millions of tonnes of imported bird guano from the coast of Chile, which had built up over millennia into great islands. This nitrogen-rich rocket fuel powered the fields of Industrial Revolution Britain, though at great ecological cost to the landscape of Chile. And ancient bird guano was, of course, a particularly finite resource.

We've already discussed the value of organic fertilisers in a healthy crop rotation. Why are they so important? They provide two vital elements: short term – essential nutrition for the growing crop; long term – health benefits for the sustainability of soils. The key nutrient which growing crops require is nitrogen (N), a major component of chlorophyll and of protein-building amino acids. The issue for plants, however, is that despite nitrogen being one of the most abundant elements on earth (seventy-eight per cent of our atmosphere consists of it) it is not readily available in its unreactive gaseous form, with no significant sources of it in the soil. Although rainfall and certain algae and bacteria can convert atmospheric N into an organic, reactive version available in the soil, this process takes a very long time and the volumes involved are comparatively tiny. Certain crops – primarily legumes such as beans and clover – are also able to 'fix' atmospheric nitrogen via their roots through a symbiotic association with Rhizobium bacteria in the soil. The remarkable thing about these crops is that not only do they require no additional nitrogen to flourish, but they will also leave spare nitrogen in the soil for the next crop. This is very handy – as farmers like free – but it's only very few crops which have this special talent, and the amount of N they leave in the soil isn't enough to carry the entire rotation. As a result, where spring crops are grown, some farmers are increasingly planting nitrogen-fixing 'cover crops' in the autumn to draw it down from the air and into the soil over the winter, before destroying them in the spring to make way for a cash crop which can utilise the free N. It's a roundabout means of farming, but it is an attempt to take advantage of natural processes to grow more climate-friendly food. But again, this fixed nitrogen is not enough to grow a high-yielding non-organic crop, so additions are required.

Manures are naturally rich in ammonia-based nitrogen, and some ninety million tonnes of farmyard manure are used annually in the UK in addition to that excreted by animals directly onto the fields.[38] The application of this manure is one way to get the extra N into the soil required by high-yielding crops which cannot be achieved naturally. Manure-based nitrogen is at the heart of organic farming practice. But on a conventional farm, even this is not enough to produce bountiful and profitable crops, and this is where one of the biggest scientific innovations of the twenty-first century comes in – the Haber-Bosch process and the creation of synthetic nitrogen in the form of ammonia in 1910. I won't go into the details (mostly because I don't understand them) but two very clever Germans (as Germans tend to be) established a technique to draw nitrogen out of the limitless supply of the atmosphere and fix it in solid form to be used as fertiliser (or, during the Great War, more famously to make explosives). Today, some 230 million tonnes of such fertiliser are produced globally each year in a process which consumes three to five per cent of the world's natural gas production – hence the associated carbon footprint of nitrogen fertiliser.[39] But also why, it's estimated, we can grow the current amount of food produced in the world on one quarter of the land area which would otherwise be required were we still at 1900-era yields – with huge implications for global land use and biodiversity retention.

Since the middle of the eighteenth century, the world's human

---

38 Soffe & Lobley (eds), op. cit., p. 38.

39 'Haber process', *Wikipedia*.

population has exploded from some 600 million to more than 7.5 billion today. At many points in that exponential growth there have been dire predictions that rapid population expansion would outstrip the ability of farmers to feed the world. Yet, despite the continuing occurrence of terrible famines in various parts of the globe, the volume of food produced has always exceeded total demand, even if it does not get shared evenly or fairly (a continuing stain on our common humanity). To a large extent, this has been possible because of the ever-increasing areas of land in agricultural production, yet by the twenty-first century we find virgin, productive farmland increasingly difficult to come by (though the spectre of climate change may alter this, while also making some currently marginal land unviable). Thus it has always been that advances in agricultural technology and practice have also allowed for greater volumes of food to be produced, whether the innovations of pioneers like Leicestershire son Robert Bakewell in the field of cattle breeding, or those of twentieth-century American crop-breeding hero Norman Borlaug who was responsible for the development of new, higher-yielding dwarf crop varieties which directly led to the ability to feed one billion people who would otherwise not have lived since the 1960s.[40]

The Haber-Bosch process, however, is thought to put even this accomplishment into the shade: up to half of all the people alive today are estimated to owe their existence to the food produced through the application of artificial nitrogen to crops.[41] This is a staggering thought. But there's no such thing as a free lunch, and there is an environmental cost which we have increasingly come to recognise over the decades. As mentioned, the Haber-Bosch process generates a significant carbon footprint through the

---

40 'Green Revolution', *Wikipedia*.

41 'How many people does synthetic fertilizer feed?', *Our World in Data*, 7 November 2017.

burning of natural gas to produce the fertiliser. Once applied, it can also be a significant source of both air and water pollution, as not all the nitrogen is efficiently converted and absorbed by the crops onto which it is spread and can escape into the atmosphere as ammonia or nitrous oxide (contributing to particulate pollution) or as nitrate into watercourses (contributing to eutrophication and damage to marine life). Indeed, it's estimated that British agriculture accounts for eighty-seven per cent of ammonia emissions in the economy (though we only contribute ten per cent of total GHG emissions) and artificial fertiliser to grow crops is a significant proportion of this.

Farming is a complex series of trade-offs such as this, usually pitting the environment against the ability to feed people, and to do so affordably for the consumer and profitably for the farmer. Farms are, after all, businesses whose primary role is selling the food we produce into an increasingly globalised marketplace where there are few financial rewards for doing 'what is best' for biodiversity or the climate. All too often, society then blames the farmer for the damage wrought on their behalf or at their direction. The sad fact is that our entire global food system is geared towards lowest-cost production and a never-ending race to the bottom on price. Such competition takes few prisoners, and as the factory floor, it's the global countryside which often suffers. Over the decades, Britain's landscape has taken its own share of knocks in the drive for ever-cheaper production, but rarely have we given in to the worst excesses of the global food production machine and our recent and ongoing record is something of which to be proud: British farmers have never made such a conscious effort to farm in harmony with nature as we do today, and with our net-zero ambition for 2040 we aim to constantly and significantly improve.

The use of artificial fertiliser in the UK has in fact decreased by around a third from the high watermark of the 1980s while crop yields have steadily risen.[42] This is indicative of an increasing appreciation of the ecological cost of the overuse of these products and a combination of regulatory and voluntary measures to utilise them more efficiently (as well as reflecting wider factors such as improved crop genetics leading to higher yielding plants). Most of the country is subject to the rules of being in a 'Nitrate Vulnerable Zone' (NVZ), which places restrictions on the volumes of fertiliser which may be applied, as well as the minimum buffer zones which must be observed around high-risk features such as watercourses or boreholes, and taking into account natural slopes and the risk of surface run-off. On-farm, a range of technologies is now available to make most efficient use of the fertiliser we use. Many of these rely on GPS to establish which parts of which fields would benefit from either more or less fertiliser. Some systems rely on satellite imagery or drone photography to take regular measurements of the 'green-ness' of the crop and establish an application rate accordingly, while others rely on tractor-mounted cameras to make real-time decisions as it moves through the crop. For non-nitrogen fertilisers, physical soil sampling is used, and the digital maps thus created are fed into the fertiliser spreader via tablet with the machine automatically adjusting its spreading rate as the tractor moves along. Clearly, these technologies have a cost (which can be prohibitive for smaller farmers, especially) but can have a beneficial impact on the environment and on the long-term finances of the farm: artificial inputs are expensive, and becoming ever more so. No farmer wants to use more of them than they must. But again, we return to unpalatable trade-offs: the demand is for ever-cheaper food; to reduce fertiliser use beyond a certain level leads to uneconomically low yields for the individual farmer, and – taken to its logical conclusion – a greater land requirement

---

42 Department for Environment, Food & Rural Affairs and the Scottish Government, *The British Survey of Fertiliser Practice*, 2020, 108pp.

to produce the same amount of food. Is that better, or worse for the environment? It's also worth mentioning that it's not only artificial nitrogen which poses a potential environmental risk: organic manures too are regulated in their storage and application, as they are similarly liable to pollute when not utilised appropriately.

Through the course of the spring and early summer, I will make multiple applications of nitrogen to my crops rather than just hoofing their entire annual requirement on in one go. This is to make sure that, at every stage of their growth cycle, they have the nutrients they need – no more and no less; a little and often. This also reduces the amount of fertiliser which will not be utilised by the crop and lost instead to the environment. On my farm, I apply fertiliser as a small granule a couple of millimetres in diameter which arrives in bulk six-hundred-kilogramme bags. These little granules are then dissolved by moisture in the air and washed into the soil by rain, before being taken up by the plant roots. Again, climate change clearly has spoiling potential here: our recent run of very dry springs has led not only to water shortages at critical growth stages of our crops (including grass) but also to a lack of nutrients being absorbed at key times. It's important to only undertake this operation on still, dry days to reduce the potential for the product to stray from where you want it to go, and to keep the machine well calibrated to make sure it's as accurate as possible. Some farmers apply fertiliser in liquid form through a crop sprayer: this has the benefit of being absorbed more rapidly through the leaves themselves, as well as being even more precise in its application, but does tend to be more expensive and on a sunny day can scorch and damage the leaves.

Nitrogen is not the only nutrient which I apply on an annual basis, the other major ones being phosphate (P) and potash (K). These are essential for supporting plant processes and stimulating growth and development, such as energetic rooting and stem extension; as such they're absorbed and removed from the soil with every crop and need to be replaced to maintain productivity. Organic manures can be a good source of either P or K (farmyard manure is rich in phosphates, human biosolids are rich in both smell and potash) but the main source of these minerals is from mined deposits which are subsequently refined and spread as granules on the land in the same way as nitrogen. Ninety per cent of the world's phosphate reserves are located in Morocco, while Canada is the world's largest producer of potash, with Russia and Belarus possessing the next largest deposits. People who think about such things might point out the potential dangers of these vital global resources being controlled by very few countries; for now, perhaps, it's best if we don't fall out with Canada.

As with nitrogen, there are risks to the environment of excess phosphates especially reaching watercourses; not only do they damage the aquatic environment and biodiversity, but they also require expensive removal from drinking water. Some sixty per cent of nitrate and twenty-five per cent of phosphate pollution can be attributed to agriculture. But again, the needle is moving in the right direction, with agricultural phosphate applications dropping by fifty-six per cent since 1985.[43] I test my soils regularly to make sure a field actually requires P or K and in recent years have utilised GPS-based precision applications to optimise what I do apply.

Lime is another nutrient which is closely monitored. This controls the pH of the soil, with most tending toward the acid the more they are used. (During planting, when I'm often to be found with muddy hands, I find that they become dry and crack as a result. Farmers hands are as a rule at the opposite end of the skin-scale to babies' bottoms.) As a result, we apply ground limestone

43 Defra 2019, op. cit.

(this, mined all over the UK) to our fields to keep soil pH as close to optimum as possible. As my hands can attest, most things don't much enjoy growing in acid conditions (it retards nutrient uptake for a start) so it's an important job to keep on top of, though as with soil P and K levels it is a very slowly moving index (unlike nitrogen, which like sugar gives plants an immediate and short-lived boost).

Sulphur is the final major plant nutrient which I apply as a fertiliser year-on-year, usually in conjunction with one of the nitrogen applications. The interesting point about sulphur is that my predecessors did not need to apply it; remarkably, industrial pollution from emissions created by the burning of fossil fuels throughout the twentieth century created a 'free' source which was sufficient for farming needs. Improvements in environmental air quality regulations now mean sulphur must be manually applied to crops to enable them to more efficiently metabolise the other nutrients they require. Talk about unintended consequences!

The organic farmyard manure (FYM) which we produce on the farm is a valuable commodity. Although I've explained why it's essential that we also use artificial fertilisers, we use the comparatively small amount of FYM we produce over the winter in a targeted fashion to do most good. It's not just the nutrients which are useful, but also the ability of the organic matter of which the muck is composed (straw and excreta) to help build long-term soil health and structure. The key attribute of manure is that it helps build soil organic matter in a way that synthetic fertiliser cannot. And this is important, as it's this organic matter which is vital for soil fertility and productivity. It encourages the development of soil microbes, which influence a soil's ability to store and recycle nutrients, and decreases the 'bulk density' of the soil, which improves its ability to absorb water and gases and allow easy rooting of plants. It encourages proliferation of soil fauna, especially the all-important earthworms which do so much to improve our soils with their constant subterranean activities, which many consider to be the hallmark of healthy earth. And in raising the organic-matter content of our soil, we can increase the amount of atmospheric carbon which is sequestered therein. This is the natural process whereby growing plants absorb CO_2 from the air during photosynthesis and retain it as biomass, primarily in their root systems. As roots grow, they capture more carbon and store it underground; eventually, when the plant dies, that subterranean carbon store is converted into humus, a stable organic medium which binds the CO_2 in the soil.

This can seem a bit baffling, but the key point is this: soil can act as a carbon sink, absorbing atmospheric CO_2 and holding it below ground via the crops farmers grow. The addition of organic manures increases the amount of carbon which can be stored in this way. It's estimated that 8580 gigatonnes of organic carbon are stored in our global soils – ten times the amount in the atmosphere[44], with one kilogramme of soil organic carbon equal to 3.6kg of atmospheric CO_2. Ninety-five per cent of UK land carbon stock is held in our soils.[45] So adding manure to my soil is not only good for its fertility and productivity, but also offers one way to combat fossil-fuel induced climate change by increasing the amount of warming carbon sucked from the air.

Sadly, this is a process which has been largely forgotten in recent decades. As the finances of farming have tightened, traditional mixed agriculture has been replaced on many farms with straight, continuous arable and horticultural cropping with too little organic matter being returned to the soil as crop after crop is harvested with nothing physically being returned to the fields, a trend which

44 'Carbon sequestration', *Wikipedia*.

45 Defra 2019, op. cit.

has seen the organic-matter content of some arable soils decline along with their general health, productivity and ability to sequester carbon. (Root vegetables are particularly rough on soil health, and tend to be grown infrequently in any one field.) I've recently tested for soil organic matter for the first time; that of our long-term arable fields is around two to three per cent; of our long-term grass pastures on which we graze our cattle, five to six per cent. It's calculated that the average arable field holds forty-three tonnes of carbon per hectare, the average field of permanent pasture eighty-three tonnes. Long-lived, deep-rooting perennial grass has a much greater capacity to store organic carbon than short-lived, shallower-rooting arable crops, but the cultivations which we visit on our arable land also release some of the carbon stored. There are now many farms which look to reduce the cultivations they employ, while increasing the volume of organic manures (augmented by leafy cover crops which are reincorporated into the soil) they use – the 'regenerative' principles of which we have already learned. 'Where there's muck there's brass' has never been more accurate, as farmyard manures have become a much sought-after commodity in the British countryside, with a healthy bartering system in place in some localities with livestock farmers swapping manure for clean straw from their arable neighbours. This is an area of exciting developments for the future, with the potential of British farms to act as carbon sinks for the wider economy as we learn to 'carbon farm' alongside producing climate-friendly, sustainable food. It even raises the possibility of farmers regularly trading in carbon credits, as polluters in the economy look to offset their emissions in a carbon-negative countryside.

I've already mentioned how biotechnology has the potential to help us move towards a more sustainable food future. The volume of CO_2 in our atmosphere is the most pressing issue facing humanity, and I believe our soils – rather than epic engineering projects – offer the best opportunity to mitigate that threat alongside a reduction in emissions. One of the strands of research currently being undertaken is for gene-edited crops with a significantly higher proportion of a naturally occurring cork-like substance called suberin in their roots, which will also grow wider and deeper than in standard crops.[46] Suberin locks up huge amounts of carbon and is very stable in soil; projections are that if seventy per cent of food-producing crops such as cereals and oilseeds globally could be converted to such GE varieties, as much as one third of global GHG emissions could be sequestered in our farmed soils annually, with concurrent and reinforcing benefits for soil health and structure. In a world still overwhelmingly reliant on fossil fuels for its energy, potentially game-changing innovations such as these must at the very least be considered as part of a sustainability strategy which stretches far beyond farming, into the future of our planet itself.

SPRING FIELD OPERATIONS

Spring sees a return to drilling on many farms, as we look to plant in fields left fallow or containing cover crops over the winter. Spring cropping is something some farmers swear by and others avoid altogether. Over the years we've dipped in and out as circumstances have dictated; historically I've preferred to get planting done in autumn, and to trust in the greater yield potential of winter crops. But the impact of climate change on autumn operations in recent years has led me to introduce more spring crops to add more flexibility into our farming system; putting our eggs in more baskets and spreading our risk. From the point of view of someone moving

46 'Harnessing Plants Initiative', Salk Institute for Biological Studies website.

actively toward net-zero farming, spring cropping is also more attractive as it requires less inputs to get to harvest, while cover crops established over the winter in those fields have the potential to benefit soil health, lock up nutrients and even act as a food source to livestock which can be adding organic goodness back into the ground between crops.

The big risk of spring crops is the narrow window in which they can be planted compared to their winter counterparts, and the fact that there's no backup plan should they fail: planted (ideally) in March, harvest is only five months away, so there's no time for do-overs. The dry springs we are increasingly experiencing can bring disaster to little plants with shallow feet; at least winter crops will be well established with robust roots by this point, and somewhat more resilient to climate extremes or pest attack.

Spring is also the season in which the majority of plant protection products are applied, as crops move rapidly through their growth stages. From now into the early summer the primary applications will be fungicides (to control disease) and plant growth regulators (to control crop height and manage leaf canopy, hopefully maximising yield by encouraging the crop the put as much energy into its grain – and not its stalk – as possible). There are certain points in the lifecycles of crops where it's to be expected these products will be applied, but these aren't set in stone and are highly dependent upon the weather: the cooler and (especially) drier the conditions, the lower the urgency or even requirement for fungicides to be applied as crop disease tends to thrive in warm, moist circumstances. At each fungicide stage, I may also apply a herbicide, an insecticide or micronutrients to address specific issues. I must admit, the temptation used to be there to apply herbicides for 'cosmetic' purposes, to make a crop look clean and spotless for the neighbours – but these days I take more pleasure in seeing a bit of a scruffy edge to my fields, with spring weeds only treated if they're likely to sap yield or create an increasing seed-return burden which would require more expensive rectification at a later date.

We've discussed why PPPs are an important element of modern agriculture, but of course farmers such as I recognise that it's better not to use them if at all possible. Any unnecessary input into the environment is better avoided, and given their increasingly exorbitant prices and the importance of safeguarding the chemistry by avoiding their overuse and risk of resistance (as with antibiotics), nobody can afford to use them unless necessary. Some organisations decry any use of PPPs on an extreme interpretation of the precautionary principle. They argue that there may be consequences to their use which we cannot currently detect. This is to overstretch the science base on which decisions as important as our food supply must be taken: to take an ideological stance against all pesticides without first explaining how plentiful, safe and affordable food can be produced in their absence is irresponsible. Even accounting for potential reductions in whole supply chain food waste (waste which would be increased on-farm without PPPs) we would still need a huge increase in the global area of farmland were we simply to discontinue their use tomorrow.

But what do I do to reduce the amount of pesticide I use? The first step is having the mindset that there are a lot of actions to take before reaching for the chemical can. All farms have an Integrated Pest Management (IPM) plan detailing how they can take steps to avoid their use until necessary through prevention of the circumstances where PPPs would be needed, observation of the results and, finally, intervention (both chemical and non-chemical) only if required. A big part of this for me is crop variety selection; as we've seen there isn't just one 'wheat', there are dozens of varieties I can choose from, demonstrating different genetic traits. My personal preference is not for top yield or grain quality, but for maximum natural resistance to or tolerance of disease. This can lead to big reductions in both fungicides (to control disease) and insecticides (to control the pests which can spread plant viruses). Varieties with shorter, more robust stems are also likely to require less growth regulator. Although good varietal selection doesn't guarantee that PPPs need not be used, it does at least allow me to adopt a more relaxed approach to their application (to wait for a perfect spray window) and hopefully a reduction in volume.

Cultivations have a part to play; ploughing provides a clean seed bed in which to plant crops without recourse to a herbicide and tends to reduce the prevalence of slugs (though, as we have seen, this has consequences for soil carbon and potential run-off). I can plant some crops later in the year (November rather than September, perhaps) to give weeds, insects and diseases less opportunity to attack before the onset of winter. A healthy crop rotation keeps the soil disease burden low and reduces the need for chemical controls. Increasingly, more progressive farmers are trying to directly harness the biological power of nature to use its natural defences against pests, by either directly introducing or encouraging the spread of beneficial insects such as ladybirds into crops to prey on destructive species such as aphids. There's also increasing research into and use of biologically rather than chemically based PPPs – 'biopesticides' – utilising bacterial, fungal and other biological actors to either augment natural plant and soil processes or target specific pests. Many farmers apply more micronutrients to their crops than used to be the case, with research indicating that a healthy, balanced biome is more resistant to disease and less requiring of fungicidal intervention. Every year, I will walk every tramline of every field and pull out certain weeds by hand as harvest approaches, bagging and burning them to destroy their seeds. There are sprays I could use, but I choose not to and instead get myself a solid farmer's/trucker's tan for a few weeks, walking mile after mile in the June sun. Some farmers hire gangs of seasonal labourers to carry out this 'roguing'. (In the past, farmers burned their stubbles, which created perfectly clean seed beds. I can just remember it; gangs of men with water bowsers and shovels, their faces streaked with soot and sweat, coaxing fire across the fields. It was a spectacular, dangerous sight, unsurprisingly banned in 1993 due to the air pollution it generated. But the ban did result in greater reliance on herbicides.)

Generally, it's not me who makes the call finally to use a PPP. I employ a crop health specialist called an agronomist who advises me on pesticide and fertiliser application. Some farmers are qualified to do the job themselves, but it's such a complex arena that I find it useful to have a second eye on things. An agronomist will walk crops and make recommendations based on observed thresholds for most PPP applications: for example, 'We will not spray an insecticide unless we can see X number of aphids per plant'. This can be a nervy business, watching your carefully nurtured crop crawling with little chewy bity things which seem to be devouring it before your eyes, but decades of research (should) mean that your crops can withstand a certain level of damage before it begins to impact on profitability. In recent years, I've been trying to adopt a more relaxed tolerance for this kind of risk in an attempt to cut down as much as possible on PPP use: trust the thresholds, go home, have a beer and try not to think about it …

And, when it comes to it, not just anyone can operate the crop sprayer; I must undergo training and exams to apply PPPs on-farm, be registered professionally and undertake further training annually to keep abreast of developments and best practice around applying pesticides. What I've been applying, how and where is also an element of my annual Red Tractor audit. Ironically, you can go to Tesco or B&Q and purchase some of the same pesticides I use (Roundup glyphosate-based herbicide, metaldehyde slug pellets or lawn feed and weed, for example) and use them indiscriminately with no training, oversight or the personal protective equipment required of professional operators. On-farm, half a dozen slug pellets per square metre is sufficient to address matters; I've seen gardeners turn their borders blue with a solid mat of the things, only for them to wash off down the road in heavy rain. In the same vein, the neonicotinoids banned from agriculture to great cost are still the major constituent of flea treatments for pets, and new research indicates that the widespread and prophylactic use of such things in our largely urban pet population is continuing to cause neonic pollution of watercourses – pollution previously blamed on farming.[47]

Every crop sprayer in the country is required to undergo an annual MOT from a qualified technician to ensure that it's in good working order, with no leaks and operating to all the correct pressures and volumes. Again, this is ensuring that – to the greatest extent possible – the PPPs which we do apply are applied safely, precisely and in the quantities specified. Indeed, each product will have its own list of instructions about the conditions under which it may be used: some are to ensure that no crop damage occurs, but others are to minimise any undesirable impact on the natural environment – and especially entry into watercourses. It's remarkable how sensitive water testing now is, so that the equivalent of a teaspoon of active ingredient in many kilometres of stream or river can be detected and traced back to an offending farm were a breach of the regulations to occur. I also make sure I have emergency action plans in place to deal with any spillages of chemicals, especially as they're being loaded into the sprayer. This is done above a bunded (i.e., sealed) containment tank, while the

47 'Pet flea treatments poisoning rivers across England, scientists find', *The Guardian*, 17 November 2020.

store in which I keep the PPPs is locked, fireproof and able to retain far in excess of whatever volume of chemicals stored therein were some Hollywood disaster scene to occur and every single container were to split and empty itself onto the floor.

The process of using PPPs is as safe and low impact as we can reasonably make it. Do I try to reduce my use of them where at all possible? Yes. At times, has this bitten me in the rear, and the pocket? Yes: in giving a threshold the benefit of the doubt and taking a gamble on whether this or that application was **really** necessary, I have been caught out and it has cost me financially. But I would rather risk not doing something than risk doing something unnecessarily and it was the forcing of my hand to repeatedly utilise insecticide on my faltering crops of oilseed rape which convinced me to stop growing it. One of its replacements, winter beans, are a revelation: come their first spring, they've had a single herbicide and no insecticide and look the absolute picture of robust health. But the catch? Well, they're just not very profitable – there's a finite market for baked beans, and imported soya is – as we've seen – much more desirable for animal feed. Here, then, is another of our farming trade-offs. I replace a profitable crop which the market values with an unprofitable one which it doesn't – but is better for the environment. What value on environmental sustainability if I can't make it pay?

LIVESTOCK AND THE ENVIRONMENT

In recent years one issue has come to dominate discussions of food and farming in the media: the environmental sustainability of red meat production. The casual observer could be forgiven for thinking that agriculture in general and beef production specifically are almost solely to blame for our warming climate, or for the destruction of natural habitat around the globe. So often have I heard variations on the phrase 'the single biggest thing we can do to combat climate change is adopt plant-based diets' that I no longer wonder why this has become so widely accepted by influencers in the media, despite lacking the benefit of being true. I know what you might be thinking: a beef farmer defending the production of beef; how very unsurprising. But let me explain why I'm proud to produce the quality British meat which ends up on many a plate, and why it can be enjoyed with confidence – and a clear conscience.

Let's start with the basics. Producing your food has an impact on the environment. If we're just looking at greenhouse gas emissions, then British agriculture is responsible for ten per cent of our national total – some 45.6 million tonnes of carbon dioxide equivalent (CO2e) per year. This 'equivalent' measure is a means of attempting to directly compare the emissions of different GHGs on the basis of their global warming potential over one hundred years (GWP100) by converting amounts of other gases to the equivalent amount of CO2 with the same GWP. In agriculture, this is important because only twelve per cent of our emissions are CO2; thirty-one percent are nitrous oxide and fifty-six per cent are methane.[48] Nitrous oxide is primarily released by both organic and inorganic fertilisers but methane is primarily the responsibility of ruminant livestock such as sheep and cattle, producing some fifty per cent of the country's total methane emissions.[49] This matters because methane is a potent GHG, some twenty-five times more warming than CO2. This then, say critics, is evidence enough that we must move away from livestock farming in the UK towards greener plant-based diets to save the planet.

48 NFU 2020, op. cit.

49 Defra 2019, op. cit.

As with almost any human activity, there's a sliding scale of sustainability in global agriculture. In the same way that there are more and less sustainable ways of producing energy or travelling, there are more and less sustainable ways of putting calories on your plate. But when it comes to the food we eat and the future of our environment, it's not as simple as accepting that plant-based equals good and animal-based equals bad. As with all things, such a false binary obscures a reality composed of many shades of grey. A few years ago the BBC broadcast a programme entitled *Meat: A threat to our planet?*, which was billed as an exposé of the global meat industry and left the viewer in no doubt that by purchasing their weekly beef joint or lamb chop they were personally contributing to the annihilation of the planet's biodiversity and natural resources. This sparked outrage among the UK farming community, but not because of what it showed. Most were in full agreement that the practices the programme highlighted were representative of the very worst of our global food system: deforestation in the Amazon driven by cattle ranching in Brazil; the leaching of huge amounts of antibiotic-rich raw sewage into watercourses from vast housed-pig factories in the USA – the same country in which you can visit huge desert feedlots crammed with tens of thousands of cattle fed a diet of harvested grains and piped-in fresh water. What angered farmers in this country was the inference that all livestock production around the world was the same; that British farms were also hellscapes of unsustainability and low regulation driven by a race to the bottom on standards to turn a faster profit. This is far from the case.

British red meat production is among the most sustainable in the world: its emissions' footprint is half the global average; that of British milk production is just forty per cent.[50] If every dairy cow

50 NFU 2020, op. cit.

the world over were as efficient as its British equivalent, the number of cattle required would drop from the 278 million in existence today to 76 million producing the same volume of milk. At the core of this achievement is our national benediction of lush green grass. As we've seen, the British climate and topography are ideally suited to its growing – in fact, sixty-five per cent of our farmland is not suited to growing any other crop. Realistically, the only alternative use for much of our permanent pasture would be to plant it up with trees and largely abandon it from agriculture, but for generations British farmers have produced high quality milk, beef and lamb from such fields instead, as ruminant animals are uniquely suited to converting that otherwise indigestible plant into delicious food and drink. Nationally, grassland provides the majority of the nutritional requirements for ten million cattle and thirty-five million sheep.[51]

What if we did not produce livestock (or produced far fewer) on those fields, instead perhaps 'rewilding' them in an attempt to lower our carbon footprint? Realistically, consumers would look to imports to replace that which we were no longer farming domestically; there is no shortage of willing sellers keen to gain access to the UK market, from the US to Australia. What would we be achieving by ceasing production of some of the world's lowest-carbon meat and dairy, only to import it from places with significantly worse statistics? We would be doing nothing but exporting our environmental conscience abroad, out of sight and out of mind, while convincing ourselves that we were doing a good turn for the environment. Our contribution to climate change doesn't stop at our borders – we all live under the same sky – and any sustainable solution to the challenges posed by our food system must be global rather than parochial in scope.

51 Soffe & Lobley (eds), op. cit., p. 181.

As we've seen, all soil is capable of sequestering atmospheric carbon, but it's permanent pasture which does it best. It's never cultivated and the long-established plants and root systems continue building organic matter in the soil, augmented by the organic manures returned to the land by grazing livestock. The very action of grazing increases the vigour of the grass to grow both above and below the surface, thereby helping it lay down even more SOM. There are some remarkable images of the deep black soils and incredible grass root systems of the old American prairies where the great herds of buffalo grazed for millennia until they were brought to the brink of extinction by European settlers. Grazing livestock are good for soils, and good soils are good for the environment and our climate. And we can quantify this. According to the Climate Change Committee, ruminant livestock are responsible for some 5.7 per cent of total UK emissions, or approximately 26.2 million tonnes of CO_2e per year primarily as a result of the enteric fermentation in their stomachs and subsequent burping of methane. However, our ruminant-supporting grasslands are sequestering some $9.2mt/CO_2e$ per year, offsetting some of those emissions, which brings the total contribution of cattle and sheep production down to 3.7 per cent.[52] Now, some people may say that's still 3.7 per cent of emissions we can simply cut by switching to plant-based diets, but this is to take far too simplistic a view. As with any issue, livestock production cannot be judged on a sole metric. Grazing livestock and their manures play an invaluable role in healthy crop rotations and soil health: the lesson of the past fifty years is that we need to increase, not decrease their numbers to maintain more sustainable soils. A future devoid of such animals would lead to the increased and increasingly futile use of synthetic fertilisers to compensate, with all their associated complications.

52 NFU 2020, op. cit.

Our British climate (for which, read: wet) also means that we are at the sustainable end of the spectrum when it comes to water usage and livestock. Seventy per cent of the food which the average British cow eats is grass, rising to ninety per cent for sheep. It's been calculated that, of the 17,000 litres of water required to produce one kilogramme of British beef, 84.4 per cent is consumed from rainfall captured within grass, with only 0.4 per cent 'blue water' from a running tap. The figures for lamb are even more favourable, at 96.6 per cent and 0.1 per cent, respectively. This compares very well with nuts and fruits grown in vast monocultures in some of the driest places on earth, irrigated with water from depleting aquifers or shrivelling rivers and exported around the world. Indeed, a litre of British milk consumes eight litres of blue water in its production; the average litre of almond drink consumes one hundred and fifty-eight litres.[53]

Of the average British cow's remaining diet, seventeen per cent is forage from other crops such as the maize which we used to grow and feed our dairy cows. A further six per cent are the by-products from other crops which are unfit for the human food chain: cattle are great recyclers. This could be straw, vegetables which haven't made the supermarket grade, or the leftover 'brewers grains' from brewing and malting. Cattle upcycle these 'waste' products into delicious, high-quality protein rather than see it buried in landfill.

It's no state secret that meat and dairy make up a valuable part of a healthy and balanced diet; in fact, the NHS suggests minimum intakes of them. Red meat is one of the richest sources of essential nutrients such as iron, zinc and B vitamins as well as a significant source of protein. Dairy, too, is an amazing source of protein, as well as potassium, magnesium, zinc and phosphorous. For most

53 ibid

people, it's the main source of iodine, which is difficult to source naturally from other foods. The nutrient density of meat and dairy, as well as the bioavailability of the nutrients they contain, is also really high. So red meat is a product I'm happy to stand by – especially in relation to many of the highly processed 'fake meat' alternatives, which don't hold a candle to it nutritionally and often contain unhealthy levels of fats and salts, along with a list of ingredients and E numbers which would make your head spin.

And this is all before we address the intellectual elephant in the room, the CO2e metric. As it stands under GWP100, because methane is twenty-five times more warming than CO2, one kilogramme of emitted methane is treated as twenty-five kilogrammes of emitted CO2. But this ignores key points. The first is that the CO2 (and methane) released from the burning of fossil fuels was previously buried, inert, in the ground and causing no warming. Thus released into the air, such CO2 becomes an incredibly stable 'stock gas' which remains in the atmosphere and will continue to contribute to warming for centuries. Conversely, the methane produced by grazing livestock is part of the biogenic carbon cycle whereby CO2 is naturally removed from the air by plants through photosynthesis and converted into carbohydrates such as cellulose. This is then grazed and broken down by enteric fermentation in the ruminant's stomach, a portion of which is emitted as methane. However, unlike fossil-fuel emissions this ruminant methane is considered a 'flow gas' which remains only briefly in the atmosphere as part of the continuous biogenic carbon cycle. After a decade, it is converted back into water and CO2 through hydroxyl oxidation, before once again being absorbed by photosynthesis and beginning the biogenic cycle once again.[54]

Consider this: every tonne of CO2 released into the atmosphere since the start of the industrial revolution is still there, overwhelming

54 'Rethinking methane: Methane has been the Achilles heel for cattle emissions, but it may be part of a climate solution', CLEAR Center, UC Davis, 4 November 2020.

the ability of our soils, forests and oceans to absorb it and exerting a continuous warming effect. But the methane my cattle emitted ten years ago has already oxidised and been absorbed once again by my pasture, meaning that after a decade my herd is contributing no net warming to the atmosphere so long as it doesn't increase in size. In fact, due to an increase in the productivity of our national dairy herd – leading to a decrease in overall cattle numbers yet an increase in volume of milk produced – dairy methane emissions have dropped by twenty-four per cent since 1990, a trend which will continue as farmers look to move with purpose towards net zero by 2040. Were humanity to cease burning fossil fuels tomorrow, we would see no reduction in atmospheric CO_2 levels for centuries: the damage has already been done, with **any** continuing CO_2 emissions merely adding to atmospheric stocks. But any reduction of methane emissions from livestock will contribute to an atmospheric **cooling** effect within a decade as the potent gas rapidly breaks down and is once again photosynthesised.

This highlights the inadequacy of the GWP100 metric to measure the genuine contribution of biogenic methane to global warming. As such, a group of leading climate scientists from across the world is calling on governments and climate organisations to adopt instead the GWP* metric which takes into account the differences in stock and flow gas contributions to real-world warming.[55] Clearly, continuing to reduce emissions from livestock is desirable, and this will be a major initiative on British farms in the coming years. But to abandon ruminant agriculture altogether would be to ignore the critical wider benefits it brings, while ultimately reducing biogenic methane emissions cannot solve our climate crisis: only aggressive reductions in the stock gas emissions resulting from the burning

55 'Guest post: A new way to assess "global warming potential" of short-lived pollutants', *Carbon Brief*, 7 June 2018.

of fossil fuels will achieve that.

In fact, many British farmers are optimising their grazing systems to increase the amount of soil carbon absorbed. The principle behind this returns to the prairies of old; huge numbers of bison moving across the landscape trampling, grazing and fertilising intensively before lumbering on. This focused activity maximises the ability of the pasture to regenerate and sequester CO_2, and can be replicated on farms (in a system known as 'mob' or 'rotational' grazing) by allowing livestock to graze only a small part of a field at a time (usually with some temporary electric fencing) before moving them on and allowing that part of the sward to rest and regrow, utilising the high concentration of livestock manure left behind. We've started to experiment with this in recent years, in comparison with the more traditional 'set stocking' whereby you tip a load of cows into a big field and let them get on with moving back and forth at random in a low-impact way. What we've immediately found is that we've reduced our requirement for nitrogen on those areas we've mob-grazed, as the greater and more even concentration of excreta has benefitted the grass much more than if spread randomly and more sparsely across the field, leaving the odd molehill-like tufts of greener growth you may be familiar with.

Grazing livestock can also benefit ecological biodiversity and are often the most effective and natural way to maintain certain habitats with a diverse range of plants and animals. By utilising livestock with different feeding habits (say a mixture of cattle and sheep), a range of sward heights is maintained and fast-growing vigorous species are not allowed to out-compete less competitive ones in open, shrubby habitats. Some of our rarest and most valuable ecosystems are thus maintained, which would otherwise revert to overgrown grasses or even forest. Native breeds, such as the Longhorn, are thought best suited to this task due to their hardiness and amenity in extensive grazing, thriving on low-input pastures and mimicking the habits of their ancient ancestors in roaming the landscape. They, and other striking British breeds such as the Belted Galloway, Highland Cattle or Soay sheep, certainly look the part and it's a joy to see them playing such a vital and modern role in the health and well-being of the countryside.

I could go on. But the key point is this: addressing the issue of food sustainability by reducing it to a simple binary narrative of plant = good vs meat = bad based on the sole (and flawed) metric of CO_2e is to do nobody any favours. It distracts us from the real issues which need to be faced, not just around our dietary choices (where the real narrative should be sustainable and healthy = good vs unsustainable and unhealthy = bad) but around the bigger issues of the globalised economy in which more than eighty per cent of GHG emissions are the result of the burning of fossil fuels for energy. Eating a few less burgers per week is not going to put that genie back in the bottle, nor significantly contribute. (It's estimated that adopting a plant-based diet may save the individual 0.82 tonnes of CO_2e per year, based on crude international averages; compare that with 1.47t by switching to green energy, 1.6t by dropping one long-haul flight, 2.4t by living car free – and 58.6t per year by having one fewer child.[56]) Are there inexcusably unsustainable farming practices involving the production of beef cattle? Yes: it's never going to be acceptable to slash and burn rainforest to provide packs of cheap burgers for the barbeque. But livestock production as part of a sustainable food system is a necessity, and between disseminating best practice, improving scientific understanding and continuing technological developments I

56 'Serious about stopping climate change? Have one less child, UBC study says, *National Post*, 12 July 2017.

hope that British ruminant production will only improve in sustainability in the coming years.

Personally, I believe that people should eat whatever makes them happy, but that they should do that based on facts and evidence rather than spin and ideology. Hell, British farmers produce plenty of plant-based foods which I would heartily encourage anyone to eat more of – we need more fruit and veg in our diets, in particular. But, like many farmers, I bridle at the sight of cheap plant-based ingredients (often imported and of questionable environmental provenance themselves, such as soya and palm oil) being highly processed and highly packaged and then sold at highly inflated prices in the name of sustainability. The cynic might suggest that profit, and not planet, are at the forefront of many of these products and of retailers' determination to stock more of them.

Or what of the unhumble avocado? The UK imports an estimated twenty-five million cubic meters of water annually (10,000 Olympic sized pools) contained within avocados, typically grown in some of the driest places on earth and irrigated from natural water sources, with each 170g fruit requiring 320kg of water to grow. There are accusations of illegal deforestation driven by the global demand for avocados in countries such as Mexico, where they are grown in vast plantations utilising large quantities of pesticides illegal in the UK – and often allegedly under the control of criminal cartels – before being shipped more than 5000 miles to our homes.[57] This isn't to demonise a tasty and healthy snack, but to demonstrate that food sustainability is a complex issue, and I'd argue that my red meat is greener (and more ethical) than their avocados. Besides – what's more plant based than pasture-fed cows?!

57 Sustainable Food Trust, 'Why our love for avocados is not sustainable', 31 January 2020.

SHEEP

Sheep have come and gone on our farm over the years, often fitting in around the other enterprises: whereas dairy production, for example, requires significant capital investment (in a milking parlour, for starters) sheep are hardy animals who thrive living out at grass and require little additional resources that a livestock farm doesn't already possess. Sheep are traditionally a route into farming for many people who haven't been lucky enough to inherit a place on a family farm as they can be inexpensive and grazed on small areas of often poor-quality rented grazing while the young farmer becomes established. You can even pick them up by hand if needs be, which makes them somewhat handier than cows.

British sheep farming has developed over the centuries in harmony with our landscape, split into three main regions: the hills, the uplands and the lowlands. Each region has unique characteristics, traits and breeds suited to the conditions of terrain and weather in the 'stratified' system. But all are also interconnected. Under the harsh conditions of the high hills, ewes (female sheep) do not thrive for more than three or four seasons and tend to move down to the relatively more comfortable upland farms for a further few years of productive retirement. Cross bred with a 'longwool' lowland ram (male sheep) these ewes then produce lambs with different qualities than those required in the hills, which are attractive to lowland farmers with a kinder climate and more fertile soils. Many hill and upland farms also struggle to finish castrated ram lambs on their thin grass, so often choose to sell these to their lowland counterparts. In marginal hill and many upland areas, sheep are the only thing which can be farmed, producing top quality and sustainable meat from otherwise unproductive land, but roaming over large areas to do so.

In the past we've had our own breeding flocks on the farm,

both bog standard 'commercial' breeds and rare native types like the Portland and Jacob depending on the passions of the people involved. We'd run the ewes with the ram from October; an 'experienced' ram would serve anything up to one hundred ewes in a season, which you might agree is quite an achievement. It's common practice to strap a paint pad to the ram's chest to see which ewes have been receiving his sheepy felicitations from the dye on their backs. One can only hope it doesn't generate any ovine jealousies; it would certainly cost him the air of plausible deniability. Sheep are pregnant for about 145 days (five months) so are looking to lamb from around March to take advantage of plentiful spring grass. The aim on a lowland farm is to have twins, taking advantage of the good quality pasture and relatively gentle climate compared to the hills where one lamb is probably as much as a ewe can cope with. But some sheep will only have a single larger lamb, while triplets are relatively common and quads or even quins are not unheard of. When a ewe produces more than two, it's common to remove the additional lambs and either attempt to foster them onto another sheep with a single or no lamb, or bottle rear them by hand; most sheep simply wouldn't be able to produce enough milk for triplets.

Sheep can be lambed either inside or out; hardier upland breeds with excellent mothering instincts tend to get on with it themselves outdoors, but it's common for lowland sheep to be brought indoors for the lambing season. I remember machinery sheds being subdivided up into dozens of small pens with the time-honoured system of shipping pallets tied together on their ends with orange baler twine and bedded down with straw. As each sheep lambs, she's taken out of the larger pen and placed on her own with her offspring to bond and ensure they get their first drinks of nutrient- and antibody-rich colostrum. This is vital for the health and wellbeing of each lamb. Unlike with most cattle breeds, lowland sheep always seem to struggle with lambing themselves: lambing season (March–April on most units) can be a busy and exhausting time with sheep seeming to favour the 12am–4am window. Somebody needs to be almost constantly on hand to help with backward, twisted and stuck lambs, and the midnight oil can be well and truly expended at this time of year. It's not uncommon for struggling lambs to be brought into the farmhouse and placed beside the stove on a cold night until they gain their strength, or stuffed inside the jacket of a farmer when out in the fields.

Sheep thrive outdoors rather than in, so mother and babies are let out into the fields as soon as possible, with each being marked with a can of spray paint to make sure we know who belongs to whom. The lambs grow fast and are weaned off at around eight weeks of age. Over summer, they will grow on the plentiful lowland grass before being ready for slaughter between five and eight months of age depending on the breed and conditions. Within any group of lambs some will become ready ('fit') before others, so around August or September we would collect them all together several times and select out those with the most body condition who were ready to go to market, leaving the smaller lambs to put on more weight. Forty kilogrammes would be a reasonable size to send a lamb off for killing – so when you think 'lamb' as you're picturing where your chops came from, think of a six-month-old, ninety-pound lump of a sheep which would do some serious disservice were they to stand on you with their pointy little toes (which they do, frequently). We've never had a sheep dog, so this could be an interesting process involving much running, shouting and falling over as we attempted to connive a group of unruly lambs into a temporary pen which we would have built in one corner of the field. (Being so young and remaining on the farm for so short a period, the hefting or familiarity of routine which you would see in our cattle just didn't apply.) Sheep dogs are remarkable when they're in action: obedient, intelligent and quick as a whip. They know what the sheep are thinking and seem to have an almost supernatural ability to anticipate what they'll do next. I, on the other hand, was more likely to go left when the sheep went right, and had Ted and Toby been with me at this point in my career I can confidently predict they would have been a hindrance rather than a help. Every year, some of the older ewes would need to be culled, perhaps because they could no longer produce lambs or due to poor health, so we could either buy in replacements or keep back some of the females for breeding rather than meat.

Because it's so dependent on taking advantage of our climate, lamb production in the UK is pretty seasonal: though some is produced throughout the year, most farmers look to take advantage of plentiful and relatively inexpensive spring and summer grass to produce really tasty meat. As a result, peak lamb season falls in the late summer, meaning that we rely on imports – primarily from New Zealand – for much of our lamb into the new year and early spring. So, despite being more than one hundred per cent self-sufficient in British lamb, its seasonality (and the fact that certain cuts are not very popular to British consumers) means that a big glut is produced in the autumn which needs to be exported (primarily to Europe), to be replaced with imports only months later.

Sheep farming is an acquired taste. As a rule, sheep exist solely to find new and exciting ways to both escape and expire. You would be surprised at how high a sheep can jump to clear a wall when it thinks it might be able to kill itself on the other side, or how tenacious they can be in getting their heads stuck in fences, trees, gates, buckets, holes in the ground, other sheep; you name it, they'll throttle themselves in it. When heavily in lamb, they even have the remarkable tendency to roll onto their backs and beach themselves ('casting'): unable to roll back over, they can self-suffocate in the middle of an open field. (If you see a sheep in this state, please intervene and roll it over.) It's often remarked that sheep live to die. If they weren't such prolific breeders, I wouldn't wonder that they would become rapidly extinct. Baby lambs can also frequently fall prey to rural predators such as foxes or badgers, but crows and magpies are also famed for cornering them and pecking out their eyes. Eagles carry them off in Scotland. Nature can be cruel. It's the reason many sheep farmers in the wilder parts of the UK are against the reintroduction of predators such as lynx and wolves, which would see lambs and even sheep as a tasty meal. Sheep can also be cantankerous: when last we had a ram, he liked nothing better than to sneak up behind and butt me squarely in the rear, knocking me flying. I have never known a bull to attempt similar.

Sheep are walking carbon sponges. Forty per cent of the weight of a fleece is pure biogenic carbon – that is, carbon consumed in grass and turned into the amino acids of the wool fibres. So in a world of micro-plastic pollution from synthetics, why not give fresh thought to one hundred per cent organic, natural and biodegradable wool, a remarkable product not only for insulating ourselves (instead of nylon) but also our homes (instead of fibreglass) and our shopping (instead of plastic). Sadly, despite once being the mainstay of the English economy upon which much of our former wealth was built, wool is now so valueless that the cost of shearing often outweighs the value of the fleece, driving farmers to compost or even burn their annual crop rather than pay to transport it to market. Though the days of it enriching the entire nobility, church and merchant class may be long gone, it did until recent years often serve at least to pay the rent on many a small family farm. In 1970 a fleece was worth £1.40; adjusted for inflation this would be £22 today, instead of the £1 which is the going rate: in the 2020s a fleece is worth less than five per cent of its value of fifty years ago. This is a sad state of affairs in a world searching for more sustainable solutions, though sometimes I am forced to wonder – how earnestly? But sheared they must be, in late spring or early summer. It's a skilled job which skilled operators make look easy (and quick) which must be carried out before the weather becomes too warm and the sheep runs the risk of becoming 'flystruck', that is, flies laying eggs in the warm, greasy fleece which then hatch out maggots which eat into the sheep's flesh. This is ghastly: shearing is a welfare necessity, regardless of its finances.

We haven't had a breeding flock on the farm for some years, but more recently we've welcomed sheep back onto the land in the form of offering temporary 'grasskeep' to neighbours who are looking for an extra bit of grazing. This gives us the benefits of having more livestock on our land, adding nutrients to the soil while paying a small grazing fee, but without the hassle of owning and caring for the animals ourselves. Plus, as we've seen, sheep inhabit a different ecological niche to cattle, which is beneficial to the health of our pastures. Farmers across the arable regions of the country are increasingly turning to this sort of arrangement, which benefits all parties – especially youngsters with sheep but lacking in land looking to make a living. For the established farmers, reintroducing livestock onto arable fields – either just for the winter or even onto a temporarily established annual grass 'ley' – has massive benefits in improving the fertility of the land, while also bringing arable weeds under control and reducing their farm's carbon footprint. But, sheep being sheep, they'll almost certainly have to put up with finding them upside down in the middle of their farmyard at three in the morning. Nobody ever said mixed farming was easy. At least, not when it involves sheep. At least they taste good.

VETS AND ANIMAL HEALTH

All livestock farms will have a relationship with a local veterinarian: unlike with pets, where a visit to the vet usually heralds an infrequent calamity (and may even raise the question: 'Where's the nearest one?'), vets will be frequent and well-known visitors to the farm. Many farms will have a contract with a local 'big animal' practice for a certain number of scheduled visits per year at an agreed price, with other visits almost inevitably on top of that. And big animal is an important distinction: vets, like doctors, have specialties, and while vets are able to treat a wide array of different species for most things that ail them, most will specialise in either small (domestic) or large (farm and equine) practice. One of the easiest ways to irritate a large animal vet who has just performed an intricate caesarean section on a half-tonne, conscious cow is to ask them to check out your dog's weepy eye. You may as well ask them to fix your sink. But, farmers being farmers, we still ask – because it's a fifteen-minute drive to the pet vet, and to us an eye is an eye. Some farmers have even been known to ask for personal diagnoses rather than visit a doctor.

Much of the routine medical treatment conducted on-farm is done by the farmers themselves; there are various courses available to us on the safe and correct application of vet meds and through the year we'll apply fly repellent (generally poured onto the animal's back), wormer and general parasite control (generally applied down their throats as a 'drench') and vaccines, antibiotics, analgesics and anti-inflammatories (usually injected). These products will mostly be purchased through the vet and, especially when it comes to antibiotics, their use will be closely monitored, with certain critical-use products only to be applied by the vets themselves. Under Red Tractor standards, all farms must write a livestock health plan with the help of their vet to strictly lay down the circumstances under which such drugs can be used. This is reviewed annually to make sure that usage is not unusually high, which might indicate either bad decision-making on the part of the farmer (did that animal really need any medication?) or failures in the farm which are causing bad health in the livestock which must be addressed. Regular vet visits will take place to review such plans, to conduct pregnancy testing, to carry out artificial insemination (if the farmer isn't themselves trained), and to carry out tasks such as ringing a bull's nose and registering him for breeding.

These final tasks are linked. Only bulls intended for a life of breeding – the best – will have rings in their noses, which are to keep very large and wilful animals under control when being led from pen to field on a halter. These are put in at perhaps twelve to eighteen months of age when it's clear whether the bull has made the grade or not, and it's a similar process to having your ears pierced – though I wouldn't advise it. But to officially register the bull as a breeding animal, a vet must inspect him to make sure that he carries no obvious genetic defects which might cause harm to a herd were he to sire any offspring. The vet will check on things such as his gait and teeth, but the obsession always seems to be with his genitals (perhaps, understandably) and particularly the size of his balls. Tape measures are produced; measurements are taken; scrotums are handled; tongues are tutted; chins are tapped. It's all very high tension, but apparently there's an honest-to-goodness correlation between scrotal circumference and fertility which can keep many a good cattle breeder awake at night. The stakes are high – there's only a few centimetres difference between prize bull and meat pie.

Vets will also be called out in emergencies, of course: cattle who take ill for no discernible reason (perhaps they have a twisted gut or internal infection) have somehow injured themselves on their surroundings and require patching up, or perhaps it's a particularly difficult calving which requires the practised skills of a professional either to deliver it naturally or perform a c-section. Most farmers have learned never to underestimate the petite young female vet who turns up on nights like this; they are usually the most skilled, strong and tenacious when it comes to safely delivering the most seemingly impossible baby.

LIVESTOCK AND DISEASE

But there's also another task on which vets are regularly dispatched, one which few of them relish: testing for bovine tuberculosis (bTB). This is a chronic respiratory disease which is endemic in the British cattle herd, and has blighted the industry for decades. It's notifiable, which means there's a legal requirement to report any cases of it; in fact, there's a vast national testing regime in place which means all cattle across the country are periodically tested for the disease. It's particularly prevalent in the South West, West Midlands and Wales (which means herds in those 'high risk' areas are tested every six months) while tests across the middle of the country (the 'edge areas', which include us) are conducted annually; in the lower risk areas to the north and east (including Scotland), it's once every two years. A vet conducts the test in two parts: on day one the entire herd is injected on the neck with tuberculin; four days later their immune response is measured based on the size of the resultant lump at the injection site. A large lump indicates that the animal is likely infected with bTB. Each and every animal with a strong immune response to the injection is then required to be killed, and the entire herd is placed under long-lasting movement and trading restrictions until at least two further clear herd tests have been passed.

Government takes this disease so seriously because it's zoonotic – it can be passed from animal to human, though in reality the likelihood of this is very low: milk, even from infected animals, is safe to drink as long as it's pasteurised. Why do we require a test, and can't just see the infected animals? It takes a long time for the health of an infected cow to visibly decline; they could live with the disease for years before it poses a clear health issue – though they would be infectious in that time. It's thus particularly cruel that animals selected for culling invariably seem fit and healthy, with only a lump on the neck to betray them.

Across England and Wales, some 40,000 cattle are thus slaughtered every year across some 3000 herds at an average cost of £34,000 per 'breakdown'.[58] Stepping back from the statistics, bTB is an ongoing tragedy which brings more fear and anxiety to most cattle farmers across Britain than any other issue. Imagine yourself in the place of a family which has spent decades building a business, carefully breeding and perfecting a herd of pedigree cattle, and who knows every animal by name and temperament. Once every six or twelve months, those animals are forcibly tested over the course of a sleepless week: this time, perhaps, it's an all clear. Phew. But perhaps one is infected. Perhaps twenty are. Or forty. And some of them are heavily pregnant, or with young calves. It doesn't matter: within days, they've been 'destroyed' on the premises (and you've likely had to help), their stiff bodies dragged away in the knacker-man's lorry. Yes, you'll receive some compensation for each animal, but for most farmers the emotional scars of this experience (which can happen over and over) can't be assuaged with a small cash payment. For most, it's an irremediably traumatic experience which leaves them living in fear of the next

58 'Bovine TB statistics and epidemiology', TB Hub website.

visit, and able to take little future pleasure in their own cattle under the stress that this will happen again.

Why does this continue to happen – indeed, to have gotten worse over the past decades? After all, in the early 1980s there were mere hundreds of confirmed cases per year, all in the far south west. There are extensive restrictions on cattle movements (we cannot sell an animal to anyone, nor even move it between two places without it undergoing a TB test before and after, and entering a period of isolation). Many farms, including our own, operate a 'closed herd' policy whereby nothing comes on or off the place, except perhaps as a straw of semen or embryo in a flask of liquid nitrogen. And bTB is spread through nose-to-nose contact, or through infected faeces and urine. So how do closed farms continue to suffer devastating breakdowns?

There is another major carrier of bovine TB, and that is the ubiquitous British badger. Protected since 1981 (to combat their targeting in cruel bloodsports) their numbers have since exploded, along with their role as a reservoir of the disease in nature (and predator of ground-nesting birds and hedgehogs). Uniquely among developed countries, the UK struggles with the issue of bTB in its national herd because successive governments have refused to seriously address the uncomfortable truth that it will never be conquered until the disease is aggressively pursued in both cattle **and** badger populations. The disease had, before the protection of the badger, been nearly eradicated through the culling of infected setts, but with its protection it has spread unchecked across half the country causing untold misery to farmers – and endemic sickness in the badger population. Emerging at night, the main route of badger to cattle transmission is thought to be through their excreta emitted onto grazing pasture or stored foodstuffs on farmyards. There are clearly things which farmers can – and mostly do – do to minimise the risk from badgers, but there is no way to completely separate them from this natural reservoir of disease in the countryside which they share.

In recent years, government-sanctioned culls of infected badger populations have led to the first significant drop in herd breakdowns to be seen in decades (by up to sixty-six per cent in cull areas[59]) but these are widely unpopular with a British public which has a national love affair with its wildlife, and there's no doubting that the badger is an enigmatic and alluring creature. The culls – in which trained marksmen are licenced to shoot the animals in prescribed zones – are frequently targeted by campaigners who not only attempt to disrupt the marksmen but have also been known to intimidate and threaten the farmers taking part. Naturally, this adds another layer of stress and anxiety to an already horrible situation for many farmers. To be clear: nobody takes any pleasure from seeing badgers culled, but in the real world it's a necessary if unpalatable requirement if we are to stop the needless slaughter of 40,000 cattle per year and the devastation of thousands of farm businesses and the mental health of their owners. Many a farmer has been reduced to futile tears as their cattle are killed before them, and suicides are not unknown. Vaccination (of either badgers or cattle) is not a viable technique; for now, the culling of both is the bluntest but most effective of instruments we have to control this insidious disease. But the culling of one without the other is a futile circle without end, like bailing out a boat without patching the hole. The farming community dreams of a day when the disease is expunged from our shores, and we need no longer to live in fear of the Damoclean sword constantly hovering above our heads.

There are many other diseases which can afflict livestock in the UK to a greater or lesser extent, some of them endemic

59 Downs, S.H., Prosser, A., Ashton, A. et al., 'Assessing effects from four years of industry-led badger culling in England on the incidence of bovine tuberculosis in cattle, 2013–2017', *Scientific Reports* 9, Article 14666, 2019.

throughout our national herds and flocks. Not only can disease become a welfare issue for individuals or groups of animals, but some are not easily detectable and can lead to significant lowering of productivity (say, lower growth rates or higher abortions) which can cost farms considerable amounts of lost income. So it's important for farmers to keep their herds and flocks as 'clean' as possible. As discussed, we operate a closed herd: on the rare occasions when we do buy an animal in, it's subjected to a full battery of blood tests and placed in isolation for several weeks on arrival to make (almost) certain that it doesn't carry disease. Vaccination is also an option for some pathogens. But, as with bTB, some things are out of our control: a protozoal disease called Neospora (which causes repeated abortion) is primarily spread in the faeces of dogs, which is a huge issue for farms with footpaths and public access. Airborne midges, blown across the Channel from the Continent, have brought two new diseases to the UK in the past twenty years – bluetongue (a virus which causes lameness and fever) and Schmallenberg virus, which can cause severe loss of condition in adult cattle and abortions or birth abnormalities in calves, which are sometimes horrible to witness. There's a lot of risk in farming, but when it comes to disease – as with the weather – sometimes it just feels like we're in the hands of the gods.

This was never better exemplified than during the 2001 foot-and-mouth epidemic which ravaged the British countryside between February and October of that year, having originated at a pig farm in Northumbria which was using illegal untreated food waste as feed. A foot-and-mouth outbreak is the farming equivalent of a national outbreak of bubonic plague or Ebola; it's that serious. It's highly infectious and affects cloven hooved animals (such as pigs, sheep and cattle), causing painful blistering of the mouths and hooves as well as fever and severe loss of condition; frequently, it's fatal. It is not a disease normally found in the UK, so any outbreak (the previous had been 1967) is treated with extreme gravity. It was soon clear that the 2001 outbreak had spread widely before restrictions on livestock movements could be introduced; it was then decided that culling was the only possible control method. But, unlike with bTB, it wasn't just the infected animals on each farm which were killed, but **every** animal on that farm **and** every animal on **every** farm within a two-mile radius, such was the fear of the disease. There were so many bodies that the army dug mass burial pits in which hundreds of carcasses were burned in the open air on their own farms, the black pillars of smoke rising for mile after mile all through the livestock-producing areas of the country. In the end, six million animals were culled – all because of one infected batch of pig swill on a single farm which hadn't followed the rules.

This was an event which traumatised a generation of farmers; on 2000 farms up and down the country a lifetime's work was destroyed in a day in the most brutal way imaginable. I was sixteen at the time and remember being removed from school for several weeks as my parents put the farm into a total lockdown, with nobody allowed in or out; footpaths were closed, disinfectant was everywhere. But for many farms, this was not enough: so infectious is foot and mouth that it was carried by wildlife, on vehicles, on shoes – even on the very wind. And if the farm two miles away caught it? Well, then the game was up for you, too.

Lessons were learned from 2001: many of today's rules around cattle passports, movement restrictions and traceability are a direct result of those harrowing months after it was realised that the disease had spread across much of the country before the first case was identified. No longer can you just turn up to a farm, buy an animal and drive away, no questions asked. But it also left huge scars among the farming community; some couldn't bring themselves to go back into livestock after the events of those days for fear of it happening again; some couldn't bear to rebuild; many lives were ruined; much irreplaceable genetic bounty was lost.

But 2001 wasn't an isolated incident. The threat of disease is a spectre which hangs over farmers the world over. Visit a pig or poultry farm anywhere in the UK and you'll be amazed at the high levels of biosecurity controls in place. All incoming and outgoing vehicles will be sprayed with disinfectant (often from fancy automated systems); you will not be able to wear your own clothing on the unit – if you're allowed on at all. Sheds (each requiring their own set of clothing) may be built to hold positive atmospheric pressure to keep non-filtered air out; levels of hygiene, especially between batches, are off the scale. All this to keep out diseases which have as devastating an impact as foot and mouth, such as avian influenza or African swine fever. An outbreak of the former led to nationwide restrictions being placed on the UK poultry sector in 2020, with all birds at infected sites being culled. An outbreak of the latter from 2018 has caused tens of millions of pigs to be culled around the world, especially in Asia.

As always at such times, questions have been asked of the sustainability of the global livestock industry in the face of such outbreaks. Are we intensifying too far, creating the perfect breeding grounds for disease and losing our respect for nature? With Covid-19, we have experienced the unimaginable impact of a new pathogen making the jump from animal to human. Does this call into question the entire concept of animal agriculture? I would say no; livestock are at the heart of sustainable farming and a healthy, balanced diet. But there would be few British farmers who would look at the market-driven extremes to which animal agriculture has been taken in some parts of the world and wish that upon ourselves or our animals: we would hope to export not just our produce, but also our production values and ethics: sentient beings are not crops.

But this is the precarious existence of much of farming life: a life lived out in the open, with a million moving parts, over very few of which we have control. Even with the best laid plans, and best will in the world, in farming everything can change in an instant.

SUMMER

• JUNE • JULY • AUGUST

BOUNTY

'Summer's lease hath all too short a date.'
William Shakespeare (1564–1616), *Sonnet 18*

SILAGE AND HAYMAKING

T HERE ARE MANY harvests across Britain throughout the year, though in your mind's eye you may imagine only the combine harvester collecting crops such as wheat and barley in the high summer months. Potatoes, carrots, beetroot, mushrooms and apples can be grown and stored throughout the year thanks to the varying climate from one end of the UK to the other, or covered production indoors or under plastic polytunnels in the fields. Sugar beet, that eponymous and unrivalled raw material for sustainable and ethical British sugar production, is harvested throughout the autumn and winter, along with the humble British pear. For a dairy farmer, every day is harvest as milk flows from the parlour to your glass within twenty-four to forty-eight hours. But on our farm, the first major harvest of the year isn't our arable crops but the grass from our pastures, collected and stored from the excess grown over the summer to keep our cattle over the long winter to come, as the seasonal cycle begins again.

Silage and haymaking are one of my highlights of the year; there's nothing quite like the sweet smell of dozens of acres of freshly cut grass lying out in the late afternoon sun. The process begins earlier in the spring, when we select which fields we'll use to take a cut of grass, as these will be left to grow instead of being grazed at turnout. At some point, we'll use heavy water-filled metal rolls towed behind the tractor to flatten molehills and push loose stones back into the ground, and chain harrows to pull out loose weeds and dead grass to leave the sward as clean as possible for cutting. The last thing you want is a stone smashing the grass mower or forager, or soil getting into your silage and making it rot in the clamp. In this regard, moles can be a serious issue in grass fields, and not just the unsightly pain they are in your lawn; when I was younger and somewhat keener on such things, my grandfather taught me how to catch moles with spring-loaded traps. Quite lethal traps, it must be said. This method of moling is a countryside dark art like hedge-laying or wall-building, but far preferable to my mind than the alternatives – poisoning or, remarkably, sitting in the middle of a field with a shotgun, watching the mole hills rise before taking a best-guess aim at their centres. Can you actually imagine. When I was a child (yes, this was considered child's work) I was paid one pound per mole produced, like a modern-day, underpaid, underage bounty hunter. The trick was to find not the mole hills, but the tunnels linking them, and there to lay the traps, but without leaving any trace of scent or of disturbed earth in the tunnel. Moles may be nearly blind, but they aren't dim, and many was the time I would find they had either bypassed my ambush points or pushed soil into them to set them off. Grisly or not, I was proud of this skill I had been taught as a youngster and my parents duly arranged to have stuffed and mounted on a small log by a professional taxidermist (yes, that's still a thing) the first mole I ever caught. A macabre trophy it may have been but as a fourteen-year-old I proudly took it to school for a class show and tell. As you can imagine, it went down rather poorly in an urban classroom with both teacher and the majority of children, and led to one of the more sustained periods of bullying that I experienced in my time there. It was a lesson, perhaps, that the things I as an individual had been brought up to think were normal on a farm were perhaps not always viewed that way by others: that there are ways and means of broaching certain subjects – such as the importance of pest control in the food chain.

To generate the greatest volume of grass before cutting, like most farmers we'll apply nitrogen in the spring to boost its growth. The amount of N used on grass has fallen significantly across the UK from a high point in the 1980s, but the question remains to what extent we actually need to apply it in a more sustainable future. The national grass stock consists primarily of ryegrass, a hugely popular variety adapted to mild and wet climates, which is well suited to ruminant grazing and forage conservation. Old permanent pastures such as ours (forty-nine per cent of the national stock) will be perennial (i.e., long-lived) ryegrass which can last for decades yet still produce decent quantities of grass. Of the small (c. ten per cent) of the grass stock which is 'temporary' (less than five years old) much will be sown Italian ryegrass – a shorter-lived version which produces even greater volumes of grass in its more truncated life. What both have in common is a penchant for artificial nitrogen to produce bumper yields, yields which have seen ryegrass popularity soar in the last fifty years. But, increasingly, farmers are questioning whether we can return to traditional techniques whereby nitrogen-fixing legumes such as clover provide the grass with the nutrition it needs. In addition, can we use a greater variety of forage species in the grass sward to achieve resilience in the face of climate change, rather than relying solely on ryegrass? After all, this continues to be the basis for more regenerative organic production.

I believe the answers are yes, and no. Much of the wide diversity of the traditional British meadow was lost from the middle of the last century in the push for production. The advent of new grass varieties, artificial inputs and a continued emphasis on ever-increasing yields saw the loss of something like ninety-five per cent of our wildflower meadows which had previously been grazed and used for hay production. The development of ensiled silage was also well suited to the rise of ryegrass. Nitrogen-fixing clovers and older grass varieties such as fescues, Timothy, cocksfoot and lucerne were side-lined, though are still prevalent in unimproved rough grazing (of which we have some, and from which we still take an annual cut of hay). Yet these secondary varieties demonstrate remarkable characteristics such as deep-rooting drought tolerance and anthelmintic (medicinal, antiparasitic) qualities which would give me grass fields better able to withstand the furnace-like droughts of years such as 2018 – when all of our ryegrass pasture turned brown and died – and enable me to reduce my medicine use, with livestock known to browse for the plants they instinctively require. (It's why I can watch my cattle straining to pull at bracken or branches just the other side of a fence despite standing in a field of lush ryegrass; sometimes they know they want something different.)

We currently run a low-intensity, extensively grazed beef herd of native suckler cattle. But in the past we owned a high-intensity herd of high-performance Continental dairy cows. The two are very different. With our Longhorns, there's no doubt that we can drastically cut our fertiliser use and increase our grass resilience by reseeding or overseeding (i.e., stitching into the existing pasture to avoid cultivation) our ryegrasses with legumes and other heritage grass species. We recently reseeded a field of permanent pasture and did just this. It's thought that the clover thus added to the new sward will provide up to 150kg of nitrogen per hectare per year, free, from the air!

Yet, with our cattle largely at grass through the year and with a relatively large area on which to graze them, we don't need to be producing the volumes of forage that others do. Had we still had our old dairy herd, this wouldn't be practical. Provision of 150kg/ha of nitrogen is significant, but it is much less than will be applied to high-yielding ryegrasses which may be harvested three or even four times over the spring, summer and autumn to produce enough grass for a high-performance herd that may spend little time outside. Ryegrass also has the characteristic of being very palatable, very digestible, high in sugar, great in bulk and easily conserved, unlike many of the other grass varieties which are compromised in these areas. Simply put, without ryegrass and nitrogen there wouldn't be enough high-quality forage to sustain more intensive cattle units (though of course some of the nitrogen used will be manures, collected over winter and spread in the spring and summer). Even grazed herds will require significant amounts of grass growth to keep them fed at any sort of high stocking density. This is another example of the production vs cost vs sustainability conundrum in which farmers find themselves: their ability to make a living farming through more 'traditional' methods is compromised by society's demand for ever cheaper food and the ever-tightening screws of the big retailers and processors. You may be surprised to hear that in dairy, especially, some companies are allowed access to the financial records of their farmers to enable them to gauge just how much (or little) they can get away with paying as they engage in round after round of retail 'price wars'. This is not a healthy or sustainable way for our food system to operate, but neither government nor consumers are wont to demand higher prices. What needs to happen is a fairer distribution of the already healthy profits being generated in the food chain, with more trickling past institutional shareholders and chief executives and into the hands of those who prop the entire system up from the bottom.

One final question you might ask: if you **can** make changes to your sward to make it more sustainable, why haven't you done so before? There's an element to which more traditional species – and clover especially – are quite delicate unless treated with caution; they're susceptible to damage by artificial nitrogen and most herbicides so that their management can be much higher maintenance than simple ryegrass leys. But, in large part, it's also inertia and tradition. Previous generations have relied on the current way of doing things and have always been pleased with the results, such as they were: we've certainly seen a huge boost of productivity in the last fifty years, and more grass equals better, right? In some circumstances this does hold true, but I would hope to see more farms such as mine – where the capacity exists to reduce the gross output of the land – to move toward more sustainable means of farming.

Silage and hay making are two of the most high-tempo periods of the year. From the moment the trigger is pulled and grass is cut and laid down in the field, the clock is ticking and nothing must be allowed to stand in the way of getting the crop harvested successfully in good conditions. Even more so than during the arable harvest, the exact proclivities of the weather are now a matter of extreme interest every hour of the day: if a standing wheat crop gets wet, it will dry. If lain grass gets hit by a storm, there's very little that can be done with it. These are critical days.

There are two major types of conserved grass forage in the UK – silage and hay. Although you may be less familiar with the former, it accounts for ninety per cent of the winter grass fed in our isles. Although the concept of conserving moist grass dates from the late nineteenth century, it wasn't until the 1950s that the concept really began to take off and replace the production of hay on a large scale. Why? As any chocolate box image of hay making will show you, it requires days (even weeks) of uninterrupted hot and dry weather to make good hay; dull, overcast conditions will do little to dry the grass, while rain runs the risk of ruining an entire crop, which can rot in the field. British summers are not the most trustworthy of hay-making companions. Silage requires a much shorter window of good weather (perhaps forty-eight hours) because the grass goes into the clamp, pit or bale still moist after only a short period of wilting; it's a lower-risk crop to make. It also became commercially viable with the increasing availability of the large quantities of plastic sheeting required to store it. This move, of course, was another nail in the coffin of the traditional species-rich hay meadow, as the bulk and species of grass best suited to silage production are very different from those for hay.

We generally take our first and often only cut of silage in mid-June, having given the fields thus set aside a long period in which to bulk up as much as possible. The grass will also, however, likely have gone past its lush, leafy best and have advanced to a stemmier form as it begins to 'head' and go to seed. As dairy farmers, this would be far from ideal, as it's in its lusher form that the grass has a higher 'D-value' – the digestible organic matter as a proportion of the 'dry matter' of the grass – and this value falls with advancing maturity. The higher the D-value, the more like rocket fuel the grass and resulting silage is for the cows. But our native Longhorns would gorge themselves on such rich food and soon become very fat without expending the huge amounts of energy that high-production dairy cows do to produce such large volumes of milk every day, so a coarser, lower-energy grass suits them well. Think dry toast over croissant.

They're grand old days on the mower tractor with Ted and Toby, generally trying to keep the rows of cut grass as straight as possible on a point of professional pride as they let me know at the appearance of every hare, rabbit or pheasant that hops out of the long grass as the sun drops from its zenith. We look to start cutting after lunch so the grass has absorbed as much of the noon sun as possible, the process of photosynthesis turning that sunlight into sugars in the mini solar panels each leaf represents, literally harvesting the fusion energy of our star. Cut too early in the day and the quality of the resulting fodder will be much reduced, while the dawn dew will likely also be clinging to the thick sward, resulting in an overly wet swath which will not ensile well. Many farmers will cut three sides of a field before working their way towards the uncut headland, allowing any wildlife hiding in the tall stems to exit under the fence or hedge without exposing themselves to the predators, both on the ground and in the air, waiting for them to make an appearance. These are the small gestures which can make a difference. Our prime silage fields are also our rockiest pasture; one of my spring jobs (before the grass grows tall) is to mark with canes all the myriad jutting rocks which have, over the years, reduced many a mower to a twisted pile of wreckage at precisely the wrong time; these things never go wrong when parked in the shed, after all. Inevitably, the moles have been busy in the intervening weeks between rolling and mowing; every molehill struck by the spinning blades of the mower sends a cloud of soil bursting into the air like a small artillery explosion, occasionally rattling a handful of pebbles off the back window of the tractor and breaking my reverie.

And this is where I leave the silaging process. Like most farmers, we do not own the machinery to gather our own grass but rely instead on teams of contractors who criss-cross the regions of the UK for months at a time collecting farms' grass for them. When I was young, we employed a local chap who came with his little tractor and forage harvester and used our trailers, which we carted back to the yard ourselves. The whole process took perhaps a week, with regular tea breaks in which I vividly remember my mother coming to the field with jugs of ice-cold orange squash poured into polystyrene cups. Today, a team of half a dozen turns up on an arranged day with monstrously large equipment and clears our entire silage harvest in (I think the record stands at) four hours from first load to last. This is farming at an epic scale and pace; there's no time to sit and enjoy the smell of warm grass or the taste of orange squash in the sun once these guys turn up. Why use contractors? Given the few days of the year we need the equipment, it doesn't make sense to own; better to employ someone else to come and do the work for a set fee and offload all the costs and risks of owning the machinery onto them. And they will need to do a **lot** of work to make the machines pay for themselves.

This speaks to something broader about the economics of farming which has developed in recent decades. The value of agricultural produce has been driven consistently lower while costs have vertiginously risen above the rate of inflation. Decades ago, many mid-sized farms might have owned their own foraging gear, or failing that turned to a neighbour who did, pottering about for a few weeks of the year in their local area. Today, you need to be farming on an epic scale to be able to afford all manner of farm equipment (the latest 'big' tractor or combine harvester will set you back £500,000); large contractors have proliferated, needing to devour huge areas over large parts of the year to justify the outlay for big new kit (much on credit) which in turn they run into the ground and must regularly replace. The competition between such contractors is fierce, locked as they are into a cycle requiring ever more acres to farm to justify their existing costs; this means their own margins are ever thinner as they cut prices to secure work, thus requiring yet more acres to drive enough turnover to cover their costs. Increasingly, small farms are being swallowed by larger neighbours who similarly need to secure more land to justify their current area and costs, driving land prices and rents yet higher. Questions can justifiably be asked about the care with which some of this land is then farmed; does everyone have the time, the money or the inclination to keep short-term contracted land in good heart?

Let's look at some examples.[60] In 1970 a tonne of wheat was worth thirty-two pounds. Adjusting for inflation, a tonne of wheat in 2020 **should be** worth £506 just for its value to have stagnated in the past fifty years. In recent years it's been closer to an average of £150. A litre of milk sold for four pence in 1970; today it should fetch sixty-three pence but is closer to thirty. A wool fleece would sell for £1.40 in 1970; today it should fetch around twenty-two pounds, but as we've already seen is virtually worthless at around a pound – less than the cost of shearing. A finished lamb costing £8.25 in 1970 does not today cost the £110 it should, but is closer to seventy-five pounds.

And costs? A sixty-horsepower tractor of 1970s small farm vintage would have set you back £1350; its 120hp equivalent today should cost £21,000 adjusted for inflation, but instead will set you back to the tune of £62,500. To have kept pace with inflation, farm labour should cost around £5.50 per hour, though today's living wage (below what most farm employees will earn) is almost nine pounds. An acre of prime agricultural land is not the £4100 it would be in 1970s money, but £9100.

On income, in 1970, my grandfather would needed to have sold

60 'Taking Stock looks back on 50 years of farming', *Farmers Weekly*, 20 December 2019.

165 finished lambs to afford a new tractor; today I would need to sell 865. Thirty-two of them would have bought him an acre of land; today it would cost me 132 – and this doesn't account for the greater profitability each lamb would have brought Gramps in the 1970s compared to today, which would stretch these figures even more. Slowly but surely, over the past fifty years, the value of the produce I grow has fallen while my costs have risen out of all proportion with inflation in the wider economy, and although agricultural productivity has improved by some sixty-four per cent in that period, this is mostly as a result of shedding workers and increased reliance on machines which have become in many cases the single biggest over-inflationary cost to farms. Between 2020 and 2021, the cost of farm machinery increased by an average of five per cent when consumer price inflation was a mere 0.9 per cent. When the forage harvester, five big tractors, trailers and other implements brought by my silage contractor might have a total value in the region of £1.2 million, that is a big additional cost.

Today, I can only dream of 1970s figures for farm income. Yet who reading this would be happy to merely earn the same today as they were fifty years ago? But, in reality, the value of my milk has dropped by fifty-five per cent, my wheat by more than 300 per cent, and my wool by a staggering 2200 per cent. In comparison, labour and land cost more than twice what they ought and tractors three and a half times. Other costs are similarly out of kilter. It doesn't take a genius to extrapolate that the pips on farms are being well and truly squeezed after decades of declining margins. Every new innovation, every boost in yield, every flashy piece of kit; none of it has improved the long-term profitability of the average farm business. This isn't to say that other metrics – around the environment, welfare or staff wellbeing – haven't improved (and I wouldn't begrudge others a better standard of living over these last decades), but, when we look at sustainability across the food chain, we can't just think of the environment: the financial sustainability of farm businesses must be addressed if we are to survive into the future to care for the environment and to produce the climate-friendly, affordable food the British public has come to expect. It's impossible to be green if your finances are in the red.

Our food system is currently defying gravity; when you consider collapsing farm margins versus the fact that the average household's income spent on in-home food has dropped from thirty per cent in the 1950s to less than ten per cent today (the third cheapest in the world) and the fact that farmers take home only seven per cent of the value of the food they produce (the rest going to retailers, processors and the like) you realise that eventually something must give, especially given the volatility of farm incomes. The total national income from farming fell from nearly £8bn in 1997 to a mere £2bn in 2001[61]; such a vertiginous fall can be reflected on my own farm from year to year, influenced by factors as diverse as the weather, foreign exchange rates, global shocks or gluts or individual farm tragedies such as disease outbreak. This is a situation which will only be further exacerbated by our exit from the EU: with sixty per cent of the average farm's income deriving from support payments – to be phased out in England by 2027 under new government plans – the financial situation for many farmers is soon to reach crisis point.

Charities offering help to those in agriculture have never been busier, whether those disbursing grants to families who have fallen on especially hard times (with one in four farming households living below the poverty line) or those offering mental health support – a largely taboo subject in agriculture which has only recently begun to be talked about more openly. But the mental health issues facing farmers are huge, with more than one suicide per week on average;

61 Defra 2019, op. cit.

2018 saw eighty-three deaths in the industry, with a rate among the highest of any occupational group. Farming is a lonely profession, with an exhaustive average working week of sixty-five hours.[62] The work–life balance is commonly poor, holidays are often scarce or non-existent, and many farming families live a hard life on a financial cliff-edge. Add to that the vast range of factors which can negatively impact farm businesses, from the weather and disease to rural crime and commodity fluctuations, as well as the familial pressures of multi-generational expectations and involvement and the often-unhealthy blurring of the line between work and home. Many find themselves working harder, longer, and for less year after year as debts mount up and exhaustion builds. There's much that is great about farming, but we can often perpetuate a toxic cycle of overwork and depression built on a macho-culture where asking for help and taking a break can be seen as signs of weakness. It's one of the greatest challenges facing us in the coming decades – to get everyone the support they need and make the entire industry fit to farm.

The silage contractors work fast, their huge 600hp forager (a combine harvester for grass) chewing through acre after acre which has been piled into long heaped rows by a huge spinning rake pulled by a tractor. The forager chops the grass into smaller lengths and then spits it into the fifteen-tonne tractor-drawn trailer which chases alongside it, trying to keep straight and steady while the forager driver manipulates their spout to maintain an even load. The key is to keep a constant stream of tractors and trailers servicing the forager so that it never stops; time is money, and this team has another farm or even two to complete today, even if it means working late into the night. It's quite a poetic dance, truth be told, watching the successive suitors race empty across the field

62 'Fit2Farm: Hard work and long hours take toll on farmers', *Farmers Weekly*, 28 September 2018.

to take their place alongside the lumbering forager, then nip in behind the departing trailer as it strains to pull away, piled high with winter forage which occasionally tips over the side as it rolls through a hump or hollow. In a wet season, such big kit makes a mess of the ground, despite its massive tyres. Perhaps, tomorrow, we'll release some cattle into here for a few days to clear up the spilt 'aftermath' and chew off the uncut grass around the fence line so as not to let any go to waste.

The loaded trailers make their way back to the farmyard (almost invariably driven by young lads in wraparound shades who enjoy making tractors 'go fast' to the detriment of my gate posts) where we'll have prepared the clamp for its reception. These structures are usually three-sided concrete-panelled bunkers sufficient to store hundreds or even thousands of tonnes of forage. The vital element in silage production is to store the grass in the absence of oxygen, in anaerobic conditions. As such, we'll have lined the walls with thick black plastic sheeting to ensure no air can seep through into the grass. The trailers then back up, tip their loads, and shoot off to collect the next, leaving a digger to push the grass up into a gentle slope which rises as the day wears on. As the digger traverses up and down the incline it's building, ferrying more grass to the top, its ten-tonne weight is constantly compressing the grass beneath its wheels, forcing the air out from between the individual blades. Not only does this mean more can be fit into the clamp, but vitally it's also making sure that as little oxygen as possible is eventually left. Once the whirlwind of clamp filling is complete and the contracting team departs at breakneck speed out of the gate to their next job, I'll spend another few hours driving across the filled clamp at low speed in our heaviest tractor, compressing it down still further in an attempt to increase the quality of the silage.

Then, one of the least favoured jobs of the year begins –

'sheeting the clamp'. Anybody with any sense generally finds somewhere else to be for the duration, but the more hands that can be found the better. Back-breaking giant rolls of black plastic are unrolled and then unfolded across the piled and compressed grass, and pulled tight to the edges of the side sheets. Have you ever wondered why so many farms have thousands of old car tyres lying around in giant piles? It isn't some odd agricultural fetish; it is for this moment. For decades livestock farmers toured garages and wrecking yards picking up as many used tyres as they could get their hands on so they could be used to weight down the plastic sheets used to make their silage. The entire clamp must be covered to keep as much air out as possible. This generally involves a chain of hands throwing tyres from one person to the next, the water built up in them over the winter inevitably exploding out of each in turn as it lands, soaking everybody to the skin in black, stinking tyre juice. Accidental soakings are dismissed out of hand; they **meant** to splash me. Ted and Toby keep out the way, finding a quiet patch of sun to lie in. When we're finished, coated from head to toe and usually breathing hard, it's a satisfying sight to see the winter's food brought in and made safe under its blanket of plastic and tyres. This might not sound very environmentally friendly, but all farms are required as part of Red Tractor membership to participate in plastic recycling schemes: this ensures that all pesticide containers, fertiliser bags and silage plastic are disposed of in an appropriate manner. And the tyres? A lot of farmers have moved to less labour-intensive systems using heavier, reusable nylon sheets weighted down with fewer sausage-shaped sandbags. So have we; but after decades of collecting thousands of the bloody things (much to the satisfaction of the garages who were only too pleased to see the back of them) I'm now stuck with a colossal bill (two to three pounds per tyre) to dispose of them. Perhaps if I keep them for long enough, they'll become collectors' items. But we don't miss the days of multiple silage cuts per year, requiring us to remove and replace the entire sheet several times over the summer (and always beneath a blazing sun).

Under the plastic, bacterial fermentation occurs under anaerobic conditions by lactic acid-producing bacteria utilising the sugars present in the leaf. This should drop the pH of the ensiled material to around 4, hopefully inhibiting any undesirable bacteria which might cause the grass instead to rot – especially in the presence of any oxygen which might seep in. One of the issues that silage can present is the generation of 'effluent', a highly nutrient-rich wastewater which can escape as the grass ferments and which can present a serious eutrophication risk to watercourses. It's vital that farmers do everything they can to reduce its production in the first place (excess water on the grass at foraging will increase the risk, hence my aversion to dew) and to catch any which does run out of the clamp; pits are designed with drainage systems to collect runoff and channel it into effluent or slurry tanks for disposal on the land when conditions permit. However, many farms are in dire need of significant reinvestment – in infrastructure more than anything – and many slurry stores are no longer up to the job. There are incidences of significant pollution events being traced back to farms which have been overwhelmed by unseasonable rainfall in recent years. It's one of the major challenges facing government and the farming industry in the coming decade to bring everyone up to a modern standard with wide margin for error to account for our increasingly unpredictable climate.

Not all farmers clamp their silage; a common sight in summer is to see fields littered with neat rows of plastic-wrapped silage bales which are then stacked up ready for use over the winter. Each bale becomes its own personal clamp, fermenting over the course of two to three months until fit for feeding. Every farmer chooses the method best suited to them or their circumstances; generally, smaller areas are better baled (and can call on a neighbour with baler and wrapper), but at scale baling is a more expensive and labour-intensive means of producing fodder than clamping, and also generates considerably more plastic waste.

Hay making is an altogether more genteel pastime conducted later in the summer when the weather is hopefully at its best. Grass intended for hay will be left until it is well past its lush prime and is stemmy and dry. Traditional hay meadows will be intentionally left until their multifarious grass species have gone to seed, helping prolong their rich diversity. Then, with a weather eye on the coming week, the grass will be cut and 'shaken out' repeatedly over the following days with a hay 'tedder', a rake on the back of a tractor which spreads the grass out to enable the sun and wind to get at every stem and dry it down to a low moisture content to bale. Hay making is more an art than a science; walk across the field and inspect the dried grass underfoot, if you think it's ready to bale go away and leave it another twenty-four hours. It must be very dry or risk heating up and going mouldy in the bale or – worse – spontaneously combusting and causing a shed fire. The worst thing that can happen is rain just before baling; at this stage the grass has become very delicate and can easily shatter if moved again, but can't be left to dry naturally as it'll rot in the field. It's easy to see why, in the British climate, hay has fallen so far out of fashion in the last fifty years.

But, when the heavens play ball, and those sweet-smelling bales of hay come rolling out the back of the baler, there's scarcely a more beautiful sight in the farming year. I actually like the smell of silage (and farmyard manure, strangely) but the smell of good hay is like the smell of pure summer: if someone could bottle and sell it, they'd be able to retire from farming – though they wouldn't. It's always a pleasure to burst open a bale in the depths of a cold and wet winter's day as a reminder that things will, eventually, get better!

BEEF PRODUCTION

We've seen already that there are many different systems when it comes to raising livestock; some farmers only hold animals for a short period of time, fattening them up before moving them on to the next link in the chain towards, eventually, slaughter and then, finally, your plate. As a suckler herd, we see our cattle through from birth to death; we know each animal by name; know their individual foibles and quirks; have quite possibly assisted their delivery and seen them take their first breath; have seen them grow from a wobbly-legged calf to a stonking meat mountain of a bull. I wouldn't say that all our animals have personalities – though some certainly do, and can become great characters – but we come to care for all of them and inevitably an emotional attachment is formed between farmer and beast.

One of the most common questions put to me is: 'How can you bear to send animals to slaughter?' Now, as a beef farmer on social media who's proud to promote what I do, I inevitably attract the attention of so-called activists who phrase the question somewhat more provocatively: 'If you really cared for your animals, you wouldn't send them to slaughter – ergo, you don't care, and they're just a commodity to you.' I can understand what might seem the hypocrisy of someone in my position expounding how the health and happiness of our animals is our prime concern; how we have a huge amount of affection for those animals; and how we then send them (let's not beat around the bush) to their deaths, for profit. But let's not confuse farm animals with either people or pets. They are neither. From the moment it is born, I process and accept that this calf or lamb in front of me is ultimately intended to be sold and eaten. My solemn task is to give it the best possible standard of living between now and that time. I then fully expect and demand that, when the time comes, it will be given the most humane exit from life possible. Were we not breeding these animals for food, they would not exist at all. Better to have a good and happy life than no life, to my mind. And, remember, even the most profit-driven farmer will endeavour to keep his animals as happy and healthy as possible: a sick or traumatised animal is an unprofitable animal, so high standards are in everybody's interest. What those societal standards may look like vary from country to country – and therein lies one of the big strengths of British agriculture: our world-leading welfare standards, driven in large part by public expectations.

And, yes, we have the occasional animal that we can't bear to part with: a cow of long years and big personality who may stay on after her productive life has finished. But if their health begins to deteriorate, even such characters as U-Ropa, the once-bottle-fed calf, will be killed. There's nothing kind about keeping an animal in bad health out of personal nostalgia. Anthropomorphism is a human construct – one that much of the undue criticism of animal agriculture rests upon.

One of the classic images of British farming is of the livestock market, where farmers take their animals to sell. On a set day every week, livestock trailers are loaded, hitched to the backs of 4x4s and driven to the local 'mart' where each 'beast' is bid on as it's led around a ring for all to see, the auctioneer blathering a frankly incomprehensible monologue as they skilfully discern the almost imperceptible motions of the seasoned bidders perched around the ring. When a child, I hardly dared even breathe in that room for fear of accidentally purchasing a dozen Aberdeen Angus steers with a twitch of the eye. Such markets are still at the heart of many rural communities, serving as not just commercial hubs for the exchange of coin, but also as social ones for the exchange of gossip, and also where today some farming mental health organisations focus their efforts to catch farmers on the hoof. But, sad to say, many have also closed in recent years. They tended to be sited (originally) on the edges of towns and cities for ease of access of driven livestock (in the old sense, walked from farm to market along ancient country lanes) from the surrounding countryside, but over the centuries have become consumed by urban growth. Many of the sites, it was realised, were more valuable for industrial or residential development than the weekly selling of sheep and cattle. And, besides, the structure of the UK meat trade has shifted in recent decades with the impact of BSE/CJD and foot and mouth, as well as the growing power and influence of the big retailers. In 1997, fifty-one per cent of finished cattle were sold through markets; by 2017 this had fallen to sixteen per cent.[63] Today, marts are primarily places for farmers to buy and sell store cattle and breeding animals.

Ninety-three per cent of retail meat sales move through the supermarkets. Independent butchers, who accounted for eleven per cent of sales in the late 2000s account for only three per cent today.[64] Mostly gone are the days when butchers would buy animals directly from the farmer at a mart, kill them, cut them up and sell them in their shops. Today, large meat-processing companies (of whom a few dominate the industry) will have contracts with supermarkets to provide an amount of meat to certain narrow specifications. The processors will have relationships with farmers who sell them batches of finished animals which they will collect before taking them to a slaughterhouse for killing and processing, then packaging the meat up and sending it on to the retailer or large wholesalers. These giant plants (which have contributed to the demise of the many small abattoirs which once served local communities) pay not for live animals but for

63 Soffe & Lobley (eds), op. cit., p. 452.

64 ibid

'deadweight' (after organs, head and other inedible parts have been removed), which in a beef animal or lamb will be around fifty per cent of their live weight, and perhaps seventy per cent in pigs. This means that the farmer is paid on the physical characteristics of the carcass at the time of slaughter – weight, fat cover and 'conformation' (essentially how meaty their frame is). This is graded via the EUROP grid, which is a bit like the BMI scale but replacing height and weight with conformation and fatness. There's a sweet spot on this grid (known as R4L) which most beef farmers are aiming for, balancing the most desirable (from the retailer's point of view) level of carcass fat with the appropriate level of conformation. This is the 'spec' which pays the most money. Keep your cattle finishing too long, and they build up excess fat (costing you in feed and bedding) which will reduce their value (and be discarded by the processor); send them too soon and they will have poor conformation (i.e., insufficient bulk) and generate a poor score (and payment) on the EUROP grid.

The travesty of this system is that it's designed with supermarkets in mind to improve the efficiency of their marketing; to ensure a consistency of product which will always fit neatly into the same packaging and look the same week after week to the same customers, who it's believed value familiarity over all else. The EUROP system takes little account of taste or texture which, when you think about it, is surely the most important aspect of the eating experience. This situation is, in part, what's driving the current proliferation of interest in farm shops and meat boxes bought directly from the farmer where **flavour** and not exact **size** and price is the priority to ensure that the customer **enjoys** the meat they're eating and that this – and not familiarity – drives customer loyalty. Don't get me wrong, you can get good meat in a supermarket (and a lot of the final experience comes down to the skill of the cook) but British consumers have been skilfully convinced that they aren't primarily interested in taste: just low prices and consistency. I think if most people took the time to consider, they wouldn't be so sure.

When we send a prime beef animal – likely a bull or steer (a bull castrated at a young age) – it will be between sixteen and thirty months old; as we've seen, 'commercial' breeds finish more quickly than our Longhorns, though we would argue the taste of the Longhorn is superior. (Indeed, the eating qualities of different breeds of livestock can be very noticeably different; I urge you to try as many as you can, most likely through a local farm shop or farmers' market.) These quality animals will be processed into all manner of end products, from prime steaks to roasting joints to mince, depending on the tenderness and quality of the different parts of the carcass: there are only so many fillet steaks on any one animal, and always more of the lower-value cuts. But when we send an older 'cull' cow into the food chain, her long life will have rendered her meat less tender and she will likely fall far off the ideal spec. Her meat will still find a place, but more likely as lower-value and processed cuts (such as mince) which will find their way into the hospitality, convenience or export market.

I've visited a slaughterhouse and seen it in operation. It seemed only right to see for myself the place my animals end their lives. I won't claim that it's the sort of place I would take someone of a delicate disposition or who has an aversion to gore. It really was quite an experience. The speed with which each animal was dispatched and subsequently disassembled into its constituent parts was remarkable; mere minutes on a production line of dozens of skilled workers processing animal after animal without pause, a reverse assembly line of remarkable efficiency and precision where everyone had their own specific role to play, sharp blade a blur in their hands. There was no emotion involved; the modern slaughter business is just that – business, with no more room or time for reflection than in any other high-tempo workplace. If you have concerns about the rights and wrongs of killing animals for meat, this probably isn't the job for you. However, what I was struck by was the professionalism of the slaughter process, and most importantly the first step: the humane stunning and killing of the animal. I can only justify being in the business of livestock farming if I can justify the quality of life I can provide to my animals, from farm to fork. It wouldn't be enough to say that I gave my cattle a good twenty months of life before waving them off to suffer a traumatic end. They might not be pets, but they are sentient and deserve better than that. And I was satisfied that each animal neither knew nor felt a thing as it was despatched at stage one of the slaughter process.

How is this achieved? All animals must be stunned before they're killed to ensure they don't experience any pain. With cattle and sheep this is carried out either by passing an electrical current through the brain, or using a captive bolt – a percussion gun used against the head. Pigs and poultry are generally stunned with gas, such as carbon dioxide. After stunning, the animal is then checked for signs of consciousness and immediately bled to death by cutting its carotid arteries; thirty seconds after the bleeding stops, the animal is checked for signs of life before the 'dressing' or butchering process is allowed to begin. There is, it must be pointed out, an exception to these rules: animals intended for religious slaughter – halal and kosher – are not required to be stunned before bleeding. There is a certain amount of controversy around the implications of this derogation to rules otherwise designed with the welfare of the animal as their primary concern.

From movement to 'lairage' (rest and recuperation) before slaughter, it's important that animals are calm and stress-free: as the consumer, you would know if they were not. Livestock experiencing anxiety before slaughter will generate adrenaline and, subsequently, lactic acid in their musculature which won't have time to break down before death, which will render their meat tough and even bitter to the taste. Clearly, this is in nobody's interests and therefore great lengths are gone to from loading, through transport, unloading and lairage to ensure that each animal is calm in the hours before slaughter. When transporting animals in lorries or with our own cattle truck, there are strict regulations regarding the maximum permissible length of the journey, rest stops, ventilation, stocking densities, food, water and much else. As a farmer, the killing process is not something I like to dwell on too deeply, but I am satisfied that here in the UK we legislate as well as we can to make it as humane as possible. In recent years, for example, CCTV has become mandatory in all abattoirs to monitor the line. Are there examples of where those high standards are subverted, and abuses occur? Yes, and these are universally to be abhorred. Every system is only as good as the people who operate it, and people are imperfect. Where rules designed to safeguard the welfare and dignity of animals are ignored, the people (and organisations) responsible must always be held to account: that's our solemn responsibility as a modern, moral society. Personally, I welcome new measures to increase the transparency and accountability of all elements of the food supply chain to increase the trust our consumers can have in us – especially when it comes to animal welfare.

HARVEST

For any arable farmer, harvest is the culmination of a year's blood, toil and sweat. (There are enough sharp corners on any farm to ensure a profusion of the former while achieving the latter.) The final fertilisers and PPPs will have been applied many weeks before, and through June into July it's a case of sitting back and watching the grains and pods grow full, before leaves start to yellow and curl, stems begin to die and the fields turn from lush green to brown and gold as the sun ripens the standing crop. This is when it's at its most vulnerable: a storm can flatten fields of cereals, top-heavy with grain, or shatter the brittle pods of oilseed rape or beans and scatter their precious bounty on the ground. Wheat and barley so flattened are difficult to harvest, and much is inevitably lost — especially after pigeons (a perpetual menace!) descend in clouds onto the flat areas to peck out the grains and in so doing enlarge the areas blown down. An increasing hazard are sky lanterns: what goes up, must come down, and naked flames landing amidst fields of tinder-dry straw have predictable consequences. (In pastures used for hay and silage too: their metal wires and sharp bamboo frames are known to cause agonising deaths to livestock which subsequently eat them. I would urge anybody to think before they use them.)

But, jangling nerves aside, there's always a sense of anticipation as harvest approaches, the great endeavour for the year. There's plenty to do beforehand; grain stores to be made spotless, spare parts ordered, machinery serviced and checked over — the last thing you want after having had eleven months to find and fix a problem on the combine harvester is for it to break the first morning in the field (which it inevitably will anyway). Grain trailers are washed and cleaned; the final pre-harvest haircut might be taken (though such things seem less pressing in a post-lockdown world). When the crops are ripe and the weather set fair, I want everything ready to go.

Harvest doesn't begin everywhere at once; the south coast is generally a fortnight ahead of the Midlands, who are a fortnight and more ahead of the north of England and Scotland. Britain is long and thin, and the extra sunshine and warmth the south of the country receives compared to the north makes a big difference in the development and ripening of crops. The first combines reported 'rolling' in the farming press or on social media always give rise to some subconscious fidgeting and a trip out to the fields to check that nothing is ready to cut just yet. To be the first to start harvest in the local area is treated as somewhat of an informal competition; I think some farmers get the combine out and drive it around just to be mischievous and see if they can trick a neighbour into cutting green crops through an acute attack of FOMO (Fear of Missing Out). One year, we did have a brief and optimistic foray into a field of winter barley (usually the first crop to ripen, in early-mid July) but stopped after a few minutes: it was a week off yet. The next day, at an agricultural show, I was on the edge of a conversation between a group of farmers who were grousing that 'Stanley's have already cut all their barley'. Agriculturalists rarely let the truth get in the way of a good yarn. And farming, it must be remembered, is a competitive sport.

Combinable crops must reach a certain level of desiccation before harvest: as they naturally die off and dry in the warm summer sun, their grains harden from green and full of milky sap to golden and rock hard. Cereals must be sold below fifteen per cent moisture content, and oilseeds nine per cent; there's no point attempting to cut them before they've ripened, as they just won't be acceptable for the market. So you may as well be patient. Different crops generally ripen in sequence through the summer; winter barley and oilseed rape will be ready to cut first, followed by winter wheat, spring crops and then finally beans and linseed; this is useful in spreading the workload through a longer cutting season rather than having everything come ready all at once. Some crops may be helped on their way by applying a herbicide to ensure faster and more even ripening; there will always be a minimum period observed between spraying and harvesting. Once each crop is ripe, summer becomes a constant race against the elements to gather it in, with weather apps being checked for rain ten times per day. The dream is of long, hot days to harvest at leisure and bale the resulting straw, but the British reality is more often short windows of dry weather punctuated by days of drizzle and rain. Each time the crop gets wet, it takes twenty-four to forty-eight hours for it to dry sufficiently to go again – crops will not pass through a combine unless they're dry (or at least dry-ish) and you don't want to be the chump in the guts of it with a big spanner trying to unblock it after pushing too soon. Trust me; there's scarce a sadder sight than a ripe field of grain with a combine harvester parked up in it under leaden clouds and persistent precipitation. With our increasingly extreme climate, I feel I've experienced more than my fair share of wet harvests, with ground (which should be baked hard) becoming so saturated that machinery sinks up to its axles and crops begin to rot in the fields before we can harvest them. We've even been driven to attach a second set of tyres to the combine to spread its weight. Nobody much enjoys those years.

The combine harvester stands at the heart of harvest, both physically and in our collective imaginations. It's the machine most associated by any schoolchild with farming and that which causes most excitement even in groups of grown adults who visit the farm; politicians, soldiers, pilots and businesspeople all want to have their photos taken in, on or near our mighty yellow beast. It's a remarkable machine, to be sure, guzzling thirty feet of crop at a time at five kph and processing it into threshed grain and winnowed straw at a rate of perhaps forty hectares per day; that's a lot of rugby pitches, and many loaves of bread. Operating the combine was the job I always dreamed of as a child when riding along in the cab (on the patiently amused forbearance of the driver), suspended above the cutter bar and watching the crops being gobbled up by the main augur, only to reappear through the glass window in the grain tank behind. Night-time was even more exciting, operating by the glow of powerful floodlights which attracted legions of moths bouncing off the windows, making exiting the cab at speed a necessity. As an adult, the excitement has admittedly passed (though I still recall the thrill the first year I drove it unsupervised) but has been replaced with the quiet satisfaction of an important task I'm lucky to have. Harvest hours being what they are, some of my fondest memories of recent years have been 'date nights' when my wife has come to the combine after getting in from her own work replete with picnic hamper so that we can at least spend some 'quality' time together – or at least so that she can see Ted and Toby. Unlike the machines of my youth, where a rolled up coat on the floor served as my eyrie, modern combines have a comfortable cab complete with passenger seat for wives and (when not present) dogs. Coming from a non-farming background, I'm not sure exactly how surreal the whole thing feels to her, but in contrast to my inner certainty when a teenager I am sure of one thing: chicks categorically do **not** dig tractors. If anything, Kathryn endures our marriage **despite** my occupation, and certainly not because of it. But she does love a good picnic. And I came with (particularly endearing) dogs.

As a farmer I do feel kinship with all the countless generations of those working the land before me who have bent their backs and furrowed their brows to feed their fellow men and women; what I achieve with my modern machine is little different to what my predecessor of a hundred or a thousand years ago would have been doing in the same spot – I just get to do it from the comfort of an airconditioned cab. There are no more satisfying moments than those rare seconds of fleeting perfection when the evening sun slants down through the gathering dusk to illuminate the long, straight rows of cut straw and filled grain trailers in the glory of the British countryside at summer. With my canine companions by my side (who love the high platform of the combine cab) and the satisfaction of a year's work well done, I could at times almost weep with the inherent beauty of it all – that I am fortunate enough to be the person who gets to experience that unique moment in time and space. Alas, there are few enough farmer poets.

It's rare that we'll be able to harvest at the moisture required for storage and sale, so when the trailer takes a load back to the farmyard from the field, odds are it'll have to be dried. There are many different methods of achieving this, but on our farm we own a kerosene-fired grain dryer: essentially, wet grain is fed in at the top of a tin tower holding twenty tonnes at a time and trickles down either side of a central burning chamber in which a high-temperature flame forces warm air to circulate through the grain. As the grain slowly filters through the dryer, it loses moisture before it's cooled and shot off into the grain store down a series of air-blown pipes. It's a noisy, dusty, humid place to be. It's important that grain is both dry and cool before it goes into storage, as otherwise it's almost certain to sweat and become a perfect environment for beetles and moulds which will make it unfit for the food chain. Cool, dry grain can be stored almost indefinitely. On really hot days this can lead to the frustrating situation of having to cease harvest because the grain is coming out of the field too warm, and waiting instead until nightfall. Drying is an expensive, labour-intensive process, as tedious as it is important. As a youngster my main role at harvest was grain store operator at the various farms we then rented. I was dropped off at the start of the day and picked up again by the final tractor on its way home at night and managed to chew through many books – good, bad and indifferent – over the course of many hundreds of hours spent watching grain slowly circulate through various dryers. Today, I'm increasingly conscious of the carbon footprint of burning hundreds, even thousands of litres of fuel every year to dry our crops. But, at harvest, opportunities to cut dry grain are few and far between, and the financial consequences of losing a crop for the sake of waiting for perfect conditions don't bear thinking of.

Our grain dryer is forty years old, a relic which is in turn housed inside our oldest shed, dating from the 1700s. Operating it is more art than science, based on many years of experience. Everything still works (just) but each additional year brings the whole shebang ever closer to a final, inevitable and catastrophic breakdown. Parts of it are so old that no spares exist, so we don't touch them and hope they just hang on. Imagine being a taxi driver and your entire business resting on the perfect reliability of your hard-driven 1970s Ford Cortina. Such a situation is common across the farms of the UK, where infrastructure installed in the good years of the 1970s–1980s is being pushed further and harder than was ever intended. There are many modern, progressive, well capitalised (and generally larger owner-occupied) farms and estates out there. But on smaller, predominantly tenanted family farms such as ours, the generally poor financial returns of the past two decades and lack of a significant asset to borrow against have led to the big investment decisions being pushed back year after year; banks aren't willing to lend on the basis of future farming cashflow when recent history has shown it to be so volatile. This clearly has implications for the productivity of many businesses, operating with obsolete, dilapidated (and frequently dangerous) machines and buildings, just looking to get by for another year, in hope more than expectation of an upturn. On many holdings, modern farming has outgrown the physical limits of the previous generation, while many businesses are trapped in the past. Combined with the reduction in financial support for farming with our exit from the EU, this has huge implications for the financial sustainability of many farms in the coming decade.

I shudder to recall the number of times I've narrowly escaped serious injury (or worse) over the years at work. Much of this can be linked to old, dilapidated infrastructure either well beyond its best or dating from a time when health and safety were not major design concerns; in the past, many hands made light work – or at least watched your back – but, increasingly, farming is a solitary activity and risks are taken to get the job done. There have been times when I've feared for life and limb, often in doing the same old jobs year after year, thinking: this isn't safe, and it isn't worth it. Fatigue and stress induced by long working hours (my longest workday stands at twenty-six hours), the perpetual race against the clock and the weather, the perils of working around livestock, a macho culture – all these factors and more give agriculture a safety record to be ashamed of. As a farmer, I am **eighteen** times more likely to be killed in the workplace and twice as likely to be seriously injured than the all-industry average. Farming accounts for 1.5 per cent of the workforce but twenty percent of workplace fatalities; approximately thirty people die on-farm every year.[65] (Shockingly, more than fifty died in the twelve months to 31 March 2021.) Despite countless campaigns and the superb work done by some individuals and organisations to raise awareness and change attitudes, this tragic death toll remains stubbornly consistent, in many cases another of the hidden costs of our cheap food culture and the meagre returns which trickle down to the farm gate.

How does the grain for your bread get from my shed to your loaf? (I once spoke to someone who was shocked – **shocked** – that I should store their future food **on the floor in a shed**! That was nothing, I reassured them; believe it or not we keep it **outside** in a field for ten months of the year where it grows in manure …) The

65 'Safe farms, safe staff and visitors – a guide to legislation', *Farmers Weekly*, 1 October 2020.

UK marketplace is today dominated by a small number of large national (usually owned by international) grain-trading firms. As a farmer, I sell directly to these firms in units of twenty-nine tonnes, the size of a bulk transport lorry of the sort you see plying the A roads and M roads of the country 365 days per year. I have a number of sale options. Firstly, I can sell 'forward' on a 'futures' price; sitting in my office, I can see the price being offered for a particular crop in six, twelve or even twenty-four months and I can choose to lock in, committing a certain tonnage to be sold and moved in a certain month. This gives me an element of financial certainty, knowing I've secured a price for part of my crop. On the flip side, it's a risky business to agree to provide grain you may not even have planted yet and for which you'll stand the full price as a default if you can't provide it when the time comes. Secondly, you can sell at the 'spot price' – that is, for immediate movement at the current market value; this has the benefit of allowing you to capitalise on any spike in prices, but you're clearly also open to the whims of the markets and there's no guarantee prices will go up in any given year rather than down. Thirdly, you can commit to some contracts which will purchase the total yield from a set area of land and pay you, perhaps, the average price for that commodity between two points in the calendar. This is used for smaller tonnages of premium crops such as oilseed rape rather than cereals: you don't need to worry about providing a minimum yield (which has been a godsend in recent poor years), but you lose control over your sale price. Lastly, you can commit a set tonnage to a grain-trader's 'pool', a big portfolio of many farmers' crops which can be marketed at a greater scale than any individual farm can manage, its mass hopefully garnering a better price and the final income to each farmer deriving from an average price per tonne across the lifetime of the pool, smoothing out the biggest peaks and troughs (minus a management fee for the trader). It's perhaps the safest option, if not the most potentially lucrative.

How each farm approaches their marketing strategy is up to them, but to do it properly the farmer needs to understand not just what's going on in their own patch but nationally and internationally too. The grain price (with most crops being pegged to wheat as a baseline as currencies are to the dollar) is incredibly dependent on an almost infinite number of variables, from domestic plantings to Chinese stockpiles, the weather in Ukraine to export tariffs in Argentina, global geopolitics to the breakdown of a solitary mill on the Humber. As a farmer, it's incredibly hard to keep track of it all and decide on the best time to sell. In 2020 we decided to offload all of our grain before what looked like a certain 'no deal' exit from the EU on 31 December, which would have had a huge downward impact on prices. This turned out to be a mistake, with grain values rising considerably into 2021 after a last gasp deal was struck. But, whenever you do decide to sell, you're always going to be a price taker: the scope for negotiation on grain sales is vanishingly small, and you're unlikely to find a price differential of more than one per cent across any of the trading firms on any given day. They're all looking at the same data, and making offers in real time based on that: by the time you've called three or four and decided to call back the first and shake hands on a price, it's likely already changed for the worse. (That being said, new smartphone grain trading apps are now available which claim to be able to offer farmers a better range of options than the traditional 'phone around' method. There is literally an app for everything.) But agricultural commodities are incredibly volatile: from pork to potatoes, the annual swings in farm income can be enormous – even if shelf prices remain relatively static. It's not unusual for me to sell grain at twice (or half) the price I did in the same month the year before; between 2003 and 2016, the average annual income for English cereal farmers oscillated between £40,000, minus £20,000 and back again not once but three times – little wonder that their average income from farming between 2014 and 2016 was minus £10,000.[66] In 2019–20 the average pig farm saw its income drop by eighty-seven per cent; the average lowland grazing rise by seventy-eight per cent (to the dizzying heights of £17,000)![67] This is the sort of year-to-year volatility which farmers accept as normal, but makes business planning very difficult.

The UK is such a tiny component of the global market (and grain is a globally traded commodity) that what's happening within our shores has little effect on price: poor national harvests don't – in line with national supply and demand – necessarily mean better prices (unless in conjunction with one or more of the world's great grain baskets such as Russia, Canada or Australia), while grain is very globally mobile, either ephemerally in 'paper trades' or physically in massive cargo ships. This lack of negotiating power, and the globalisation of agricultural commodities, means that the price I receive for my wheat is some forty per cent of that which my grandfather would have known while, as we've seen, my costs have risen precipitately, not least in regulatory terms, and high standards come at a financial cost which most of my foreign competitors do not have to bear. This is a particular bugbear for British arable farmers, who are proud to produce a quality product only to see cheaper imported grain grown to standards which would be illegal here flow into the country every year to be mixed with their own, few questions asked. (British bakers demand a certain percentage of high-protein wheat which we struggle to grow in our climate, sourcing it instead from Germany, France, Canada and the USA.) This is a blatant hypocrisy in our food

66 Defra 2019, op. cit.

67 'Defra farm business income forecasts highlight tough year', *Farmers Weekly*, 9 April 2021.

system (along with importing GM foodstuffs which are illegal to produce in Europe) which nobody seems inclined to address as it helps underpin cheap food prices.

Most farms lack sufficient storage space for their entire harvest. Partly, this is a consequence of the 'green revolution' of the 1970s, which saw yields gradually double by the 1990s due to new varieties geared around new PPPs and more plentiful fertilisers. As a result, grain sheds built to take the whole harvest at that time are now woefully inadequate. Subsequently, many farmers are forced to sell a significant proportion of their crop at harvest to make space, but unfortunately this is exactly the time of year when grain is generally worth the least, with traders knowing that farmers must sell regardless of price. Plus, come harvest, many arable businesses are desperate for cashflow to pay for the costs of the crop they've just brought to harvest – even if that cashflow isn't profit. Grain traders are the intermediaries between the farmer and end user: they buy on behalf of bakers, flour mills, maltsters, brewers, animal-feed companies and biodiesel plants, as well as fulfilling export contracts for cargo ships which might be delivering malting barley to Europe or pulses to Egypt. They take samples of our wares, discern their quality, and dispatch them to the appropriate home: milling wheat or malting barley which haven't made the grade to be sold into those human consumption markets at a premium will be discounted and used instead for animal feed or fuel. Those that have will be delivered to maltsters and millers who will produce the malt and flour for our booze and bread, before forwarding their products on to brewers and bakers who in turn sell on to the retailers and, thence, to you.

Each lorry of grain leaving the farm carries its own passport certifying the provenance of the load: crop type, variety, a risk assessment on its fitness to enter the food chain, a declaration that the lorry was suitably clean and proof of the farmer's membership of the Red Tractor scheme. Upon arrival at its destination, each load will be sampled for quality before offloading. Any issues will either be rectified and charged back to the farmer (perhaps it's slightly above the allowed moisture and must be dried or has a few too many small grains and will be sieved) or the load will be rejected outright and either diverted to a different user (perhaps the animal-feed mill nearby doesn't mind that it's got a low protein content) or returned to the farm (if there is any indication of insects – colloquially 'bugs' – in the load). Anything except a clean bill of health has serious cost implications for the farmer, who will be charged any extra transport costs plus a deduction from every tonne transported. Frankly, many farmers have learned from long experience that trust is a commodity in short supply in this part of the food chain: it's perhaps too easy, fifty or a hundred miles away, to make spurious deductions on a load, while a surprising number of lorries find themselves rejected on Friday afternoons, especially around bank holidays. It isn't just the mercy of the elements under which farmers operate, and challenges often lead to such deductions and rejections being overturned.

One tonne of milling wheat will produce about 1500 loaves of bread, accounting for about eleven per cent of the value of each. To produce one tonne of malt requires 1.3 tonnes of malting barley, which in turn will produce around 15,500 pints of beer. With 1500 loaves costing around £1650 and 15,500 pints costing £62,000 at retail, it's easy to note the small return seen by farmers when a tonne of either grain is usually between £130 and £200. The real profit is in the processing, packaging and retailing, so I always look askance at reports that poor harvests leading to a twenty per cent uptick in grain prices have had a similar impact on consumer prices. Somebody, somewhere, is making a few pounds more, but it isn't the farmer.

As a mixed farm, the straw provided by our crops is also vital, providing both feed and bedding for our animals over the winter. Once separated from the grain, the combine leaves it in long rows called 'swaths' ready for baling. In our case, we don't produce enough bales to justify owning our own baler so rely on a neighbour to do the job for us. This is another weather-critical job; as with hay, straw is baled so tightly that with even a hint of dampness it runs the risk of either mouldering or spontaneously combusting. Unlike with the grain dryer, there's no cheat for wet straw if it gets caught in the rain and it's just a case of hoping there's enough sun and wind to dry it out in the swath. That's why I'm always incredibly grateful to our neighbours, who seem inclined to drop whatever they're doing on their own farm to fit us in at harvest. These sorts of relationships are the glue which holds rural communities together; networks of local farmers who operate on the basis that one good turn deserves another and what goes around comes around: somebody else's cows are always liable to escape at some point – but then, so are your sheep. You must be able to trust that your compatriots will come to your aid when you need them. Once the straw's baled, it's a case of collecting the bales with telehandler and trailer and stacking them up into great piles for easy access over the winter, indoors if possible to keep them out of the rain. (And, increasingly, out of sight of the road to keep them from attracting the interest of petty arsonists looking for a quick thrill. I remember the night we lost a large number of bales in this way; the previous evening we'd had a break-in, the culprits stealing a couple of cans of petrol with which they returned the next night to torch our bales, the empty cans left as evidence. The fire service attended, but the remains smoked for days.)

Farming has little respect for leisure hours or time with family at the best of times, but harvest usually takes it to the next level with eighty- to one-hundred-hour working weeks, snatched meals, broken sleep and an **endless** sensation of feeling itchy. Mechanisation has certainly revolutionised the process (it's thought a modern combine harvester can do the work of 1000 people!) but there's still an awful lot of shovelling, sweeping, grunting and grousing. I remember watching, as a child, a farmer on TV proclaiming that – despite the vagaries and vicissitudes of his job, at harvest – atop his combine harvester, he felt like the most important person in the world. I understand where he was coming from; what more vital task is there than the production of food, with harvest the moment when a year's endeavours come to fruition? Yet it's easy to feel more than a little jaded by such grand thoughts: caught between the Scylla of unblinking climate change and Charybdis of unfeeling global markets, it's becoming increasingly difficult to make a living from 'simply' growing food.

SUMMER SHOWS

For many farmers, the summer show season is a highlight of the agricultural calendar. Too many (especially of the older generation) consider any time away from work as morally subversive; weekends 'off' are an indulgence for the lazy, and holidays are positively degenerate. But the network of local and national shows are firm dates in the calendar which even the most leisure-shy farmer finds an acceptable reason to leave the farm (perhaps even in a jacket) to catch up with friends in the beer tent, kick tyres on the machinery stands or even participate in the competitive business of livestock showing.

For the most part, showing is the preserve of the pedigree breeds, organised by the breed societies of which farmers are members. It's like being part of a club. Taking your animals to county fairs and shows and competing against your peers is a venerable tradition dating back hundreds of years; back in the day serial champions might subsequently stand to be painted in works commissioned by proud owners looking to commit to immortal canvas the achievements of their prize-winning animals. Today, a photo taken by a professional photographer usually suffices. Or on an iPhone by one of the kids. For the pedigree breeder, livestock shows are our shop window; what better way to generate sales than to come top of the class against your competition in front of an audience of those most likely to want to buy your wares? Animals with a couple of firsts or breed championships to their name are (generally) worth more than those with no show pedigree; a herd with a proven track record of generating show winners is naturally the place to go if you're in the market for some fresh blood to improve your own herd.

For the serious contestant, the work to prepare a potential show champion starts long before you load the livestock trailer to drive to the show – years before. For an animal to be any good in a show ring, it needs to be 'halter trained'; that is, to be comfortable being led in a controlled manner by a tether over its head. It's no use having the most magnificent bovine the world has ever seen, a mooing goddess, if it thrashes around like a bucking bronco and exits through the side of the show ring with you being dragged after it: the judge can't see it if it's in the car park. (This does happen, much to the embarrassment of the farmer and the excitement of the watching crowd, many of whom – like spectators at a motor race – are only there to catch a crash, ice cream in hand.) From a young age, animals destined for the show ring are gradually trained to accept the halter and calmly follow their handler around with only gentle pressure ever needing to be applied to the rope. To be in with a chance of winning, they need to be well behaved and learn how to 'stand' in the appropriate way, much like a body builder at one of those no-less-bizarre human events, which is why handlers will carry a show stick with which to poke their feet into position and calmingly scratch their bellies. And although they won't be doused in fake tan, show animals will be very familiar with all manner of other products used to get them ring ready. After the inevitable snipping and shaving with the clippers to remove any extraneous hair, they'll be shampooed, conditioned, and even glued to make sure their best lines are accentuated; our Longhorns will even have their horns and hooves buffed to a glossy shine and their tails fluffed up like massive puff balls. It's all nonsense, of course, but just like with those bodybuilders it's the accepted routine which has grown up around each breed for the highly artificial environment that is the show ring. By the time an animal which has been destined for the stage actually reaches its first event, it'll have been washed, blow dried, polished and led – generally pampered – for more hours than it will remember.

I urge you to visit such a show when you get the chance; it's a great way to get a taste of some of the best that British livestock farmers have to offer. Whether housed in sheds, great marquees or just in lines under the sun, it's a unique opportunity to get up close to some magnificent animals and have a chat with the farmers accompanying them; they're usually happy to answer questions and welcome genuine interest from people curious about food and farming. Agricultural shows are a rare opportunity for 'town and country' to mix and become better acquainted, and nowhere else will you be able to see such a wondrous range of livestock (and vegetables) in one place. Admittedly, showing has never been a passion of mine (being designated 'poo monitor' as a child did little to ignite my enthusiasm) but my parents have had great success with our cattle over the years. I do get in on the action with my crops, though: most regions have farm competitions where you can enter everything from a bale of hay to a well-tended garden to be inspected by a travelling judge. You are reading the words of a man who has – in his time – had the **third best** field of winter wheat and the **second best** field of winter barley in the Ashby and district area. It's kind of a big deal. But these competitions do foster a sense of genuine pride in farmers for the produce they grow and the animals they breed; and that passion's no bad thing at all.

CHICKENS

Like many farms, we've always had a flock of chickens in residence to provide a steady source of eggs and brighten the place up a bit. Over the years my mother has changed breed several times, but we've always had something a bit rare and unusual from the Belgian Mille Fleur Barbu D'Uccle with their unique feathery feet to the Old English Game with their mighty spurs for fighting. Anyone who's ever kept their own chickens will know how satisfying it can be to collect your own eggs every day – they somehow taste fresher and seem yellower! Like most little farm flocks, ours are free to wander the gardens and yard, pecking up the flower borders and generally making a nuisance of themselves. Chickens have a great homing instinct, and once they've gotten used to living in a particular coop for a few days will return there every evening as dusk starts to fall, once you let them out to roam free during the day. The imperative is to always remember to lock them away at night, as Mr Fox is generally to be counted on to pay a visit on the nights we forget – and he will kill indiscriminately just for the enjoyment of it. (It's also not unknown for our poor chickens to experience death from above during the day, being pinned to the floor and carted off by various birds of prey.) Ted and Toby have also been known to make a nuisance of themselves around the chickens, chasing them hither and yon despite my yellings. It's tough being a chicken; perhaps that's why occasionally they take indignant perch atop the house.

Naturally, hens tend to be prolific layers in the longer days of summer and autumn (producing an egg a day) before trailing off and even stopping altogether in the winter. They lay regardless of the presence or otherwise of a cockerel to fertilise their eggs – the eggs you buy in the supermarket will be from hens who've never even laid eyes on a male. Ours do run with cockerels, so it's common for a hen to disappear and take up residence in a straw stack or in the dark corner of a shed and settle down on a cluster of eggs for three weeks or so to hatch them out: the first we might know of it is when she proudly leads them in rough single file back to the coops one day, sprinting from shadow to shadow to keep from being spotted from the air. It's one of the most warming sights of the farm. (Incidentally, eggs which have been fertilised are also perfectly edible – unless they're incubated by the hen for at least three days there won't be any visible change in them at all, and if they aren't incubated in those crucial early hours then the fertilisation will come to nothing.)

On a much (much) larger scale, the British poultry industry is booming with many farmers diversifying into both chicken and egg production (it's uncertain which came first) to satisfy rising demand. (Although the consumption of all meat continues to rise in the UK, since the 1990s chicken has become far and away the nation's favourite.) The margins involved per egg or bird are tiny, but the numbers in modern operations are often very large on a relatively small land area, making it an attractive proposition – especially for arable farmers who can use the chicken muck as a high-quality organic fertiliser, while using their own grain for cheap feed. In 2018 there were forty million laying hens reared in the UK (in a range of systems from enriched 'colony cage' to organic free range and others in between) and more than 900 million 'broiler' chickens bred for meat. There's no overlap between the two, with the different types of bird being antithetical to each other's task. Broiler birds particularly are a world away from the rare breeds we keep; selectively bred over the past fifty years to maximise growth rate and breast size, they're now capable of going from hatching to slaughter in a remarkable 40 days (and even less in other countries), enabling multiple 'crops' of birds in a single shed through the year. I've visited such an indoor poultry unit in the UK and was impressed by the standard of welfare afforded the birds in their short lives. But the extreme nature of this type of food production is – as always – a reflection of society's demand for ever-cheaper food. Indeed, the average retail price for a dozen eggs has dropped by around a third in the past decade, squeezing farm margins yet harder. I dream of the day when consumers might speak up en-masse and say: 'Enough! How sustainable is this?'

FARMING AND THE ENVIRONMENT

The relationship between human food production and the natural world has always been, in part, antagonistic. Even before the days of settled agriculture, our hunter-gatherer forebears are thought to have hunted whole species to extinction; the millennia since have seen humanity both harness the power of nature and shape it to our own needs, rarely considering the impact on the wider web of ecosystems on which we all ultimately are a symbiote part. Since the nineteenth century our impact on the planet has grown exponentially, the shadow of mankind's exploitative tendencies reaching from the depths of the oceans to the most remote rainforests and high into the atmosphere above. Our pollution now even stretches into orbit.

Our population explosion in the second half of the twentieth century, coupled with technological revolutions which enabled us to impact on the natural world on a scale previously unimaginable, have led humanity increasingly down an ecologically destructive cul-de-sac into which we have drawn countless pristine landscapes and exploited them for our own ends.

Britain's place in recent world history has ensured it has an outsized share of the blame for the current state of the planet, despite its diminutive size. Within our own borders, we've presided over a startling decline in biodiversity, especially in the years since the world wars pushed us into taking extreme actions to safeguard our own national existence, before the onslaught of modernity drove us to reshape the landscape in ways that the markets would better reward for their own benefit. I've already spoken of the very visible loss of farm hedgerows this drove on my own farm (with losses of up to fifty per cent in some regions being common), but other statistics are similarly grim: sixty-three per cent of farmland bird species have declined since 1970, along with seventy-five per cent of butterfly species while ninety-five per cent of species-rich unimproved grassland has been lost since 1930.[68] The factors behind national biodiversity loss are complex, and certainly can't all be laid at the door of agriculture: climate change, urbanisation and industrialisation, invasive species, light pollution, the foreign predation of migratory species – even domestic cats – all have their part to play. But modern farmers, controlling seventy per cent of our land area, are increasingly accepting of their own past mistakes and embracing the means to remedy them.

It would be too simplistic to suggest a simple generational divergence in attitude to this new farming 'environmentalism', but it is fair to say that many younger farmers are particularly energised

68 Soffe & Lobley (eds), op. cit., p. 275.

by the concept of farming in harmony with – rather than in antagonism against – nature; there is more than a hint of truth to the notion that some farming in the late twentieth century was more about pummelling the land into submission than working in partnership with it. I admit to taking my own journey in this regard; upon 'returning home' in my mid-twenties, I was broadly unconcerned with the state of nature on my own little patch but, as the years have passed, I've increasingly formed my own views and priorities on how I wish to farm in future: nature-friendly farming is good for the soul, if not necessarily the wallet. And this is an important point to make: whatever harm can be laid at the door of farmers in the past seventy years, it was largely laid there by a society more concerned with ever-cheaper food than the health of our shared environment. Too few people thought to ask how it was that food had become so affordable; like taxes which can never be avoided, only deferred, the cost of that food was and is being paid somewhere. Society has just preferred not to ask too many questions, especially of itself; too often farmers have felt unfairly castigated for doing little other than what was asked of them at the point of a financial spear.

From 2003, the European Union realised that its farm subsidy programme – which had historically rewarded volumes of production – was fundamentally flawed on a continent which no longer faced the imminent spectre of hunger. Consequently, environmental elements were added to the Common Agricultural Policy (CAP), rewarding farmers for enacting positive outcomes for nature; these were both embedded as a fundamental requirement in the basic area payments which farmers received to underwrite food production, and were also available as a distinct and separate income stream for those who wished to enact whole-farm environmental schemes across their land. My farm has participated in these schemes for many years, as well as being a willing participant of the Championing the Farmed Environment partnership, an initiative by the British agricultural sector to do further voluntary works in the natural sphere.

What does today's Countryside Stewardship (CS) scheme look like on my farm? We're enrolled in a 'Mid-Tier' scheme, the entry-level environmental programme we've inherited from the CAP with our exit from the EU. (Above it is the 'Higher-Tier', a more comprehensive – and agriculturally limiting – scheme for farms who wish to really focus on environmental works and are recognised as having high-value flora and fauna on their land.) The essence of CS is to restore and enhance biodiversity and safeguard water by the de-intensification of farmed land, or even the widespread removal of that land (especially arable) from production. Payment is then made by government for carrying out prescribed actions and achieving the stipulated results (though the historically appalling bureaucracy and mismanagement of the scheme has discouraged many from engaging).

Much of our permanent pasture is now registered as 'very low input', meaning we can no longer apply artificial fertilisers or PPPs, while at the same time we are duty bound to ensure a range of sward heights to encourage different habitats which we will manage by grazing. This variable sward composition will affect the range and number of invertebrates and birds which will populate it, as extensive grazing helps create diversity and increase wildlife value, while dung from livestock is a veritable smorgasbord of natural nutrients and habitat for invertebrates, which in turn feed other species.

We have established grass buffer strips around many of our arable fields to provide an added layer of protection to hedges and watercourses from potential spray or fertiliser drift, as well as creating a new habitat for fauna such as ground-nesting birds and small rodents to creep out of the field margins – who in turn act as lunch for airborne raptors. The hope is that beneficial insects will then increase in number, predating on pests such as aphids and reducing our need for insecticides. Other buffer strips across slopes will help to reduce soil erosion, cutting the loss of this vital resource while reducing watercourse sedimentation and pollution.

Some fields will be left as overwintered stubble, a habitat which isn't much to look at but provides an important home and source of food for seed-eating birds and mammals such as the brown hare, while spring-sown crops are excellent habitats for birds such as the skylark, grey partridge or turtle dove.

Whole fields, too, have been relinquished from production: some have been planted with pollen and nectar wildflowers to provide an abundance of food for pollinators such as bees, as well as butterflies, from spring through to late summer, and to attract beneficial predatory insects such as hoverflies. The general increase in invertebrates should then provide a valuable food source for bird populations. They look fantastic too. Other fields will be planted with legume and herb-rich swards which will provide welcome variety from pure ryegrass for our livestock while also reducing the need for artificial fertilisers and improving soil health and water infiltration with their deeper rooting systems. Yet other fields will be planted with legume mixes which may not be grazed but will provide soil health benefits, pollinator habitat and food and homes for ground-nesting birds.

On our boundaries, hedges will become less managed and allowed to grow yet wilder, providing a more robust habitat and increasing the amount of food available for birds over the winter, while new lines of native hedge will be planted to replace those lost in decades past. Fallen timbers will be left to rot down and provide valuable invertebrate and fungal habitat at the base of the food chain, rather than being cleared away for the sake of neatness.

These are the actions we've signed up to at our small farm; in our current CS scheme I chose to remove some twenty per cent of our arable land from crop production, with a third of our grass becoming very low input. How do I feel about this? Honestly, on a personal level, excited: this is the most ambitious environmental scheme we've ever implemented and I look forward to seeing the positive impact on local biodiversity as well as the reduction in our carbon footprint on the journey to our 2040 net-zero target. Much of the land taken out of combinable cropping and put into soil fertility building legume and herb mixes should, frankly, never have been cropped: the slopes were too steep, the soils too thin or too sandy; in years long past, they were home to grazed livestock. These are the fields of which I have spoken earlier, where a creeping realisation has dawned over recent years that we haven't been farming them as the physical reality dictates, but rather as the financial imperative has demanded. The payments we'll receive for taking these fields out of intensive arable will likely at best barely offset the income we would otherwise have accrued from growing cereals or oilseeds, but that intangible satisfaction of a job better done will – for me – make all the difference. In honesty, climate change has prodded us in this direction: these poor soils have suffered the most under the spring droughts which now seem to afflict us with metronomic regularity. Financially, that twenty per cent of our arable area now removed from production is barely viable if the recent climate trend maintains its course towards ever-greater extremes. Practically, growing a thin crop of wildflowers now makes increasing sense over trying to grow a crop of wheat which needs to be high yielding just to break even in the mad world of modern farm economics.

But this is a head versus heart situation. Cognitively, I worry that the increasing pressure for British farmers to remove land from production for the benefit of the environment is in fact counterproductive. For every tonne of oats I'm not producing, for every finished beef animal I'm not managing to rear on those low-input fields which require lower stocking densities, demand does not decrease. Either I increase production on my remaining land by intensification, or as a nation we will import those oats or that beef from elsewhere, from countries which likely do not have our baked-in levels of welfare and sustainability, and where our increasing demand for their produce will likely drive yet further environmental degradation of our shared global inheritance. The basic fact remains that we have a growing population to feed; the danger is that we greenwash our domestic food and farming policy and, sure, make ourselves feel better, but just export our environmental conscience abroad. This is an issue of particularly pressing urgency as we lurch into a post-CAP agricultural policy in which food features hardly at all.

I often describe myself as a 'farmer and conservationist', sometimes to the annoyance of keyboard warriors who identify strongly with the latter and believe the two descriptors to be mutually antagonistic. This is nonsense. As guardians of the majority of our natural space, farmers are (in the jargon of the times) 'key stakeholders' when it comes to the future safeguarding of our environment, and while some may consider angry social media comments to be a form of conservation, most British farmers are out there, day in, day out, taking practical steps for the good of the wildlife on their farms. Many do a lot more than me; I don't claim to be an authority. But even more striking then, that a third of my farmed area — not to mention the rough corners, woods and streams — is now officially in a voluntary conservation scheme.

British farms are home to more than 410,000km of hedgerows and twenty-eight per cent of our nation's woodlands; farm woodland area has increased from 660,000ha in 2007 to 980,000ha in 2016. In recent years farmers have planted more than 23,000ha of food sources for farmland birds and 19,000ha of pollen and nectar sources for pollinators.[69] Farming practices are improving as we all accept that the future must be more sustainable than the past. The tide has turned, with the 'bad old days' now firmly behind us – in this country at least. There are many pioneering farmers in the field of nature-friendly farming – and I urge you to seek out their stories – but the rest of us are determinedly playing catch up.

---

69 Defra 2019, op. cit.

CONCLUSION

JUNE 2016 WAS an eventful month for me. Not only was I married to my (long-suffering at time of writing) wife, but the British people also voted to leave the European Union of which we had been an integral part since 1973. Although only one of these events provided me with a large cake, epic collection of Polaroids and the first (though by no means last) opportunity to dress Ted in a bow tie (as best man in all but name), I knew that both would have a lasting impact on my future.

Around the world, agriculture is almost universally dependent on financial support from governments – that is to say, on taxpayers' money. The fifty-four largest economies spend some $540bn per year on direct payments to farmers.[70] As we've seen, in many cases – and to an increasing extent over the decades – growing food simply doesn't pay and it's in nobody's immediate interests (except the farmer's) to change that. As a result, farms in many countries are dependent on a combination of direct and indirect subsidies to remain solvent.

As members of the EU, the majority of our farming strategy was decided in Brussels as part of the CAP. At its heart was the

---

70 Hinrich Foundation, 'Agricultural subsidies: Everyone's doing it', 15 October 2020.

aim to increase European self-sufficiency in food in the wake of the devastation of the Second World War, though over time this evolved into a hybrid system also incentivising good environmental stewardship. By 2020, the final year in which full CAP payments were received by UK farmers, this money amounted to some £3bn per year, distributed according to the area of land each farmed and its productive capacity. (For a lowland farm such as mine, this equated to some £230 per hectare.)

With our exit from the EU, government embarked on a revolutionary new approach to farm support with Michael Gove at Defra (the previously backwater Department for the Environment, Food and Rural Affairs). What slowly emerged over the subsequent half decade was a dismantling of the CAP framework and its replacement with a system of 'public money for public goods' aimed at creating a 'Green Brexit' based around boosting the countryside's 'natural capital'. Instead of receiving an area payment for land farmed, farmers would receive public money only for fulfilling specific environmental services aimed at improving biodiversity, soil, air and water. Food production was explicitly dismissed as a public good, and for the first time in living memory was to become unsupported by the public purse. This is more than just semantics. The reliable flat-rate area payment of the CAP (paid on land**holding**, not land **ownership**) fulfilled a multitude of roles, from providing the liquidity for day-to-day farm cashflow and investment, to insurance against volatility of income.

The importance of this 'Basic Payment Scheme' (BPS) varied depending on farm type; the bigger the area farmed, the larger the income from CAP. Thus, horticulture, poultry and pig operations relied on subsidy payments for only some ten per cent of their income. At the other end of the scale, broadacre arable farmers depended on these payments for some eighty per cent of their incomes, and extensively grazed livestock more than ninety per cent.[71] The 'average' English farm was dependent upon BPS for sixty-one per cent of its farm business income. Despite this, sixteen per cent of farms were still making a financial loss year-on-year, and without BPS this figure was estimated to rise to more than forty per cent, with more acute pain for the smaller tenant farmers who relied most on these payments – despite government's clumsy (though effective) attempt to paint CAP as a gravy train for wealthy landowners. It's also ironic that with the withdrawal of direct payments, extensive livestock grazing is to be the most badly impacted sector – exactly that part of our farming system we need to expand to improve the sustainability and health of our soils.

The new system of public money for public goods was finally unveiled in late 2020 as the Environmental Land Management (ELM) scheme. Despite being presented as the replacement for BPS, it was in fact little more than a rejig of the existing Countryside Stewardship schemes long available as an optional extra under the CAP, which allowed farmers to render enhanced environmental services in return for additional payments on top of BPS. At the time of writing, it remains unclear what the payment rates will be for the environmental services to be provided by farmers under ELM (as the scheme is not due to commence until 2024) but the fear is that they will be little better than those under CS, calculated on an 'income forgone' model where the payments farmers receive for carrying out enhanced environmental work were **designed** not to return a profit any greater than that which would have been earned had the land been left in food production. This had obvious implications for the uptake of these schemes, which entailed a large amount of extra work and administrative effort, as well as potentially punitive inspections, for no additional return other than

---

71 Defra 2019, op. cit.

the satisfaction of being involved.

Direct area payments will be phased out by 2027 (at least in England; as a devolved power the other nations are pursuing less drastic change in agriculture). Once gone, it is hoped ELM will compensate those farmers who wish to participate for land largely removed from agricultural production and placed into stewardship. But it will explicitly **not** support food production across the rest of the farm (although it is supposed that individual grants will be available to help boost productivity, as was also the case under the CAP). For the first time since the 1930s, British farmers will be producing food exposed to the full force of the global markets, and at a time when once again government is looking to liberalise trade with the non-EU world and their cheaper, lower-standard food exports. (It also seems inevitable that larger landowners and landowning institutions will gobble up the majority of funds under ELM, with the smaller tenant farmers most disadvantaged by the loss of BPS also the least able to access the new scheme, a double whammy expected to prove fatal for many smaller family farms.)

Why does this matter? It all comes down to sustainability. Clearly, the past system of farming under the CAP was largely broken. Although we can point to environmental improvements in recent years, there is much more we could and should be doing to regenerate our natural environment. At the same time, direct area payments to farmers were keeping heads above water – but only just. One farming family in four lives in poverty.[72] In reality, many farms are themselves subsidising the food they produce by selling assets, taking no wage, working all hours and – increasingly – diversifying: two thirds now operate non-farming diversifications, from glamping to retail to commercial lets, just to keep themselves in the business of growing food. It's difficult to think of another

---

72 'Farming families "living in poverty"', *Farmers Weekly*, 30 November 2010.

industry which voluntarily funds a loss-making product, effectively subsidising the big retailers' balance sheets.

The core assumption underlying ELM is that we are a rich nation and can pay others to feed us. The last time British food production was unsubsidised – in the run up to both world wars – our national self-sufficiency collapsed to around thirty per cent. It was reasoned that feeding the nation was most efficiently left to the market, which at that time meant imports from the Empire. Today, this ideological assumption has been mated with the concept that we must react to both climate change and our historic loss of biodiversity. We are therefore presented with an 'agricultural policy' aimed at removing land from production to rebuild and safeguard our natural capital while giving no thought to the question of whether by so doing we merely offshore our food production and ecological footprint abroad. I would argue that we have a moral responsibility to both feed ourselves to the greatest extent possible and to do so in an environmentally sustainable fashion. ELM raises the spectre of greenwashing our environmental conscience by focusing narrow efforts entirely within our own shores, while giving little thought to the consequences. This is my major issue with the concept of 'rewilding', which has become a rallying cry for many so-called environmentalists, some of whom state a wish to remove farming from as much as fifty per cent of our landscape. Such projects undoubtedly have their place and can become foci of regional regeneration schemes. But climate change knows no borders, and merely offsetting our impact elsewhere achieves nothing in the long run; the chainsaws would merely intensify in some of the most delicate and valuable ecosystems of the world while we let our own productive farmland go to waste. To paraphrase the proposition: if a rainforest is cut down halfway around the world and I don't see it, is it really cut down? Well, yes, I'm afraid it is. A recent report demonstrated that the consumer habits of the average citizen of the G7 group of nations is responsible for the felling of four trees per year in the globe's tropical regions (from a range of commodities from chocolate to timber, beef to soya, rubber to palm oil). Greenpeace UK commented on the findings by saying that reciprocal afforestation in developed countries was no substitute; 'Cutting down a tropical rainforest cannot be compensated by planting a pine tree.'[73]

For years farming groups have been explaining to government the folly of slashing financial support for our high-standard, high-cost farming system and the inevitable consequences of that for sustainable domestic food production and self-sufficiency in an increasingly climatically and geopolitically unstable world. For the most part, these entreaties have fallen on deaf ears, with Defra (despite being aware of the financially precarious situation of the majority of farms) breezily proclaiming that with BPS gone, those who sell goods to farmers and to whom we pay rents will step up and take their share of the pain. Moreover, farms will further diversify to keep afloat. I have to tell you; the notion that landlords and suppliers will voluntarily join farmers in shouldering the burdens of our cheap food system is a pleasant fantasy, while the thought that this country's food security will in future explicitly rest on farmers subsidising production with second jobs and barn conversions is, frankly, exasperating and not a little worrying.

But, ultimately, this isn't my problem. Frustrating as I may find it, if government wants to pay me solely to plant trees, rewild land and flood my fields, so be it. Food security – **national security** – and the sustainability of our food system are things politicians are paid to worry about (whether they choose to or not); I'm just a simple farmer trying to support my family and do the right thing where I can. Farmers may believe that sustainable food production

---

73 'Average westerner's eating habits lead to loss of four trees every year', *The Guardian*, 29 March 2021.

and the environment **must** and **can** go hand in hand – hence the National Farmers Union's net zero 2040 ambition. But, if government is immune to reason and insists on prioritising one to the detriment of the other, I for one am not going to throw myself on a sacrificial pyre for the sake of their misjudgements – misjudgements which will become glaringly evident in short order. But, all the time, our rainforests are burning, our rivers are being drained and our atmosphere is warming – trends to which we give tacit approval by operating a 'don't ask, don't tell' policy to food imports and much else besides in our economy. Embedded carbon from imports already accounts for some forty per cent of our national footprint – but is generally not counted in official figures as the emissions occur outside our borders. The semi-detached house we share with our neighbour is on fire while we busy ourselves rearranging the garden furniture.

A truly sustainable food system must be a triumvirate of producer, consumer and state. Unless we all make sustainability a priority, nothing will change. Farmers – many already clinging on by their financial fingernails – cannot act independently as the environmental conscience of the nation: not while we take home only seven per cent of the value of the food supply chain. Consumers cannot continue to expect ever-cheaper food without asking of themselves the hidden costs behind the price tag. And no government will ever take this issue seriously until voters force their hand; it's too easy to greenwash a policy here, kick a can down a road there. Climate change is real, and the clock is ticking. We must approach this issue holistically; the provenance of our food is about more than the price of our weekly shop: it's about our health, our environment, our trade policy and our future. It's about who we want to be as a nation, and what we want to bequeath our children: a gift, or a curse? Britain can be a champion for sustainable food production; we can export our climate-friendly wares and our knowledge around the world and change things for the better. But, as things stand, we look set to become a greenwashed moral backwater with an iniquitous two-tier food structure, end market for the unsustainable dregs of the global food system for the poorest in society, with only the better-off able to afford to buy British. If we want our government to genuinely support sustainable food production, we must tell our MPs to put our money where their mouth is and support British farming. We want sustainable produce on every plate.

Food prices need not necessarily rise to fund the transformation we need to see. Indeed, despite the UK enjoying the third cheapest food in the world, there are still far too many living in 'food poverty', a reflection more of the appalling gap between rich and poor and the spiralling cost of living than the inherent unaffordability of food. (Indeed, the £3bn previously handed to farmers at point of production in direct payments is dwarfed by the £17bn in VAT breaks given to consumers at food retail.) But we must see farmers receive more of the value of the produce they grow, and this means the large retailers (the top eight of whom sell ninety-two per cent of all groceries in the UK) ending their ceaseless price wars and returning more value to their suppliers, and producers shortening supply chains and selling more food directly to the public to retain more of its value. Both of these require the buy-in of and pressure from the consumer; the great British public is the key to change – it's you who choose to buy (or not) our wares; give us the financial tools, and we'll continue to build a sustainable food system the envy of the world.

But – among all this talk of food sustainability and climate change – let us never forget that the burning of fossil fuels is responsible for more than eighty per cent of the emissions in our economy, the stock gases which are not going away. That is the elephant in the room which must be addressed, whatever good works we do in the fields.

All too often, the food on our plates is taken for granted; we are fortunate to exist at a time unique in human history when – for most – food is plentiful and affordable. But the events of spring 2020 demonstrated the fragility of our modern food system. As Covid-19 forced the nation into its first national lockdown, panic buying of food ensued and shelves in retailers across the nation stood empty (and many householders presumably built thrones of toilet paper). Although this perhaps said more about human nature than supermarket just-in-time supply chains (demand spiking dramatically to outstrip normal supply) it did demonstrate the fact that, when it comes to it, the ability to secure sufficient food is a primal human instinct, and although we may take it for granted ninety-nine per cent of the time, it takes little to raise it to the very top of our agendas. That December, the spectre of shortages loomed again with a threatened 'no-deal' exit from our transitional arrangements with the EU and with it the possibility that the huge volumes of our food imported from the Continent would become stuck at the ports. For the most part, this disruption was avoided through a last-minute deal, but it once again highlighted the fragility of our nation's resilience to sudden shocks when it comes to long and extended supply chains.

When we talk about food sustainability, it is not 'simply' a matter of the environmental impact of the food we consume, but also of the resilience of our entire food system. Despite the challenges I've outlined, this is why I believe it's essential that we raise our national self-sufficiency from its current level of around sixty per cent. During the Covid food crisis, I was personally proud to stretch every sinew to ensure the tiny contribution of my farm; it was a time of spring planting under cobalt skies, and national events instilled in me an authentic sense of purpose. But the reality is that farming operates to very set and slow timescales, and production cannot quickly be ramped up to meet unexpected demand: it must be part of a more concerted and long-term national commitment. I believe that we must produce more food, more sustainably – and that will include a change in the things we grow; fewer bulk commodities and more (especially) seasonal fruit and vegetables to raise our domestic production from the very low levels to which they have fallen. It would be scant consolation in a future food crisis to think of all the farmland we had set aside for nature, seeing our self-sufficiency drop and leaving us unable to feed ourselves. It's said society is only three missed meals away from anarchy; I've never seen a riot resulting from a lack of rewilding. Farming and the environment **must** go hand in hand; some of the best farming practices harness the one to optimise the other, which is at the core of regenerative principles and sustainable intensification. And we must remember that food sustainability isn't just about CO2e: it's about water use, soil health, protection of habitat, prevention of antibiotic abuse, animal welfare and ethical employment practices – both at home and abroad.

In writing this book I aimed to explain the story behind your food, the day-to-day activities of life on a ubiquitous mixed lowland farm in Britain. As I've stressed, no two farms are exactly alike but I hope to have done the subject some humble justice. It's vital that as a society we develop a better understanding of how our food is produced and where it comes from. In a world where technology, consumerism and urbanisation have in all too many instances reduced food to a sanitised, shrink-wrapped convenience delivered ready-cooked to our doors, most of us have never been further removed from the reality of the fields. And if we don't understand something, how can we make informed decisions? Too many groups take advantage of this disconnect to push narrow partisan views which at face value sound alluring; siren calls to a better world. Worried about the climate? Boycott beef! Concerned about ecosystem loss? Roll-out rewilding! (Some farmers dryly comment they'll back the reintroduction of wolves to the countryside when bears are allowed to roam Knightsbridge.) But without viewing the cause and effect of such binary solutions in the wider context of the global food system, we risk merely robbing Peter to pay Paul. The reality is that good decisions around food are more complex than such positions imply.

I'm proud to be a British farmer, and that's a feeling which permeates the industry. Nobody farms for the money (one wry joke tells of the farmer who wins a million pounds and when asked what they'd do with it responds: 'Farm until it's all gone of course'). Farming is a hard job, from the UK to the Ukraine, but still people flock to it. There's something about farming which stirs the passions and often brings out the best in people who are willing to put the hard work and honest labour in to make a success of it. A life on the land is no bucolic idyll (though at times it can cause your breath to catch in your throat) but farming gives you a sense of place, of purpose, of a home in the timeless landscape: of belonging. The smell of a field of cut hay can be intoxicating to the senses; the sight of a curtain of rain sweeping across an open landscape, transfixing. The sound of a calf's first breaths, heart-warming. No; nobody farms for the money, but farming is good for the soul.

And we need more good people in agriculture. Too often it's seen as a closed shop; something to be born into. But it's a huge industry with ever-expanding roles; away from the traditional jobs on the land we need engineers, vets, agronomists, programmers, journalists, botanists, ecologists, geneticists, mechanics, soil scientists, hydrologists, climatologists, policy advisers, biochemists, entrepreneurs and more. Many things about the coming decades are uncertain, but we know we need to produce seventy per cent more food by 2050 than we do today – and we need to do so more sustainably. Modern agriculture is awash with technology –

from apps to drones, GPS to autonomous robotics, renewables to blockchain, the STEM subjects are at our core. Long gone are the days of farming being a 'backward' industry (were that ever the case): not only do we offer solutions to some of the most pressing issues society faces, but we are a forward-looking, progressive and innovative part of the economy. And we have fresh air on tap (except when we're spreading manure). Agriculture is the biggest job on earth, and we need more talented young men and women in our ranks.

So I encourage you to take more of an interest in your food; follow some farmers on social media; engage with farming shows on TV and radio; read. Visit your local agricultural show and talk to the farmers on the livestock lines; frequent a local farm shop and buy your food directly from the source – see where it's grown and bred. Encourage your children's school to engage with the *#FarmerTime* initiative, which links primary age children with a farm by videocall once a fortnight (they love it, especially when the cow poops). Attend a local Open Farm Sunday event this June (it's free!) and have a tour of a real farm; ask questions. Don't accept a celebrity tweet or YouTube video as gospel. The better informed we all are, the better decisions we can make. As a British farmer, I'm proud of the work I do, but I'm determined to do better. If this book has done anything to help inform the conversation, then I'm proud of that too.

ACKNOWLEDGEMENTS

Writing is a great pleasure, and penning a book has been a dream for as long as I can remember. As a teenager I wrote reams, specifically, of Star Wars fan fiction, culminating with a full novel at the age of fifteen. I'll never forget the support and encouragement of my English teacher, Andrew Walsh, who even went so far as to dispatch my optimistically written manuscript to publishing houses in an attempt to fire my enthusiasm. I still remember to this day the kind and encouraging response I received from one, including the enclosed novel which they claimed was very much 'my style'. I still have it on my shelf today.

This book is the product of a lifetime's aspiration, but also of a desire to explain the reality of modern British farming – or, at least, a part of it – to the general reader. For some time I searched for a book exploring the subject in the round from the point of view of a practical farmer, rather than that of an academic or environmentalist with an axe to grind. Failing to find one, I decided to do the job myself.

To achieve this, I extend huge thanks to Martin Stanhope, my editor at *Countryside* magazine, for pointing me in the direction of Quiller, who took a chance on a first-time author with no manuscript and a rough idea of what he wanted to achieve. Thanks too to Tim Relf, formerly of *Farmers Weekly*, for giving a completely unpublished young farmer the opportunity to begin a hugely enjoyable side career as a columnist which has finally led to this book. Sue Bassett, for Quiller, made the process of editing a breeze, and her comments and suggestions immeasurably improved the end product.

My thanks, as always, go to Minette Batters for obliging me with a foreword and for her inspirational leadership around food, farming and the environment on the national stage. Without her tireless efforts in recent years, Britain's farmers and our shared countryside would be in a much more difficult place – though she would be the first to say that much remains to be done.

I have been blessed with the support of many good friends over the course of writing this book, a project which came at a difficult moment in my life. Special thanks must go to Sarah, Tom, Harriet, Mark, Ed and David B for all their wise counsel, and David L for the loan of some wheels!

Finally, where would I be without my family – Kathryn, whose support and enthusiasm have been unstinting, Ted and Toby upon whose coat-tails I continue to ride, and my little joy Edward, who has not, in his toddling, been directly helpful in the writing of this book or in allowing me the sleep required so to do, but nevertheless I hope he'll enjoy reading Daddy's book when he's old enough, just as I hope it'll do a little something to make the world a better place for him by the time he does.